FEASTING WITH MINE ENEMY

FEASTING WITH MINE ENEMY: RANK

AND EXCHANGE AMONG

NORTHWEST COAST

SOCIETIES *by ABRAHAM ROSMAN*

and PAULA G. RUBEL

COLUMBIA UNIVERSITY PRESS

NEW YORK AND LONDON   1971

Copyright © 1971 Columbia University Press

ISBN: 0-231-03483-0

Library of Congress Catalog Card Number: 74-133033

Printed in the United States of America

THIS BOOK IS DEDICATED TO THOSE GIANTS

OF AN EARLIER PERIOD —

FRANZ BOAS, EDWARD SAPIR,

AND JOHN R. SWANTON

ACKNOWLEDGMENTS

THIS BOOK is part of a larger project involving an investigation of the relationship between forms of exchange and types of social structures. The research was initially supported by the Social Science Research Council, and subsequently by the National Science Foundation (grant number GS-2567).

A number of friends and colleagues have been most helpful with comments and suggestions. We would particularly like to thank Morton Klass, Robert F. Murphy, David M. Schneider, Helen Codere, Harvey Pitkin, George Bond, Joyce Riegelhaupt, and Judith Shapiro.

We have used the resources of several archives, and would like to thank the libraries of the American Philosophical Society and the University of Toronto for their assistance. Dr. David Sapir kindly permitted us to consult Edward Sapir's field notebooks on the Nootka, and to quote from them, for which we are grateful.

Acknowledgment is also made to Beacon Press, for permission to quote from Claude Lévi-Strauss's *The Elementary Structures of Kinship;* to the American Philosophical Society, for permission to quote from the material in the Boas, Swadesh, and Sapir Collections; and to Thomas F. McIlwraith, for permission to quote from his field notes on the Bella Coola.

We extend our gratitude to Suzanne Youngerman, who worked as our research assistant throughout this project. We would also like to thank Jennifer Oberg for her assistance with the Nootka material.

Columbia University
June, 1970

ABRAHAM ROSMAN
PAULA G. RUBEL

CONTENTS

TABLES

DIAGRAMS

CHARTS

FEASTING WITH MINE ENEMY

Friar Lawrence: That's my good son; but where hast
      thou been, then?
Romeo: I'll tell thee, ere thou ask it me again.
      I have been feasting with mine enemy,
      Where on a sudden one hath wounded me,
      That's by me wounded;

ROMEO AND JULIET, ACT II, SCENE III

CHAPTER I. *INTRODUCTION*

When a great man gives, it is a sign of magnanimity; when a poor man gives, it is a sign of his bondage.   IBN KHALDUN

THE POTLATCH was recognized from the time of first contact with it by early observers as a unique phenomenon. It has always been the embodiment of the rich ceremonial and religious life of the societies of the Pacific Northwest Coast. The sumptuous feasting and giving by which people enhance their rank has occupied the attention of many generations of anthropologists. Two prominent features have demanded explanation. Why should important individuals reduce themselves to penury by extravagant giving? Why should important individuals be shamed by the necessity to accept gifts from other important individuals? Numerous explanations of the potlatch and its attendant activities have been advanced. These explanations proceed from different theoretical premises. Some are psychological in their orientation; others are economic and ecological. All of them are either inadequate or incomplete as explanations, leaving the potlatch only partially understood.

In the analysis of the potlatch which follows, we have adopted a very different approach which incorporates and builds upon structural theory and theories of exchange. The most significant theorist for us has been Marcel Mauss, who, in his classic work, *The Gift,* identifies kinds of exchange systems which are characterized by different modes of distribution. Implicit in the distinctions which he makes is the idea that these different systems are paralleled by different social structures. Our general approach involves a demonstration of the relationship between kinds of exchange systems and kinds of social structures. The potlatch is one example of such a relationship. Our ideas about exchange are embodied in the following set of propositions.

To give, to receive, and to repay constitute the basic elements of the exchange process. This process necessarily involves social interaction. The very act of giving by an individual is a recognition of his separation from others, just as giving between groups defines the separation between "we" and "they," in effect defining group boundaries. The decision to accept or receive what is offered is an acknowledgment of separation. Repayment is necessary in order to have exchange; without repayment one would have transfer but not exchange. In addition to defining separateness, the sequence of these acts of giving, receiving, and repaying serves to create bonds between individuals and groups. Both bondedness and separateness are thus inherent in the exchange process.

In initial encounters, exchanges serve to create relationships. In illustrating his principle of reciprocity, Claude Lévi-Strauss uses the example of strangers who sit at the same table in a cheap French restaurant and are impelled to offer each other wine and thereby establish a relationship which bridges their discomfort at being strangers to one another (Lévi-Strauss 1969:59). This relationship is ephemeral if no further exchanges take place. In his study of informal social behavior, or elementary social behavior as he calls it, George C. Homans defines social behavior as exchange. By concentrating on informal social behavior, in terms of the strategy of the manipulation of exchanges, he attempts to show the way in which patterns of relationships develop out of continuing exchanges (Homans 1958; 1961).

Where preexisting social relationships are present, for which Homans uses the term "social institution," continuing exchanges serve as expressions of those relationships. In these cases, the exchanges serve not to create relationships but rather to reaffirm ongoing relationships by expressing them anew.

A principal theme in anthropology has been the manner in which the exchange of women creates and maintains social relationships. This approach has been referred to as alliance theory. The major proponent of this kind of theorizing has been Lévi-Strauss, who is in the mainstream of the French anthropological tradition. Beginning with the concept of the division of labor, as developed by Durkheim (1893), French anthropologists have been concerned with how the segments of a society relate to one another. Exchange has proved a pivotal concept in this approach. Mauss's work on the gift illustrates the way in which a series of exchanges of goods, services, and women serve to integrate groups, while at the same time maintaining separateness and even hostility between them (1925). Selecting from and elaborating upon the work of Durkheim and Mauss, Lévi-Strauss (1949) concerns himself with the exchange of what he considers the most valuable commodity—women. The exchange of women is seen by Lévi-Strauss as creating and maintaining alliances.

Alliances are usually characterized as relationships between groups which imply support and solidarity in time of need. Indeed groups which are bound as affines to one another may count upon one another for such support. Affines are bound together by the exchange of women, and, as noted above, exchanges of any sort can serve to create and maintain relationships. Alliance theory also recognizes that the relationship between affines, who at times may be allies, may also involve hostility and conflict. Thus, alliances imply support as well as conflict. Just as exchanges imply separateness as well as bondedness, so too alliances built upon the exchanges of women serve to outline the boundaries of units and set them off against one another, sometimes in a hostile fashion, while they at the same time create links between the units. It can be seen that there is a very close linkage and overlap between alliance theory and exchange theory.

In addition to his pivotal role in the formulation of alliance theory, Lévi-Strauss has been closely identified with the development of structuralism. The concept of structure derived from Lévi-Strauss (1953) is central to our analysis. We deal with the development of structural models inductively arrived at from the examination of a fixed corpus of previously gathered ethnographic materials which includes a statement of ideal rules as well as information about actual events. Our method in developing these structural models has been to follow the procedures used by Lévi-Strauss in *The Elementary Structures of Kinship* (1969[1949]). These structures are constructs of the analysts. The question of whether such models exist in the mind of the native informant, either consciously or unconsciously, is irrelevant in our approach to structure.

Lévi-Strauss has demonstrated that groups which exchange women according to a specified marriage rule indicating who the preferred spouse shall be will stand to one another in certain fixed patterns of relationship. The analyst therefore can build a structural model which represents a particular pattern of exchange of women between groups. The marriage rule characterizes that pattern. In what follows we have made mention of a marriage rule generating a structure. It is not our intention to imply causality in the use of the term "generate." By the analysis of recurrent exchange behavior, the analyst is able to construct a structural model. Following Lévi-Strauss, we began by concentrating upon the exchange of women. Marriage rules are concise statements of how women move from group to group. It is in this sense that we have used the expression "marriage rules generate." The verification of the structure developed by the analyst consists of examination of other kinds of exchange behavior in the society in terms of the structure developed by the examination of the exchange of women. The kinds of exchange behavior which can be examined with a view toward confirmation of the structure are the exchanges of goods and services in ceremonial contexts other than marriage.

The procedure which we used begins with an analysis of the marriage rule. For example, in the case of the Tsimshian, we began with an explicit statement of the preference for marriage with mother's brother's daughter. Following Lévi-Strauss (1969 [1949]:

422-55) and Edmund Leach (1961a[1951]:54-104), we proposed a structural model to represent this pattern of exchange of women. We then sought confirmation of this structural model in accounts of life-crisis events in which a variety of exchanges took place. The most significant of these events in the Tsimshian case constituted potlatches. By ordering the data on Tsimshian potlatches in terms of the structural model developed from the marriage rule relating to the exchange of women, we found that the Tsimshian potlatch became comprehensible. This procedure constitutes a verification of the structure proposed for the Tsimshian. At times, this verification involves a modification of the structure, as in the case of the Haida and Tlingit to be discussed below.

In the above example, we were concerned with the relationship between Tsimshian structure and the specific form which the Tsimshian potlatch takes. The six Northwest Coast societies discussed in this book are all characterized by ceremonial events accompanied by the giving away of enormous quantities of goods. All of these societies have features in common which will emerge in the course of our discussion and which will enable us in the conclusion to talk about the potlatch type of society. At the same time the potlatch in each of these societies represents a specific type of exchange system which is directly related to the structural model built for each society.

The ethnographies on the societies which we have selected for examination—Tsimshian, Tlingit, Haida, Nootka, Kwakiutl, and Bella Coola—are particularly rich, perhaps the richest in the ethnographic literature of North America. Among the ethnographers who produced them are some of the early leaders of American anthropology, men such as Boas, Sapir, and Swanton. The area has continued to be investigated since the time of these men; the results are voluminous and include data on every aspect of culture.

One could examine this material with a view toward elucidating some of the significant theoretical developments in American cultural anthropology in the past fifty years. Early issues such as the "evolutionary" sequence of matrilineal to patrilineal descent which concerned Boas and others were played out in this material. The construction of a methodology by which a time perspective might be developed for aboriginal cultures; the relationship of primitive art and mythology to other aspects of culture; and the relationship between individual personality configurations were developed by people who primarily utilized Northwest Coast materials. It is interesting to note that the work of Mauss, who also drew heavily upon Northwest Coast material in discussing various kinds of exchange in his *Essai sur le don,* was largely ignored by American anthropologists.[1] Though American and French anthropologists relied upon the same ethnographic material, it is clear that they had little effect upon one another.

There have been a few attempts to study the Northwest Coast in a comparative framework, systematically examining the regional variations (Boas; Sapir). In our comparative investigation of the variations within a single type, we have followed the method of controlled comparison advocated and used by Eggan in his study of the western Pueblos and by Richards in her study of variations occurring in the matrilineal belt of Central Bantu societies (Eggan 1954; Richards 1950).

Despite the fact that four different language families are represented on the Northwest Coast, this area has nevertheless been considered as a unified culture area by all analysts. The six societies discussed below include members of all four families. The central unifying feature of the cultures of the Northwest Coast is the potlatch and its associated phenomena, but there are also critical similarities in the economic basis, art styles, mythology, and religious ceremonialism. With respect to social organizaton, however, there are major differences. Of the societies analyzed below, three have matrilineal descent systems—Tsimshian, Haida, and Tlingit— and three have ambilateral descent systems—Nootka, Kwakiutl, and Bella Coola. The matrilineal societies are clear exemplars of the

[1] Only Barnett cites Mauss's work (1938b).

most extreme form of the matrilineal complex, though none were treated in detail by Schneider and Gough in their work on matrilineal kinship (1961). The presence of inheritance and succession from mother's brother to sister's son, of avunculocal residence, and of Crow kinship terminology (for two out of three of our examples) makes these matrilineal societies extremely interesting in relation to recent thinking about the structural features of matrilineal descent. No less interesting are the three ambilateral societies. When these societies were first investigated, the concept of an ambilateral descent system and ambilateral descent groups had not been developed. Since then Davenport, Goodenough, Murdock, and Firth have sharpened the understanding of this type of descent system (Davenport 1959; Goodenough 1955; Firth 1957, 1963; Murdock 1960). The three ambilateral societies support the contention that groups based upon ambilateral descent are transgenerationally stable. The structural implications of ambilateral descent emerge clearly from our analysis.

The six societies discussed here may be examined with regard to another interesting variable—that of the marriage pattern. In Lévi-Strauss's terms three of them exhibit elementary structures and three of them exhibit complex structures (1965). The three matrilineal societies all have preferential cousin marriage and thus constitute elementary structures. However, among these three, the Tsimshian have matrilateral cross-cousin marriage while the Tlingit and the Haida have patrilateral cross-cousin marriage. An avalanche of theoretical debate has been engendered by the subject of cross-cousin marriage rules and their implications. Occurrence of matrilateral cross-cousin marriage in a matrilineal society is very rare and raises the issue of the structure of affect in relation to the structure of authority (Homans and Schneider 1955). The relation of matrilateral cross-cousin marriage to rank and hierarchy posed by Leach will be seen recapitulated in the Tsimshian (Leach 1951). Patrilateral cross-cousin marriage, as found among the Haida and the Tlingit, has also been the subject of much discussion. Needham

has questioned the very viability of such a system, while Homans
and Schneider and Lévi-Strauss have debated its association with
matrilineal descent (Lévi-Strauss 1963:322; Homans and Schneider
1955). Lévi-Strauss has also contended that with patrilateral cross-
cousin marriage one gets only short cycles of exchange, while matrilateral cross-cousin marriage produces long cycles of exchange,
providing the basis through marriage for long-term alliances (1969
[1949]:ch. 27). Needham has argued that, logically, patrilateral
cross-cousin marriage reduces a social structure to a moiety system.
Lévi-Strauss has also discussed the relationship between moiety
structures and three-sided structures. We shall show that patrilateral cross-cousin marriage among the Haida and the Tlingit gen-
erates a structure which is stable and has transgenerational integrity, and that Needham's announcement of its nonexistence was
precipitous. The structural implications of patrilateral cross-cousin
marriage in these two societies make it very likely that such a
marriage preference can only be accommodated in a matrilineal
descent system. Lévi-Strauss's premise concerning the necessity of
short cycles as a structural concomitant of patrilateral cross-cousin
marriage is based upon the view that alliances rest solely upon the
exchange of women. Our view focuses upon the exchange of many
other things in addition to women. It has enabled us to discover
that long-term alliances between groups practicing patrilateral
cross-cousin marriage exist which involve the exchanges of many
things, including women. Lastly, both two-sided and three-sided
structures exist for these societies but it is the latter, the three-sided
structure, which emerges in the potlatch, which constitutes the
significant ordering structure.

Societies with ambilateral descent systems are characterized by a
particular type of complex marriage structure. The essence of this
structure involves what we call marriage strategy. We will show
that a consistent structure underlies both ambilateral descent and
this type of complex marriage structure.

These are the variations among the six societies studied which make their investigation so relevant to theoretical concerns today and therefore justify their examination. They must be seen as variations upon a single theme constituting the single underlying structure throughout the Northwest Coast, a structure we refer to as the potlatch model.

One important issue must be discussed at this point. The ethnographic data which we utilize for our study were recorded over a span of eighty years, a period of considerable and continual change in the area. Most of the potlatches which we shall describe were not witnessed by the ethnographers but were recalled for them in detail by informants many years after their occurrence. The question of the comparability of the data arises, and also what kind of structure is revealed by those data. We do not claim that structures are characterized by eternal existence. We feel that the data reveal the variations of an underlying structure. Our examination and analysis of actual events has verified that structure. This in no way implies that the structure is pristine, or an eternal mental construct which retains its characteristics indefinitely. The conceptualization of an underlying structure satisfies the requirements of an adequate theory since it accounts for many features which have heretofore been seen as unrelated. We feel that, for the time period covered by the ethnographic accounts, the structure remained more or less in existence.

It is clear that the major focus of this book is theory. We began with an interest in the potlatch as a type of exchange, and in the process of examining the Northwest Coast materials we developed a model which we call the potlatch type of society.

The questions posed at the beginning of this chapter acted as the stimuli for our investigation. What follows in this book demonstrates the kinds of answers that a theory of structure and exchange can provide.

CHAPTER II. *THE TSIMSHIAN*

TSIMSHIAN SOCIETY is ordered in terms of a structure which relates to the presence of a rule of preferential mother's brother's daughter marriage. This marriage rule serves systematically to separate wife-givers from wife-takers, creating a structure of generalized exchange which, among the Tsimshian, involves a hierarchical arrangement of groups. Tsimshian potlatching involves the same structure.

The Tsimshian, who speak a Penutian language, inhabit the areas surrounding the Nass and Skeena rivers in northern British Columbia. They are divided into four phratries, which in turn are subdivided into clans; these are subdivided into lineages or houses (families). The kinship nomenclature is of the Iroquois type.

Most, though not all, phratries are represented in all villages (Garfield *et al.* 1951:19). Phratries are exogamic and thus constitute the reference unit with respect to marriage. They appear to have no significance with regard to political organization, economics, or warfare. They are referred to by animal names and are associated in Tsimshian mythology with animal forms which are also used as crests. These crests may not be exclusive to particular phratries. Though members of a phratry speak of a common origin which is referred to in their myths, in behavioral terms they do not recognize one another as kin. There is indication of unrelated clans having amalgamated in the past to form phratries (Boas 1916: 486 f.; Barbeau 1917; Sapir 1915b:20-21). There are no totemic associations with the crest animal; people are not considered to have descended from the animal and there are no food taboos associated with it. However, in Tsimshian mythology, the characteristics of the animal are associated with the phratry.

Clans are named groups that tend to be localized. Though they may be found in different villages, they are not nearly so dispersed as phratries. The clans found on the Nass River are by and large not recapitulated on the Skeena. However, some Skeena River groups do conceptualize kin relationships with certain Nass River groups, though all the clans of a phratry do not envision such relationships. Phratries within a town are ranked, as are clans in a particular phratry.[1] Where ethnographers note that a clan is dominant, we tend to find that it is also most numerous and of highest rank and its chief is the town chief. Thus the rank of a clan is dependent on the number of people in that clan within the town.

Clans, like phratries, are also associated with particular crests. The crests owned by many clans within a phratry are those which have reference to the phratric totem. Crests are also owned by the individuals in the several leadership positions within clans or localized sections of clans.

The lineage or "house" is the basic residential and kin unit. It consists of people who occupy a single house and are under the political leadership of a house chief. The lineage constitutes an

---

[1] Both Barbeau and Sapir present the ranking of clans for particular tribes which inhabit winter villages (Sapir 1915b; Barbeau 1917). For example, the following table presents the clan composition of the Gilodza tribe (Boas's Giludzar) from Barbeau (1917:402-3).

Rank	Lineage	Number of houses	Clan	Phratry
"Royal Family"	Nialslkamik	3	Sky	Fireweed
"Councilors' Class" (relative rank fluctuates greatly)	1. Niasq'amdzis (before advent from abroad of present royal house this family is said to have enjoyed royal standing)	3		Eagle
	2. Niaskse'net	3	Gitlaxksadin	Fireweed
	3. Niaskwe'xs	6	Gitksadzc	Fireweed
	4. Niaspints		Gitlaxksadin	Fireweed
	5. Niaskimas	4		Raven
	6. Lais	3		Wolf

Plus several families of lower rank from the extinct Gitwilksabe tribe.
Boas refers to the Fireweed phratry as the Bear phratry (Boas 1916:480-82, 483).

economic unit under the direction of the chief, the occupants of the house being subordinate to him. All resource properties belong to lineages. The lineage constitutes the unit which potlatches under the direction of the house chief, who marshals its resources. By virtue of the rule of avunculocality, the lineage usually comprises the chief, his immediate family, unmarried children, his married maternal nephews, and their nuclear families.

This kinship structure of phratry, clan, and lineage or "house" is cross-cut by a system of residential subdivisions. The tribe is the largest residential unit. It occupies a particular area and has a winter village or town which is its population center during that part of the year. At other times the people disperse to fishing stations, berrying grounds, etc. The tribe functions as a political unit with a head chief.

Ethnographers who have studied the Tsimshian have uniformly supported their division into ranked strata. Garfield (1939:177) has referred to these strata as virtual castes, though Boas (1916:498) refers to them as classes and Barbeau (1917) uses both terms interchangeably. Unquestionably, rank differences exist in this society and are related to differential control over resources and command over personnel. However, ranked strata fixed in their relation to one another, as suggested by Boas, Garfield, and Barbeau, are not evident when the ethnographic material provided by these investigators is examined and reanalyzed. Their ethnographic material supports, rather, the following picture.

With regard to rank, its indicators in terms of names, crests, and other nonmaterial privileges are usually passed on in family lines. However, their acquisition must be validated by ceremonial means. These indicators of rank are limited in number. They are embodied in the leadership positions of the kin units of various magnitudes—head of the "house," whose name is that of the house, and heads of the clan and tribe. The head of the tribe is the head of the dominant clan of the village. These leadership positions should pass from generation to generation according to rules of succession which in turn are also bound to the ceremonial system of exchange constituting the potlatch. Further, these positions of leadership in the various levels of kin units are in turn ranked with respect to one another (Boas 1916:496 f.; Sapir 1915b:4; Garfield *et al.* 1951: 26 f.). But a central feature of the Tsimshian rank system, according to our analysis of the ethnographic data, is that there are areas of flexibility which permit the possibility of manipulation by the distribution of property.

The following are those features regarding marriage among the Tsimshian which the ethnographic sources consistently agree upon. Each of the four named phratries is exogamous. The sources consistently speak of a preference but not a prescription for mother's brother's daughter marriage (Garfield *et al.* 1951:23; Garfield 1939:231-32; Boas 1916:440). Marriages are spoken of as alliances between lineages or kin groups. Mentioned, but not stressed, are a number of subsidiary points. For example, sister exchange is mentioned in two separate contexts, the first involving the exchange of sisters by two great chiefs (Boas 1916:510), the second in a genealogy (Garfield 1939:279). There is also a tendency for chiefs to marry outside of their tribal villages.

Given these ethnographic features, a particular structural model generated by preferential matrilateral cross-cousin marriage seems to suggest itself. This kind of structure has been proposed by Leach in his discussion of the Kachin (1951). It consists of an arrangement of groups interrelated by matrilateral cross-cousin marriage, in which particular groups are defined as wife-givers and wife-takers in relation to one another. We will borrow the Kachin term and refer to this as the *mayu-dama* type of structure. The term *mayu-dama* has several connotations. One is marriage between equals; the other implies rank differences between marriage partners. Among the Tsimshian the structure is characterized by a consistent difference between wife-givers and wife-takers.

This view is supported by the following evidence. Each village or tribe has its own particular ranking order. (See footnote 1, p. 11.)

Since equals usually marry equals, tribal chiefs or head chiefs of
villages will probably marry women from other villages. The son
of a chief will move to his own mother's brother's village, succeed
to the mother's brother's position of leadership, and marry his
daughter. A circular marriage pattern may be present involving
the chiefs of different villages and, by definition, of different phratries. This last must encompass at least three or all four of the
phratries. Sister exchange is also a possibility (which means that
mother's brother's daughter would equal father's sister's daughter).

Intravillage marriage, in line with the ideal of mother's brother's
daughter marriage and the evidence of the ranking of those phratries and clans present within a village, logically implies a ranked
type of relationship in which lineage alliances through marriage
between greater chiefs and lesser chiefs reflect the differences in
rank which are present. It appears likely that women marry upward, that wife-receivers are of higher rank than wife-givers, and
that people at the bottom rung are marrying slaves (see Diagram
A). It must be kept in mind that the units involved here are lineages from different phratries, since phratries are exogamous. Several
kinds of evidence support the view that women marry upward.
Among the Tsimshian, the father's lineage performs a number of
significant services at birth, initiation, and burial for which the
members are reciprocated with property (high rank offers services,
low rank returns property). At the lowest stratum of society are
slaves, and there are frequent reports of men of the lower stratum
marrying slaves. We hypothesize that slave men have no regularized
access to women.

Though there is little direct information on specific marriages
to demonstrate conclusively the existence of this model, the available evidence on marriage presented supports it, as does the material on rank which follows.

The picture presented by earlier ethnographers regarding rank
was in terms of rigid castes or classes of chiefs, commoners, and
slaves. The data on social organization, however, present a very

Diagram A. MoBrDa Marriage, Tsimshian Pattern

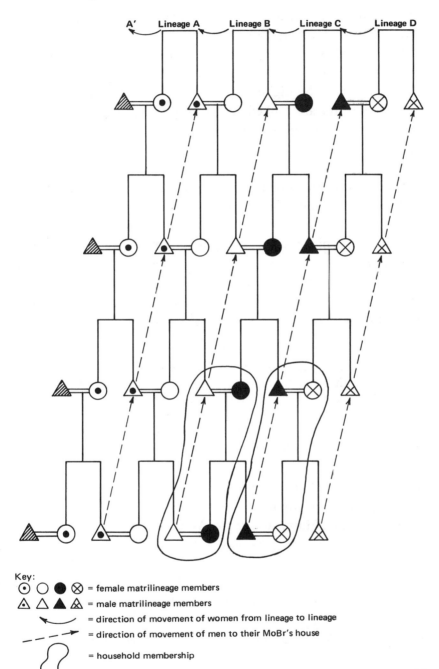

Key:
⊙ ○ ● ⊗ = female matrilineage members
△ △ ▲ △ = male matrilineage members
↶ = direction of movement of women from lineage to lineage
⇢ = direction of movement of men to their MoBr's house
⬤ = household membership

different picture, in which groups at every level are ranked with respect to one another. Thus in a tribe members of a house are ranked, as reflected in the names they hold. The highest-ranking name is the chief of the house. Houses within a clan are ranked and the chief of the highest house is the chief of the clan. Clans within a phratry are ranked, as are phratries within a tribe. The ranking of the phratries within two adjacent tribes may be very different. However, in all cases the chief of the highest-ranking phratry is the chief of the tribe. The picture of fixed classes presented by Boas and Garfield is inconsistent with our postulated model since a mother's brother's daughter marriage rule with fixed classes would produce a caste structure with no intermarriage between strata. Their picture does not conform to the ethnographic data. The ordered hierarchy of groups which is found among the Tsimshian is completely consistent with a *mayu-dama* structure. The marriages of particular concern are those of the chiefs at all levels, since such marriages represent alliances of special significance.

The head men of the tribe advised the chief in his choice of a wife or wives, arranging matches to increase the wealth and prestige of the chief, cement friendship and gain allies in case of warfare. A chief whose own kinswomen were the wives of another chief was reluctant to raid him or make trouble for him. . . . When the chief married, his leading tribesmen carried out the negotiations and made the marriage arrangements instead of his lineage (Garfield 1939:234).

Polygyny existed and chiefs could have as many as twenty wives (Garfield 1939:234; Boas 1916:420). Chiefs took wives from other tribes. These were women from another phratry, from the head lineage of that phratry and tribe. With matrilateral cross-cousin marriage, women would be moving in one direction, in a circle. There is a suggestion of this in Boas's statement that "during the past century the sister of each Legex [highest-ranking Tsimshian chief] married Dzebasa, a Gispawadweda [phratry], and chief of the Gitqxala [tribe]" (Boas 1916:522, footnote 3). Given polygyny, high chiefs must have also taken additional wives from lineages of other phratries within their own tribes. Lesser chiefs in a tribe took wives from lower-ranking lineages, women moving upward from lineage to lineage in a step pattern reminiscent of Leach's picture of the Kachin. In this case, surplus women at the top of the rank system became the wives of polygynous chiefs. In the material to follow, we shall note the way in which goods also move up, since a father's lineage is frequently recompensed in goods for services performed at various *rites de passage* throughout the lifetime of the individual.

Marriages sometimes occurred between people of widely differing ranks. They reveal the significant role which a father may play in raising the status of a child. Garfield notes that "a child who had one parent of a chiefly rank and one of common rank could not hope to secure recognition as a member of the higher class except through the most lavish giving of potlatches by his parent and himself" (Garfield 1939:232). Further, she mentions the marriage of Legex, the highest-ranking chief of the Tsimshian who married a beautiful commoner and "later elevated his daughter by a series of potlatches and power initiations until all the tribes grudgingly admitted that she was 'as high as the chief!' The Tsimshian still hold to the ideal of marriage between social equals but they fall far short of it in practice" (Garfield 1939:232-33).

Garfield at one point states that marriages between commoners and slaves are forbidden (Garfield *et al.* 1951:29), yet she elsewhere notes that a special term is applied to children, one of whose parents is of commoner rank and the other of slave status, indicating that mating occurred and possibly even marriage (Garfield 1939:178). Garfield also cites the existence of a term for individuals who had one chiefly parent and one parent of lower rank, and notes: "If either parent married beneath the chiefly rank the children automatically lost status, which may only be regained for them by liberal potlatching by their parents or 'uncle' " (Garfield 1939:177).

The model suggested herein for Tsimshian society is one in which wife-givers and wife-takers are clearly separate. Ethnographic evidence supports this construct. Initially, in the life cycle, an individual is involved in the interactions between two lineages, his own and his father's. After marriage, a third lineage enters the picture, that of his wife and his children. We have postulated that wife-takers are superior to wife-givers and thus one's father's lineage would be superior to that of one's wife and son.

Examination of the ethnographic data relevant to *rites de passage* reveals the following concerning lineage interactions. An individual is physically born in his father's house. The duties of tending his mother, severing the cord, and bathing him for the first time devolve on the father's lineage, that is, on his father's sister. She and the women of his father's lineage are recompensed by his mother and the women of his mother's lineage. Such compensation in the form of gifts which are given in return for services is not reciprocated by return gifts (Garfield 1939:220). This basic pattern of relationships with father's lineage, as will be seen, is recapitulated at *rites de passage* during the course of one's life. Father's lineage provides services which result in honor accruing to the child and the father's lineage is in turn given property.

The announcement of a birth is made by a male relative of the father's lineage or by the chief of the father's tribe. Groundhog skins are given by the announcer to each lineage head as the birth is announced. These groundhog skins are provided by the child's own lineage, which also pays the announcer directly for his services (Garfield 1939:221).

The first name given to a child is the property of his own matrilineage and phratry, though it may refer to the totemic symbols identified with or belonging to his father's phratry. Thus personal names frequently reveal father's lineage as well as the child's lineage (Sapir 1915b:27; Boas 1916:507 f.). Since a lineage controls a pool of such names, referring to father's crests, this would support our view concerning continuing alliances of wife-givers and wife-takers. This first name is formally announced by a member of the father's own lineage, who is compensated for his services with items such as a slave, a large canoe, or costly garments (Boas 1916:511; Garfield 1939:222). A child's name is changed on several subsequent occasions: at the age of two when his hair is first tied, when he becomes a youth, when he becomes a man, and finally when he takes a chief's name. At these times, a member of his father's lineage announces the new name and he is always recompensed for this service by some type of gift (Boas 1916:511-12). Services are performed by members of the father's lineage at the ceremonial tattooing of hands or body (Boas 1916:512), at ear perforation for a girl (Boas 1916:531), at lip perforation for a girl (Garfield *et al.* 1951:25), and at initiation into secret societies (Garfield 1939:301), these services being reciprocated with gifts.

Marriage represents the point at which the linkage between ego's lineage and his wife's lineage is renewed. When mother's brother's daughter marriage occurs, the alliance recapitulates one made by mother's brother in the previous generation, ego's lineage continuing to stand as wife-taker. By this time, ego has already shifted his residence to the home of his mother's brother. This shift places him physically in the same location as the male members of his lineage. Though he moves from the location of his father's lineage by virtue of this shift, he continues to maintain ties with his father's lineage throughout his lifetime, and these ties are perpetuated after his death in the funeral procedures.

A man is said to have special access to the wife of his mother's brother during the latter's lifetime (Garfield 1939:234). She becomes his wife after the mother's brother dies. Since it is likely that she is considerably older than ego, she can choose a secondary wife for him, usually a younger woman from her own lineage, who advances to the position of senior wife after the latter's death. This structurally brings about the same result as mother's brother's daughter marriage, as the alliance between two lineages is perpetuated transgenerationally (Garfield 1939:235).[2] These transgenerational alliances between two lineages as a result of marriages are

---

[2] Lévi-Strauss draws the same conclusion about mother's brother's wife marriage, noting that "among the Garo . . . the son-in-law marries his widowed mother-in-law, 'thus assuming the anomalous position of husband to both mother and daughter' " (Lévi-Strauss, 1969 [1949]:273). This only accords with matrilineal descent.

specifically referred to by Garfield (Garfield *et al.* 1951:23; Garfield 1939:232). Negotiations concerning a marriage are conducted by the boy's maternal relatives, his father having only a peripheral role in the negotiations though he does perform services at the celebration and may exchange gifts with the father of the girl (Garfield 1939:233; Boas 1916:532). The initiative is on the part of the boy's maternal kin who begin their negotiations by a gift offering, which constitutes part of what the ethnographers refer to as the purchase price. Its acceptance signifies the girl's relatives' acceptance of the suit. Then the boy and members of his lineage go to the bride's house: a mock fight of considerable severity ensues. Eagle down is then spread to signify peace. Dancing and a feast follow at which time the boy's lineage pays the remainder of the "purchase price." However, according to Boas, "In the evening the girl's clan relatives give a considerable amount of property to the bridegroom which he distributes among his own clan relatives according to the amount which they have contributed to the purchase money" (Boas 1916:532; see also Garfield 1939:233).

As a result of the marriage, the boy's lineage obtains the services of a female for sexual and economic purposes. Though children do belong to the lineage of the wife, their economic contribution as juveniles to their father's lineage is referred to. A woman, however, continues to be counted as a member of her own lineage after marriage and is not incorporated into that of her husband.

A man's children are born in his lineage house, at which point his own lineage becomes a "father's lineage" to the lineage of his wife and children. If he has married his mother's brother's daughter, then his own lineage continues in his generation to be father's lineage (superior) to the lineage to which they were father's lineage in the generation of his mother's brother. This further supports our hypothesis of transgenerational alliance of lineages through marriages. (Note: wife does not shift residence in this system.)

The building or repair of a house is another point which shows the interaction and interplay of lineages (Garfield 1939:276; Mayne

1862:264). The members of the lineage having their house built provided the bulk of the material and labor as well as the gifts and the food to be distributed when it was completed (Garfield 1939: 276). However, there were certain services and prerogatives alloted to the lineage of the father of the clan house-head and that of the fathers of other men holding important names who were to live in the house. These were: preparation of the site, carving of the house posts, and, most importantly, the right to carve a totem pole to stand in front of the house (Garfield 1939:276, 326; Barbeau 1929: 7). These various services performed by father's lineage were reciprocated with gifts from ego's lineage at the potlatch held after the completion of the work.

The final event at which father's lineage plays a critical role is at burial. The services involved in burial are provided by the father's lineage. The women of the father's lineage wash the body of the deceased and wail for him while the men of the father's lineage prepare the coffin and dig the grave (Boas 1916:512). They receive marmot skins and blankets for these services (Boas 1916: 534).

The relationship between ego's lineage and that of his wife and children—the lineage toward which he stands as wife-taker and father—is characterized by the same kinds of exchanges of goods and service, except that ego's lineage in this context stands in the superior position of father's lineage.

During childhood, while a son remains in his father's house, the father may occasionally sponsor or contribute to the son's ceremonials. However, the role of mother's brother in regard to his sister's son becomes the crucial relationship as the child grows older, his own lineage becoming solely responsible for his social welfare (Garfield 1939:196; Garfield *et al.* 1951:25). The social position of the children remains of concern to the father. A son has access to any resource area where his father had hereditary rights as long as his father is alive. This is for his own sustenance but not for use in potlatching (Garfield *et al.* 1951:17). From the point of view of sentiment, the Tsimshian conform to the classic matrilineal pattern. Fathers are said to love their sons, as Boas notes: "It is rather striking that in hardly any of these cases is there any mention of an intimate love between the uncle and nephew. On the other hand, the relations between parents and children, particularly between father and child, are described as most intimate" (Boas 1916:425-26).

Examination of the major ceremonial institutions involving exchanges and distribution of goods not only serves to illuminate aspects of the social structure which may not be clear from other contexts but also presents the dynamic organizational aspect of that structure. In accordance with the procedures outlined in our introduction, we must now examine the potlatch among the Tsimshian in order to confirm our theoretical model of this society.

The term *ya ku*, or potlatch, as used among the Tsimshian has been variously defined by ethnographers. The parameters of the meanings attached to the term vary. For example, Boas limits the term "potlatch" to those "great festivals to which outsiders are invited" (Boas 1916:537), although in another section of the same report he refers to such great festivals only as festivals and not as potlatches (Boas 1916:439). Garfield points out the difficulty of distinguishing between potlatches and supernatural power ceremonies. In the ethnographic data certain elements are basic to the potlatch: a series of ceremonial events and multipurpose rituals take place in which a host and his kin group, contributors of various kinds of goods, and invited guests interact according to specified roles; public announcements are made and events such as a *rite de passage* take place at which the social standing of specified individuals is advanced; and goods are distributed.

The essence of the potlatch is that it is a ceremonial event, employing every mode of symbolic expression in Tsimshian culture to make statements about the panoply of social relationships and statuses in that culture, including the changes in status as individuals go through the life cycle, the ordered relationships between kin groups, and the system of rank difference in and between groups. During the potlatch ceremonial these three types of relationships are intimately interrelated.

The most important potlatches invariably involve a memorial for a dead chief and the erection of his grave post, the succession to his chiefly office, and the assumption of his chiefly names by his successor. These events usually occur as part of the same potlatch. Other events which may be included in the same potlatch, or may instead be the occasion for separate potlatches, are the building of a new house, initiation into secret societies and acquisition of supernatural power, and a change of name. Though the public ceremonies attending the perforation of ears, nose, and lips resemble the potlatch, there is no clear indication of whether they are part of the potlatch or constitute separate ceremonies. Wiping out an insult or shameful event is also the occasion for a potlatch.

Several feasts and exchanges mark the occasion of a marriage. Garfield notes: "Gifts were again exchanged between the in-laws and food and gifts were provided for guests. . . . Speeches were made by relatives, who vied in the recital of their family histories. Songs, dances and dramatic skits entertained the guests and reimpressed them with the importance of lineage possessions" (Garfield *et al.* 1951:24). Structurally, therefore, a marriage seems like a potlatch.

Chart A is a schematic representation of an actual potlatch held by Nisgane to mark the end of a mourning period for his predecessor and the assumption of the latter's name and position; it indicates the events included in the Tsimshian potlatch best described in the ethnographic sources. The potlatch of Nisgane has as its formal purpose the accession of the host to a new name and status, and as its subsidiary purposes the initiation into religious societies and the establishment of "contact" with the supernatural, marking changes in status for several individuals of Nisgane's matrilineage.

If Chart A is examined in terms of interactions and exchanges,

Chart A. A Tsimshian Potlatch

| Other clans of host's tribe | Host (Raven) | Host clan (Raven) | Host's father's clan (Wolf) | = | Initiate's father's clan |

A. GATHERING PROPERTY

Invites clan to feast
to announce plan
and apportion work
and contributions ————————→

←———————————————————————— Sisters' husbands
bring canoe-load
of olachen and
firewood

Sister's son
←——————— brings olachen;
assists in fishing

Two days of berry ————————→
picking

←——————— Cloth to women
picking berries

B. OFFICIAL ANNOUNCEMENT OF POTLATCH TO OWN TRIBE

Invites to a feast
←——————— for formal potlatch ————→
announcement

Invites to a feast
to request liquor ——→

Feast ——→

Gifts ——→

C. INTRODUCTION OF THREE OF HOST'S SISTER'S CHILDREN TO SUPERNATURAL POWERS

Invites own tribe
←——————— and father's clan ———————————————————————————————————→
of initiates

Three father's sisters sing songs
←———————————————————— and dance

Father: gift for service

Chief of host's tribe
sings and blows ————————→
power on children

←——————— Blanket

Host and his brother
give to guests:

Each chief ←——————— 4 blankets

Each person of 1 blanket and
lower rank but ←— moose skin
of recognized
standing

Initiates dance ←————————————— Father's sisters assist

24

Chart A (continued)

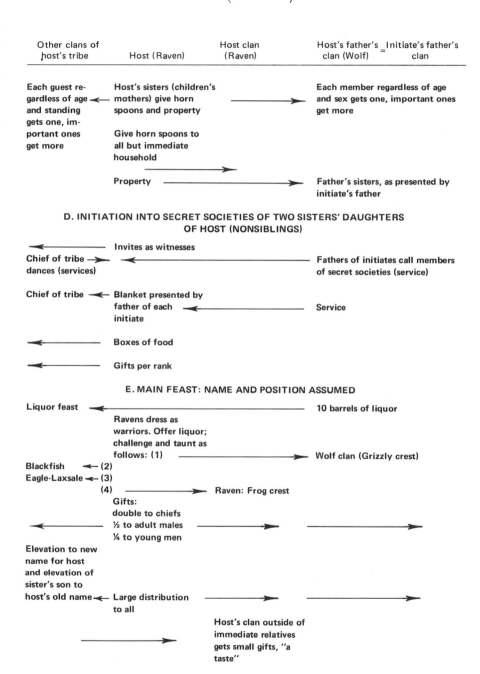

Other clans of host's tribe	Host (Raven)	Host clan (Raven)	Host's father's clan (Wolf) = Initiate's father's clan

Each guest regardless of age ◄— and standing gets one, important ones get more

Host's sisters (children's mothers) give horn spoons and property ————►

Each member regardless of age and sex gets one, important ones get more

Give horn spoons to all but immediate household ————►

Property ————————————► Father's sisters, as presented by initiate's father

D. INITIATION INTO SECRET SOCIETIES OF TWO SISTERS' DAUGHTERS OF HOST (NONSIBLINGS)

◄———— Invites as witnesses

Chief of tribe ——► ◄————————————— Fathers of initiates call members
dances (services) of secret societies (service)

Chief of tribe ◄— Blanket presented by
father of each ◄———————— Service
initiate

◄———— Boxes of food

◄———— Gifts per rank

E. MAIN FEAST: NAME AND POSITION ASSUMED

Liquor feast ◄————————————————— 10 barrels of liquor

Ravens dress as
warriors. Offer liquor;
challenge and taunt as
follows: (1) ————————► Wolf clan (Grizzly crest)

Blackfish ◄— (2)
Eagle-Laxsale ◄— (3)
(4) ————► Raven: Frog crest
Gifts:
double to chiefs
◄———— ½ to adult males ————► ————►
¼ to young men

Elevation to new
name for host
and elevation of
sister's son to
host's old name ◄— Large distribution ————► ————►
to all

Host's clan outside of
immediate relatives
————————► gets small gifts, "a
taste"

Source: Garfield 1939: 198–201, 299–301, 305–9.

the patterns of relationship between kin groups are revealed. The potlatch provides a support for the earlier points made concerning the structural relationship of father's lineage to ego's lineage. In this case, the Raven lineage of the host stands as wife-givers to the Wolf lineage, which is the father's lineage. Members of the Wolf lineage are honored as father's lineage in a number of ways. For example, they have the honor of announcing names, they have the honor of giving property, and they are first in order of receipt of gifts. Garfield notes: "A man who was planning a potlatch honoured his father's lineage by requesting assistance" (Garfield 1939: 326). The father's lineage for ego and for the initiates, his sister's children (succeeding generation of ego's lineage), is the same, reiterating our points about the transgenerational alliance between lineages through marriage.[3] The host lineage does not appear in the role of father's lineage at any point in this potlatch. Neither the host's wife nor his children are assigned any important role. At any given potlatch, only two of the three units which form the *mayu-dama* structure are interacting. Within the context of the potlatch, the services performed by "father's lineage" parallel those mentioned previously. Nowhere in the ethnographic account of Nisgane or his potlatch does Garfield indicate awareness of the structural significance of this patterned interaction between ego's lineage and his father's lineage.

The examination of the exchanges also supports the distinctions between ego's lineage, father's lineage, and spouse's lineage. Contributions of goods and services from ego's lineage are not returnable except in terms of the prestige accruing to the group by virtue of the potlatch (Garfield 1939:198, 193). Assistance and contributions from father's lineage and spouse's lineage were recompensed

[3] It is nowhere mentioned that the women of Nisgane's lineage (Raven) consistently marry Wolf men. At his ear perforation the name of his father's lineage is *not* given, but his father's name is Lais (Garfield 1939:195). Lais is a Wolf name (but of a different tribe) (Garfield 1939:206). "In distributing Chief Niaswexs received first, then all the Wolf men, as was customary when Ravens gave a feast" (Garfield 1939:301), indicating the superiority of Wolves as father's lineage to Ravens.

with goods (Garfield 1939:198, 199, 193-94; Garfield *et al.* 1951: 17).

The potlatch as a ceremony marks succession to leadership, which involves name change and movement to a position of rank as a leader. Nisgane's succession apparently was unchallenged, but the ethnographic data indicate that this is not always the case. If there were two or more contending heirs, the first to accumulate property would potlatch and gain the name, position, and rank. Obviously such an individual had the support of others in the lineage to enable him to accumulate the necessary property quickly. Garfield notes: "When there was a dispute the man who could get his wealth together first and take charge of his predecessor's funeral was most apt to be recognized. In order to do this, he had to have the support of most of his relatives, since few men had sufficient means to assume such responsibilities single handed" (Garfield 1939:181).[4] His acceptance as the new holder of the name and position comes when the guests he has invited to the potlatch accept his gifts for the service of witnessing his accession to position. Nisgane's potlatch involved his succession to a position of leadership. At the same potlatch, his sister's son took the name that Nisgane had previously held and his other sister's children acquired names and memberships in secret societies, these marking their movement in the rank system of the society, "the rank of the person being the higher the more frequently he has gone through the [initiation] ceremonies" (Boas 1890:854).

The rank positions of individuals and groups being called upon to act as witnesses are accorded recognition. As noted, witnesses receive gifts for the service of witnessing Nisgane's claim to position. Equally important is the service which Nisgane's potlatch provides for the public acceptance of the rank of guests. Chiefs of

[4] Garfield provides a case of a dispute over succession where one nephew of the deceased took possession of the dwelling of the deceased and announced his intention to take charge of the funeral. His rival was not financially strong enough to compete and, chagrined by his defeat, moved to another tribe and later became its chief (1939:179-80).

other groups are accorded honor by virtue of the roles they play at
the potlatch. Nesewex, for example, the tribal chief, plays a central
role in the acquisition of supernatural power. Differential amounts
of property are given to chiefs as compared to others. The order
of taunting at the liquor feast is an indication of the rank order of
phratries and subgroups for this particular occasion from the point
of view of Nisgane; the Wolf clan is taunted first because it is
Nisgane's father's lineage, the Blackfish clan second because it is
the clan of Chief Nesewex, the Eagle clan third, and other crests of
Nisgane's own clan last (Garfield 1939:217).

"The order in which the various houses in the tribe receive their
gifts at a potlatch is the surest clue to their respective ranks in the
native's mind" (Garfield 1939:178). At potlatches involving groups
and chiefs from more than two tribes or towns, order of distribution indicates the rank order of the chiefs and the tribes invited
(Garfield 1939:217, 204). Seating at a potlatch is also an indication
of rank order (Garfield 1939:217-18; Garfield *et al.* 1951:27; Boas
1916:541). At three points Garfield provides the rank order of the
nine Tsimshian tribes on the lower Skeena. One is at the distribution of gifts at the elevation of a great chief, occurring sometime in
the last half of the nineteenth century (Garfield 1939:204), the second at the distribution of gifts at an adoption ceremony in another
of the nine tribes (Garfield 1939:230), and the third at a funeral
potlatch (Garfield 1939:255). The list shows disagreement in the
order of rank, indicating the lack of absolute fixity and agreement
in conceptualization and operation of the rank order from the perspective of differing central personae. At the same time that they
were being taunted, the recognition of the rank of phratries and
subgroups was publicly announced. In the context of this potlatch,
and the Tsimshian material generally, rivalry, though clearly present, is subordinate to the mutual services which hosts and guests
provide each other. The individual's right to all claims, that is,
names, crests, privileges, and position, was established through the
potlatch (Garfield 1939:218). Nisgane and the men of his lineage

dress in warrior costume and taunt others in the challenge feast, symbolizing the rivalry, but the presence of others is vital to the Ravens (as Mauss has put it), for the Ravens need the others to make them great. Thus, though the Ravens taunt their guests, the latter are rewarded by the public announcement of their high rank and the recognition of respect due their rank. Rivalry, symbolic of cleavages, is one aspect of the potlatch; of equal significance are the exchanges which bind groups to one another.

A potlatch like that of Nisgane is merely one event in a continuing series of interactions between groups. At subsequent potlatches hosted by Nisgane's guests, Nisgane would be seated and accorded honor in proportion to his claim. Every group needs other groups as witnesses at their potlatches. The hosts at one potlatch were the guests at another and in this sense potlatches are reciprocal. Property distributed at one potlatch will therefore eventually be returned at another. Thus, there is an endless chain of potlatching and distributions of property between groups. A group which has been the recipient of property at potlatches is expected to potlatch within a reasonable length of time when the occasion arises. If this does not occur, then social relationships between the groups tend to become disrupted. Garfield presents an example of this in the account of the funeral of Chief Dzibasa, of the Gitxala tribe. At this funeral potlatch, all nine tribes of the lower Skeena were invited. Leaders of two of the tribes were not called upon to make speeches in honor of the deceased, and were not asked to be pallbearers as was customary. Thus, not having performed services, they were not recompensed with goods at the potlatch. This slight was the result of the fact that they had not potlatched within recent years and were felt to be in debt to the Gitxala tribe. They were not accorded the high rank which they felt should have been publicly accorded them at the important funeral of Dzibasa and directly suffered a loss of prestige by being overlooked at the funeral.

The amounts of property which are distributed at potlatches are conceptually separate from borrowing with interest, though individuals may borrow property with which to potlatch and this may be returned with interest. Careful analysis of the actual potlatches in the available ethnographic data supports this point, despite the fact that Garfield discusses interest and the "debtor-creditor" relationship of host and guest (Garfield 1939:214-15). She notes that informants would not give definite rates of interest comparable to those obtained from the Kwakiutl (Garfield 1939:214). She further notes that one of the factors determining the amount given was the relative status and wealth of the host and guest (Garfield 1939:214). An ambitious person would return a larger amount to increase the prestige of his own name (Garfield 1939:215). Garfield in her discussion of potlatch property tends to merge her discussion of the distribution of property at the potlatch proper with her discussion of the means by which property to potlatch with is accumulated.

A central feature of the Tsimshian rank system is its flexibility. Though the system of ranking within a group has been presented as one of rigid lines and fixed positions with rigid rules for inheritance and succession, the ethnographic evidence reveals a good deal of flexibility in practice.

Though Garfield's conceptualization of Tsimshian society conforms to that of Boas, emphasizing caste lines (Garfield 1939:177), she notes elsewhere that "the lack of rigid rules of pr'mogeniture prevented lineage heads, their close kin and heirs from forming as distinct a class as would have been the case had there been strict succession of the eldest" (Garfield *et al.* 1951:28). Succession is fairly flexible and is dependent upon the individual's ability to accumulate and distribute property, that is, to potlatch. Barbeau provides an excellent example of this when he indicates that "Nawle, also of the Larhasail phratry, was the earlier head chief of the Gitenmaks, whom Gitemraldo supplanted through his ability and success in the potlatch" (Barbeau 1929:67).

Garfield also notes that chieftainship shifts from house to house within a tribe and that "even middle class men have risen to prom-

'inence, as head chiefs and middle class names have become chiefly titles" (Garfield 1939:184; see also Barbeau 1929:98). Names which are symbolic representations of positions therefore rise and decline in importance according to the virtues of their bearers (Boas 1916: 510; see also Boas 1916:497-98).

Boas points to mobility in the social structure and flexibility in the rules of succession. For example, he mentions that "owing to warlike deeds and newly acquired wealth, individuals that belonged to the nobility but had the position of attendants evidently pushed forward into the head ranks from time to time; and it seems also plausible that some of the people of low ancestry may have pushed their way into the higher ranks . . . the social advancement of poor boys is an ever recurring theme in Tsimshian tales.[5] I am under the impression that the rigidity with which primogeniture is regarded, at least theoretically among the Kwakiutl, does not exist among the Tsimshian" (Boas 1916:498). Boas also mentions "the tendency for people of younger lines, or even for those whose relationship to the nobility is not known, to push their way into high and important positions" (Boas 1916:498).

The flexibility of the system is also manifested in changes of relative rank of groups (Barbeau 1917:402-3). This has varied with population movement. The historical record of movements of various tribal groups and subgroups throughout this area is reflected in the variations in rank of the four phratries as one goes from one area to another, as well as in the diachronic variations in rank mentioned in the data (see Barbeau 1917 and 1929). This is consistent with our hypothesis of *mayu-dama* marriage structure, since groups may be fitted into the structure at various points with ease.

---

[5] See Boas's recording of the tale Growing-Up-Like-One-Who-Has-a-Grandmother, in which the following elements occur: a poor orphan, the chief's nephew, goes through a series of adventures during which he performs supernatural tasks to marry a princess who turns out to be his uncle's daughter; he acquires supernatural power and accumulates goods with which to potlatch. During the potlatch, his uncle distributes goods and the "poor boy" receives a name and becomes a chief (Boas 1902:137-68).

The flexibility of the rank system is also consistent with the *mayu-dama* construct.

The underlying structure which we have presented for Tsimshian society is generated by a preferential rule for matrilateral cross-cousin marriage. The presence of this rule in a matrilineal society involves a conceptualization of father's lineage and son's lineage in successive generations. In Tsimshian society, wife-givers and wife-takers are hierarchically ordered, with father's lineage (wife-takers) the higher. This relationship between father's lineage and son's lineage is expressed in a variety of ceremonials marking *rites de passage* but finds its greatest expression in the potlatch. Ego's lineage gives women to father's lineage but in addition it gives goods to father's lineage which are conceived of as an exchange for the services performed by the father's lineage at various ceremonies. Thus both women and goods move upward. In a matrilineal society, goods are being exchanged for the fathering of children to perpetuate the matrilineage much like *urigibu* among the Trobrianders. Since women move upward, the highest chiefs have many wives and receive many goods which they subsequently redistribute at potlatches, thereby increasing their prestige. The potlatch emerges as a series of exchanges between affines. Other tribes may also be present to perform the service of witnessing and receive goods in return. Potlatches mark succession. After the death of a chief, the funeral potlatch is given by the most successful claimant to the position. He must succeed in accumulating sufficient goods from his matrilineal kinsmen in order to potlatch. Affines are not involved in the accumulation of goods or in the sponsorship of the potlatch since this is an affair of the matrilineage. The only function of affines in regard to succession is in the service of witnessing and thereby officially accepting the claimant as successor to the title and position.

The potlatch is central to the rank system. Claims to positions of rank may be validated only by successful potlatching. The lack of fixed rules of succession makes the ability to potlatch first an im-

portant requirement for succession. Several claimants may vie for
the position. He who potlatches first and validates his position
thereby succeeds to it. Individuals may also raise their rank within
their kin group by potlatching. In the few cases where great discrepancy in rank between parents exists, they may raise the rank
of their children by potlatching. Groups may raise their status by
potlatching, or it may be lowered by failure to potlatch sufficiently.
In these aspects of the rank system where mobility and shifts can
occur, potlatching is a central feature.

The ceremonial aspect of the potlatch involves the expression of
a certain amount of rivalry as revealed by the taunting songs.
Among the rivals are the lineages with whom the host lineage has
affinal connections as father's lineages—the lineages to which his
lineage gives women. The competition is mainly ritualistic in nature and does not involve destruction of property. The marriage
ceremony itself involves a mock battle, which is another symbolic
manifestation of the rivalry between affines who reappear at potlatches to be taunted.

In the Tsimshian potlatch can be seen a recapitulation of the
major structural features of Tsimshian society: alignment of kin
groups in accordance with their relationship through the pattern
of mother's brother's daughter marriage, the character of succession to positions of political leadership within the group, and the
ranking of groups with regard to one another. The lines of exchange of goods and services follow these structural alignments,
binding groups to one another while they serve to set them apart.

CHAPTER III. *THE TLINGIT AND THE HAIDA*

THE TLINGIT and the Haida exhibit many of the same structural features as the Tsimshian—rank, potlatch, matrilineal descent, and avunculocal residence. However, among the Tlingit and the Haida there is a preference for marriage with father's sister's daughter (FaSiDa) as contrasted with the Tsimshian preference for mother's brother's daughter (MoBrDa) marriage. This difference in marriage preference is related in turn to significant differences in the structures of these societies. The composition of groups, the nature of their relationship to one another, and their ranking systems reflect these structural differences. The exchanges which occur in potlatches are another dimension within which these differences can clearly be seen. Though the Tlingit and the Haida share the same over-all structural pattern, variations between them exist and are clearly revealed in comparisons of potlatching.

The Haida inhabit the area of Queen Charlotte Island and the southern tip of Prince of Wales Island. The Tlingit occupy the islands and coastal area north of the Haida, extending into Alaska. Both groups speak Athapaskan languages.

The Tlingit and the Haida are characterized by matrilineal moieties, clans, and lineages or houses. This series of kin groups, is cross-cut by residential units—towns—which are associated with a particular geographic territory. Individual rank distinctions are present and important. Residence is avunculocal and the kinship terminology is of the Crow type.[1]

The moieties into which the Tlingit and the Haida are both di-

---

[1] Murdock and Swanton differ in regard to the term for mother's brother's children used by the Haida. As Murdock's description and analysis on this point is the more detailed of the two, we are accepting Murdock's terminology and his classification of Haida terminology as Crow (see Murdock 1934b:379; Swanton 1905a:62-63).

vided—Raven and Wolf for the Tlingit and Raven and Eagle for
the Haida—are exogamous units. The clans into which these moieties are subdivided appear to have a feeling of kinship with one
another. Swanton provides two genealogies showing how the Haida
perceived the interrelations of the clans within their moieties
(Swanton 1905a:76, 93). There appear to be no other functions
beyond that of exogamy for these moieties.

The subunits within the moieties have been referred to as clans,
lineages, or houses. However, these kin units may better be seen as
ranged in several levels of segmentation reflecting greater or lesser
feeling of closeness of kin relationship. This construct more clearly
reflects the processes of fission and sometimes fusion which characterize these peoples (De Laguna 1952:3). Ownership of the same
or similar crests usually reflects close relationship. The numbers of
levels of segmentation vary for particular units. For example,
within the same moiety a particular kin unit may be found in only
one town, while another kin unit may be found to have three levels
of segmentation, being divided into several lineages or houses in
one town and several houses in two or three other towns. The term
"clan" has been used by Oberg and Murdock, the term "sib" by
De Laguna, and the term "family" by Swanton for the completely
localized kin unit as well as for that unit inclusive of three levels
of segmentation.

It is the localized kin unit, which we shall call the lineage, that
consists of one or more houses and that has rights to territories
for hunting and fishing, cemetery areas, house sites, and trade
routes, as well as the use of crests, personal names, house names,
and secret society rites. This is the unit with corporate and legal
functions which conducts warfare and participates in feuds, and
which makes alliances through marriage (De Laguna 1952:3, 4:
Oberg 1934:145 ff.; Swanton 1905a:69; Murdock 1934a:236-37).

The house unit comprises the membership of a single large
household, all living in one large dwelling under the leadership of
a house chief. The ownership of the dwelling is vested in the house-

hold, which might comprise over thirty persons including members of the chief's immediate family, the chief's maternal nephews and their nuclear families, his retainers and slaves (Swanton 1905a:69; Swanton 1905b:333). Young boys usually move to the houses of their mother's brothers whom they will eventually succeed. This rule of avunculocal residence produces a core of matrilineally related males whose spouses come from the opposite moiety (Swanton 1905a:66, 70, 50; Swanton 1905b:331). Separate houses within the same lineage may also possess somewhat different totemic crests, songs, stories, and personal names from those of the other houses within the same lineage (De Laguna 1952:4). The house chief acts as the trustee of the entailed "house" estate (De Laguna 1952:4) and directs the economic activities of his household (Murdock 1934a:237). He has absolute power over the members of his household and controls manpower. Houses may also initiate warfare under the leadership of the house chief. He outfits warfare expeditions in which his sisters' sons participate and the slaves and other property obtained goes to him (Swanton 1905a:69). The chief of the most prominent house within a lineage would be considered the chief of that lineage (De Laguna 1952:4; Murdock 1934a:237).

The town or tribe is the independent geographical unit. It consists of several lineages representing both moieties, though one lineage made up of a cluster of houses apparently dominates each town (De Laguna 1952:3). This dominant lineage is usually portrayed as the founder of the town. In the mythological past, only males of that lineage, it is said, were found in that town (Murdock 1934a: 236-37; Swanton 1905b:332; Swanton 1905a:66). The town is the largest politically coherent unit. The dispersed members of related lineages living in different towns do not unite as a single political entity, though they do have relations with one another as kin. They might join together in a raiding expedition but each war canoe represents a distinct house under its chief; the authority of all the canoes of one town is never placed under the control of a town chief. Each house retains its identity under its own leadership

(Swanton 1905b:334). In any given town, there are three levels of leadership: the house chief, the lineage chief—the most important house chief of that lineage in the town—and the town chief, who is the most important house chief of the dominant lineage of the town. The town chief among the Haida is called "Town Mother" or "Town Master." Among the northern Tlingit the power of the chief is not as fully developed as further south (De Laguna 1952:6).

Leadership within the town and lineage derives directly from leadership within a house. The rule of succession to leadership parallels the rule of inheritance, since succession to the position of house chief is coterminous with inheritance of name, wife, and dwelling of the deceased. The rule of succession ideally is younger brother followed by elder sister's eldest son. In actuality, there was a good deal of conflict and rivalry for succession to political office. Swanton notes: "I have elsewhere hinted that elder nephews succeeded to a position before younger. That was, however, rather a natural than a legal condition of affairs. In choosing a successor to any position the first requisite appears to have been success in amassing property. So it happened that elder sons were sometimes passed over by younger ones, or nearer relatives for those more remote" (Swanton 1905b:333). De Laguna also notes for the Tlingit that the potlatch is the "arena where potential heirs compete for coveted honors and where the victor triumphs over his rivals" (1952:6). The manner in which potlatch distributions are involved in succession will be discussed in detail below.

The political system apparently was a flexible rather than a rigid one, open to manipulation by rival claimants. Since the actual authority of the lineage chief depended upon his influence over his house chiefs, and ultimately upon his control over resources and his accumulation of property, "it is easy to see how a successful house chief might overshadow the nominal head of the family [lineage] and supplant him or come to found a new one" (Swanton 1905a:69; see also Murdock 1934a:237 on establishing an independent subclan). De Laguna notes that, among the Tlingit, "open and direct aggression within the group of kindred . . . lead[s] only to the splitting up of the sib and the emigration of one of the factions" (1952: 8).[2] These examples of competition for political office illustrate the process involved in lineage fission, a process well documented in the historical data concerning both societies (De Laguna 1960). The dispersal of subunits of formerly localized lineages is usually explained in the historical data in this way.

Rank differences have been associated with the Tlingit and the Haida, as they have with other societies on the Northwest Coast. Among the Northwest Coast societies, groups are usually ranked with respect to one another. However, among the Tlingit and the Haida we find that moieties are not ranked and rank differences between clans are minimal. Swanton lists for the Tlingit what he calls major clans of "national significance." He does not provide a ranking of those clans, nor of the clans he calls the highest (a slightly different listing). In both cases, these clans are the most widely dispersed and most numerous. Another group he mentions as being low caste (Swanton 1908a:408, 414, 427). Among the Haida, ranking of clans is even less specific, and Swanton notes that "one old woman said that . . . there were three Raven families [clans] that stood first, and three Eagle families" (Swanton 1905a: 70). We conclude, therefore, that ranking of clans was tenuous for the Haida and the Tlingit in comparison to the Tsimshian and certainly much less significant than for the ambilateral peoples to the south. There is no clear statement of the ranking of lineages or houses within a town, as is specifically stated for the Tsimshian, though, as noted above, the town chief was from the dominant lineage.

Within the house, rank differences are manifested in a graded series of names or titles. The highest title is the referent for the leader of the group. Those individuals holding the highest titles

[2] In the Tlingit genealogy provided by Durlach, further examples of the fission process are evident in the establishment of the Finn and Killer Whale houses (Durlach 1928).

usually carry out activities in behalf of the house group, utilizing house crests, dramatizing various ceremonial prerogatives frequently within the context of the potlatch cycle. Swanton sums up the relationship between rank, title, and position when he states that

after assuming his uncle's position,—a town, family, or house chief—he was entitled to choose one of his uncle's potlatch names. After that, he could add a new one every time he made a potlatch, but he did not take them necessarily from his uncle's list. He might make up a name commemorating some episode that redounded greatly to his own credit and reputation: such, for instance, as Unable-to-Buy, assumed by a chief whose opponent was unable to buy a copper from him; or He-became-the-Eldest, a name taken by a chief who received a place "over the heads" of his elder brothers. . . . Once acquired, all such names could be passed down as ordinary names in the family by being given to the man's son's sons, as above indicated (Swanton 1905a:118).

This quotation also substantiates our point about the flexibility of succession.

As noted above, the Tsimshian marriage structure is involved in the creation of marriage alliances which reflect differences in rank between groups. The marriage pattern among the Tlingit and the Haida, however, with its characteristic preference for marriage with father's sister's daughter, creates a different structural pattern, one in which logically consistent status difference between intermarrying lineages cannot be maintained over time.

None of the ethnographers of these two groups systematically explored the structural implications of the marriage rule, but merely presented the marriage pattern in terms of the exogamous moieties. Such a dual structural pattern in which women are exchanged between groups in successive generations is alluded to by De Laguna in her equation of mother's brother's wife and paternal aunt, implying that father's sister's daughter and mother's brother's daughter are the same person (De Laguna 1952:7). Many of the sources state that it is possible to marry one's mother's brother's daughter (Murdock 1934b:364; Swanton 1905a:70, 1905b:332). This possibility appears to be restricted only to chiefs.[3] The Haida and the Tlingit would seem therefore to conform to Needham's reduction of prescriptive father's sister's daughter marriage to a dual system involving exchange marriage between two brothers and two sisters (Needham 1958), which he arrives at on purely logical grounds. In fact, Needham uses De Laguna's ethnographic material to support his own analysis of patrilateral cross-cousin marriage. He relies solely on De Laguna and makes no reference to the work of Swanton or Durlach (Needham 1958:212). It appears that De Laguna's analysis is incorrect, for the weight of the evidence from Swanton, Durlach, and even De Laguna herself points in a different direction.

If one explores the implications of father's sister's daughter marriage as a preferred type, it is evident that ego's lineage is linked through marriage with at least two other lineages (see Diagram B). Though these other two lineages fall into the same moiety opposite to that of ego, they nevertheless retain their distinct identities. There is no overlap of personnel in them. Despite the existence of moities, it is the lineages that control and create marriage alliances. Each lineage is linked to two other lineages, different from one another, not simply to an opposite half of a moiety. With data abstracted from our analysis of an extensive Tlingit genealogy provided by Durlach and additional information on actual marriage alliances for the Haida from Swanton, we will support our interpretation of the structure.

A dual system would imply frequent brother-sister exchange, which does not appear in the ethnographic data with the exception

[3] Swanton, Murdock, and De Laguna use almost identical wording. Swanton notes: "He was expected to marry his uncle's widow when he succeeded. Often he married the daughter of the chief he was to succeed" (1905b:332). De Laguna notes: "A young man who is succeeding to the title of his maternal uncle would marry his uncle's widow, and she would be ideally his paternal aunt" (1952:7). Murdock states: "In any case, the preferred marriage is with a *sqan* [father's sister's daughter] of the same generation, though not necessarily a first cousin. A nephew who is in line to succeed to a chiefship, however, usually marries his *qagit* [mother's brother's daughter], i.e. the daughter of the maternal uncle whose place he is to take" (1934b:364).

Diagram B. FaSiDa Marriage, Tlingit-Haida Pattern

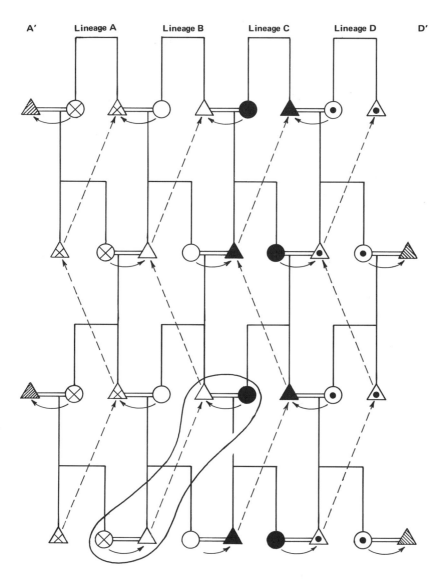

Key: See Diagram A, p. 15.

of one case in the Durlach genealogy (such a single exception is also mentioned for the Tsimshian, who have a preference for MoBrDa marriage). The data on kinship terminology support the conceptual separation of mother's brother's daughter and father's sister's daughter. The preferred marriage is always specifically stated as marriage with *at* (Tlingit) and *sqan* (Haida), who are father's sister or father's sister's daughter, and never with *kalk* (Tlingit) or *wucun* (Haida), the mother's brother's daughter.

The genealogy provided by Durlach, as one of the bases for her analysis of the kinship terminology, provides further support. It is nine generations in depth and includes over one hundred individuals. For thirty-eight marriages both the lineage and the clan affiliations of both partners are provided. The genealogy contains two actual father's sister's daughter marriages and one marriage with father's sister but no marriages to mother's brother's daughter. The ego of the genealogy is a member of the Eagle moiety, Kagwantan clan, and Finn house, while his father is of the Raven moiety, Ganaxadi-Chilkat clan, and Whale house. Table 1 illustrates the pattern of marriages for the Finn, Killer Whale, and Grizzly Bear houses of the Kagwantan clan. This clan has intermarried with

TABLE 1. *KAGWANTAN MARRIAGES*

Kagwantan clan	Ganaxadi-Chilkat clan			Luxnaxadi-Sitka clan		Lukaxadi (Chilkat) clan
	Whale house	Frog house	Sea Lion house	Whale house	Sea Lion house	
Finn house						
Female	4	1		1	1	1
Male	4	1		2		
Killer Whale house						
Female	1		1	1		
Male				2		2
Grizzly Bear house						
Female	1			1		

the Whale, Frog, and Sea Lion houses of the Ganaxadi-Chilkat clan, with the Whale and Sea Lion houses of the Luxnaxadi-Sitka clan, and with the Lukaxadi (Chilkat) clan. Table 2 illustrates the

TABLE 2. *GANAXADI-CHILKAT MARRIAGES*

Ganaxadi-Chilkat clan	*Kagwantan clan*					*Naanyaai clan*
	Killer Whale house	*Finn house*	*Drum house*	*Sitka Wolf (Juneau) house*	*Grizzly Bear house*	
Whale house						
Female		4	3	1		1
Male	1	4	1	2	2	

marriages of the Whale house of the Ganaxadi-Chilkat clan with various houses of the Kagwantan clan and with the Naanyaai clan.

Since the genealogy from which these data are abstracted derives from one ego, it is slanted in the direction of ego's own (mother's) clan and his father's clan. Nevertheless, each of these is clearly linked to a third clan through marriages, giving an over-all picture as follows:

	Ego	*Father*	
Luxnaxadi-Sitka (Raven) in Sitka	Kagwantan Finn (Wolf) in Chilkat	Ganaxadi-Chilkat Whale (Raven) in Chilkat	Kagwantan Drum (Wolf) in Sitka

This evidence must also be set against the fact that there are roughly twenty-nine clans in the Raven moiety and twenty-four in the Eagle moiety. The genealogy indicates that Finn house is a budding off from Killer Whale house, which had budded off from Grizzly Bear. These three houses are therefore closely related branches of the Kagwantan clan, in contrast to Kagwantan Sitka Wolf and Kagwantan Drum. This illustrates the process of segmentation mentioned earlier. The Finn house of the Kagwantan clan is located in Chilkat and is allied in marriage with two other houses, one in Chilkat (Ganaxadi-Whale) and another in Sitka

(Luxnaxadi). The Ganaxadi-Whale house in Chilkat, in addition to its linkage with the Finn house of the Kagwantan clan, is also linked to the Drum house of the Kagwantan clan in Sitka. Thus the data on marriages from the Durlach genealogy substantiate our view that, from the standpoint of any lineage, a tripartite, rather than a dual, structure is present. Ego's lineage is primarily linked to two others by separate sets of marriage alliances.

Essentially the same pattern of intermarriage with two other lineages occurs among the Haida. Swanton writes of this relationship: "Certain special families and towns were in the habit of intermarrying. This fact was expressed by saying that such and such a family [clan] were the fathers of such and such another one" (Swanton 1905a:67). With a consistent pattern of father's sister's daughter marriage, it is not possible for one group always to be in the position of fathers to another group, since wife-givers and wife-takers logically must reverse in successive generations. Swanton provides a series of distinct triads for the Haida; for each clan he presents the two in the opposite moiety with whom it is allied in marriage. When analyzed, the triads can be seen as linked into longer chains involving a series of seven linkages, but not forming a circle (Swanton 1905a:67). It can clearly be seen that the operative unit in marriage relations is the lineage and more specifically the house; but not the moiety. The exogamous moieties may present the illusion of a dual system, but members of opposite moieties operate in terms of their lineage identity with regard to marriage alliances. This will emerge more clearly in our analysis of the potlatches.

The Durlach genealogy presents other data which illuminate the structure of the groups and their relationship to one another. As can be seen from Diagram B, the structure generated by preferential father's sister's daughter marriage is one in which for a *particular* ego, father's, wife's, children's, and daughter's children's lineage is the same. This contrasts with mother's brother's daughter marriage among the Tsimshian where father comes from one lineage and wife from another. There is ethnographic evidence from both the Tlingit and the Haida to support this identity of father's lineage and wife's lineage. The Durlach genealogy, when analyzed, showed that for the Tlingit, in thirteen out of the twenty cases where both wife's and father's lineage affiliation was known, wife and father came from the same clan, and in six cases wife and father came from the same lineage (house) in that clan. This must further be set against the background of the knowledge that there are some twenty-five clans in the opposing moiety. For the Haida, Murdock notes in a very different context: "These songs are privileges, not of his own clan, but of a clan of the opposite moiety—his father's clan according to my informant, but possibly the clan of his wife and children, since the two are frequently the same and were confused by my informants in other instances" (Murdock 1936:8). While Swanton notes: "Thus the father of my interpreter, Mr. Henry Edensaw, his wife and children, belong to the Stastas" (1905a:68). Thus, though the ethnographers of these two societies have not recognized the over-all pattern of marriage alliances created by preferential father's sister's daughter marriage, they provide material which substantiates our analysis of this pattern.

In addition to the lineage to which father, wife, and children belong, ego's lineage is linked by marriage to another lineage which, as noted in Diagram B, contains the father, wife, and children of his mother's brother. Given avunculocal residence and succession to the position of mother's brother, this lineage is also of importance to ego. The significance of this lineage to ego emerges clearly in the analysis of the potlatch.

The inheritance of names, in both the Tlingit and the Haida, may be offered as further support of the analysis of the social structure presented here. The Haida believe that a child is frequently a reincarnation of his father's father and hence receives his father's father's name. Since names are the possessions of lineages, it follows that a child and his father's father are members of the same lineage (Swanton 1905a:117, 118; Murdock 1934a:249; Curtis 1916:122).

As regards the Tlingit, De Laguna indicates that an individual is considered the reincarnation of a maternal ancestor; father's father is not mentioned. Examination of Diagram B shows that father's father and mother's mother's brother are identical. The Durlach genealogy also provides data on the transmission of names. Out of eighteen cases of such transmission, two thirds skip one or three generations. Five out of nine male names are inherited from mother's mother's brother, who is ideally also father's father. One name is inherited from an actual father's father. This information about the transmission of names among the Tlingit and the Haida further supports our structural analysis by emphasizing the alternation of generation and the identification of one's father and one's son from the point of view of any male ego.

In the discussion of the structure of cross-cousin marriage in matrilineal societies, the question of the control over women is of significance. From the descriptions of how a marriage is arranged for both the Tlingit and the Haida, it is apparent that negotiations are primarily in the hands of the matrilineages of bride and groom. As Swanton notes for the Tlingit:

When a youth desired to marry a certain girl, or when his friends desired to have him do so, the latter went in a body to the girl's mother and her clansmen. Then his mother, sister, or uncle said, "I value the words I am going to speak at forty blankets. If you are willing, kindly accept them." The mother replied, "Perhaps two days later I will speak to you." That time having elapsed, the youth's friends went thither again and said, "Will you accept my words?" If she consented to the match the girl's mother said, "Yes," after which the boy's friends left the blankets or money they had before promised (Swanton 1908a:428).

Murdock's account for the Haida is very similar. "The mother of the youth, after consultation with her husband, brothers, and sisters, proposes marriage to the girl's mother, who discusses the matter with her husband and clansmen before coming to a decision" (Murdock 1934a:250-51). As can be seen from Diagram B, since ego marries his father's sister's daughter, his father is therefore involved in allocation of the bride. It is also important to note that, for both the Haida and the Tlingit, in this instance the initiation of negotiations is in the hands of women—ego's mother and his father's sister. This is important for the discussion of the structure of father's sister's daughter marriage, since ego's father's sister at various points in ego's life cycle plays a significant role; "a paternal aunt ushers the child into the world, severs the umbilical cord with a knife" (Murdock 1934a:248), and is equally important at funeral rites (Murdock 1934a:253). Both Leach and Needham question the possibility of father's sister's daughter marriage as a structural type primarily on the basis of their lack of belief in the significance of the role of father's sister in the allocation of her daughter. The data from the Tlingit and the Haida clearly indicate the significance of the role of father's sister in the negotiations leading to the marriage of her daughter.

The pattern generated by mother's brother's daughter marriage, as among the Tsimshian, may be related to consistent differences in rank of groups, but the pattern generated by father's sister's daughter marriage, where wife-givers and wife-takers alternate in successive generations, cannot account for consistent differences in rank between the two categories. We find that among the Haida and the Tlingit rank order of groups is hardly present; the emphasis is upon intra- rather than intergroup rank differences, and mobility is present within the group.

The features of the social structure discussed so far are held in common by the Tlingit and the Haida. Examination of the potlatch system and the exchanges embodied therein, as they relate to the kinship structure and to rank, reveals differences between the two. The most striking difference is that among the Tlingit there is one fundamental type of potlatch while among the Haida there are two (and several subsidiary types [Murdock 1936]). The difference in number and kinds of potlatches between the Haida and the Tlingit relates in turn to the nature of group interaction. Swanton notes that superficially the Tlingit potlatch resembled that of the Haida, but with the former only one motive underlay the custom, regard for and respect for the dead, and there was but one kind of potlatch in consequence. . . . Among the Haida, on the other hand, the social idea quite overbalanced the religious. When a man took the place of his dead uncle or brother he was indeed obliged to give a feast and make a distribution of property to those of the opposite phratry, and the latter acted as undertakers; but this potlatch was of very much less importance than the great potlatch which a chief made to his own phratry, which was purely social in purpose and intended only to increase his reputation and advance his standing (Swanton 1908a:434-35).

Among the Tlingit there is an intimate interrelationship between potlatch, funeral rites, and succession to the office formerly held by the deceased. No major potlatch cycle apparently occurred without a death except for two minor types of potlatches, involving shaming and reaffirmation of social status after some event resulting in a loss of dignity. It is not apparent from the ethnographic sources whether every death is accompanied by a potlatch, but certainly the death of every important male is followed by a potlatch. In addition to its mortuary aspects, the potlatch cycle involves the building or rebuilding of a house to be occupied by the successor to the deceased, the accession to formal status by children of the deceased's group who receive new names, formal display of crests and dances owned by the deceased's group, and secret society performances (Swanton 1908a:434; De Laguna 1952:5; Krause 1956:156). Thus it can be seen that the potlatch ceremonial cycle is a multifunctional institution involving activities in many spheres of life, one which utilizes a multiplicity of symbolic forms of expression to signify the individual's place within his group, as well as the relation between groups.

The presence of moieties or dual organization had led De Laguna to interpret the potlatch among the Tlingit as an interaction between *two* sides—the hosts being of one moiety and the guests of the other. Swanton, on the other hand, very specifically notes that at potlatches the hosts range themselves at the inner end of the house, the place of honor, while the guests always range themselves in *two* parties facing each other along the two walls. He presents a number of examples showing which groups would be ranged together if a Raven chief at Sitka gave the potlatch, or if a Wolf chief did so. "The division of the guest . . . [moiety] at this feast was evidently based upon supposed consanguinity. If people were invited from another town they formed one party and the town people the other; if only the town people were invited, they, of course, had to divide into two bands" (Swanton 1908a:435). Thus, instead of a simple division into moieties, it is apparent that at the potlatch there is a threefold division: host, guest I, and guest II. The theoretical significance of this point will be further explored after our discussion of the Tlingit potlatch.

Chart B is a schematic representation of the only account of an actual Tlingit potlatch contained in the ethnographic material.[4] It is an account of "a feast at Chilkat substantially as given by Dekinaku, an eyewitness and participant" (Swanton 1908a: 438). This feast was sponsored by two donors of the Raven moiety of Chilkat after the completion of the house belonging to one of them. Though the completion of the house marked the occasion for the potlatch, funerary rites for the predecessor of the man whose house was completed also took place at this potlatch. As Swanton notes, the bones of the dead were taken up and placed in a box, a carving being erected over them. "The host asked his visitors to do this and they performed the service just before the gifts were given out. That was the reason for the feast and the reason they were summoned" (Swanton 1908a:441).

In the potlatch presented in Chart B, rivalry and symbolism of competition are evident. The guests from Sitka, members of the Wolf moiety, prepare themselves before arriving at Chilkat "by fasting, abstinence, and the manufacture of medicines made of flowers, as if preparing for war" (Swanton 1908a:438). Their com-

---

[4] Fragmentary details concerning another potlatch are contained in "Speeches Delivered at a Feast When a Pole Was Erected for the Dead" (Swanton 1909:374 ff.).

Chart B. A Tlingit Potlatch

Sitka Wolf Opposite moiety (foreign town)	Chilkat (Raven) Donor's moiety	Chilkat Wolf Opposite moiety (own town)

A. PREPARATION FOR THE POTLATCH

◀———————————————— Build house for donor

◀——————— Wife goes to invite Sitka people to potlatch; "invites" people to give her property for her husband

$2,000 worth of property ————————▶

B. POTLATCH PROPER: GUESTS ARRIVE AT HOST'S TOWN

◀——————— 20 boxes of olachen grease
20 boxes of berries
firewood

Crests left overnight as sign of good faith

Display of crests

Dance ————————————————▶

◀———————————————— Dance

◀——————— Food served (favorite of deceased) on ————————▶ named dishes

Songs and dances[a] ————▶ "Your opposites are going to drive ◀——— Songs and dances your sorrow away"

Two young men take part in an eating contest and others make fun of them while eating goes on

◀——————— Food distributed in named dishes and eaten with horn spoons belonging ————————▶ to deceased

Take up bones of dead, put into box, and erect a carving ————————▶ Display of crests

Displays property left by dead brother, uncle, or mother

Nieces and nephews brought out

Chief wears earrings and other things he had received from dead members of the clan which he wanted to let the people see

"They said that 'he spent so much money to let the people see them'" (Swanton 1908a:442)

◀——————— Food of finest kind served ————————▶

Display of crests

Principal guests dance ————————▶ ◀——————— Principal guests dance

[a]Contesting sides indicate that they want to dance in peace by saying to each other, "I am holding your daughter's hand" (Swanton 1908a: 440).

Chart B (continued)

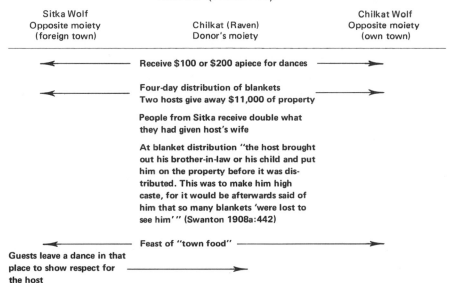

Sitka Wolf Opposite moiety (foreign town)	Chilkat (Raven) Donor's moiety	Chilkat Wolf Opposite moiety (own town)
◄───────────	Receive $100 or $200 apiece for dances ──────►	
◄───────────	Four-day distribution of blankets ──────► Two hosts give away $11,000 of property	
	People from Sitka receive double what they had given host's wife	
	At blanket distribution "the host brought out his brother-in-law or his child and put him on the property before it was dis- tributed. This was to make him high caste, for it would be afterwards said of him that so many blankets 'were lost to see him' " (Swanton 1908a:442)	
◄───────────	Feast of "town food" ──────────►	
Guests leave a dance in that place to show respect for ──────► the host		

Source: Swanton 1908a: 438–43.

petitors, however, are not the hosts of the potlatch but rather fellow members of the same moiety from Chilkat, who constitute
"the opposites" during the course of the potlatch. They compete
with these opposites in dancing, singing, and feasting. Before competitive dancing begins, there is a dance in which the contesting
sides indicate that they want to dance in peace. Following this,
highly competitive songs and dances are offered that may even result in actual violence.[5] They are followed by competition in eating. The Wolf visitors from Sitka are challenged to eat all that is
placed before them and are mocked by the Wolves of Chilkat
while they eat. Thus, the competition which occurs is between the

[5] A song leader from Sitka (Wolf) made a remark which "meant that he knew every
kind of song, and that the opposite people were good for nothing. As soon as he heard
this, a Klukwan man named Quacte turned around and asked his wife for his knife,
and a fight was imminent" (Swanton 1908a:440). The disturbance ceased at the behest
of the host, a Raven. Note that "opposite people" clearly indicates members of the
Wolf moiety, the moiety of the taunter. Both men are guests of the Raven host.

two groups of guests. "Great rivalry was always exhibited by the two parties, however, and their endeavors to outdo each other sometimes almost resulted in bloodshed. Each side attended carefully to the slightest remark made by an opponent, especially by the two song leaders with which each was provided, and the least slight, though couched in the most metaphorical language, was at once seized upon and might precipitate a riot" (Swanton 1908a: 435). The structural pose throughout the potlatch cycle is a tripartite one; hosts of one moiety form one group while the guests of the opposite moiety "ranged themselves in two parties facing each other at the sides" (Swanton 1908a:435). These two groups of guests are in fact the kinship units with which the host group is allied by marriage. Swanton has provided the names of a few participants in the "two parties" of the opposite moiety. These coincide in part with names on the Durlach genealogy and verify that the two groups of the opposite moiety at the potlatch are the two groups with which the host group most frequently intermarries: the Ganaxadi from Chilkat, the host group, intermarry with the Kagwantan of Sitka and the Kagwantan Finn house of Chilkat. It further seems likely that the two groups may be identified as the group of the donor's wife and the group of the wife of the deceased. The presence of the widow's group, while not attested to in this potlatch, is directly referred to in "Speeches Delivered at a Feast When a Pole Was Erected for the Dead" (Swanton 1909:374), where Swanton states that "the first side to dance is that to which the widower, or the widow of the deceased belongs" (Swanton 1909: 375). The alignment of the groups in the potlatch therefore confirms our earlier analysis of the structure generated by father's sister's daughter marriage, in which every lineage is linked to two other distinctly separate lineages.

In discussing Diagram B, we pointed out that the lineage of ego's wife was identical to that of ego's father and ego's children. At a potlatch in which ego is the donor, his wife's people obviously play a significant role. Further, a man's children are raised in prestige through the potlatching of their father. In the potlatch analyzed in Chart B, the host brings out his child and places him on the property to raise his status. The second lineage linked to ego's lineage contains the following relatives: sister's husband, mother's brother's wife, sister's son's wife. These do not seem to be highly significant in ego's life, but in the context of the potlatch their importance may be seen in terms of their relationship to the other unseen focal point of the potlatch cycle—the deceased. The event which leads to the potlatch is the death of a man, and this second group of individuals are the deceased's wife-father-children lineage. They are directly concerned with the mortuary rites for the deceased. Thus, the two groups which are linked with a third group in marriage alliances come together in the potlatch. A term of reference exists to express the relationship between these two groups, members of the same moiety bound to one another by links to a third group. This term—*(ax)daketqi*—reported by Durlach, is one whose meaning is not clear to her. She cites the text reference and indicates that the term is used by "the chief of the Kasqaguedi, a Raven clan, . . . in addressing the opposite Ravens. Just what is meant by this is not clear. Perhaps it means the other Raven clans present" (Durlach 1928:54). Our analysis makes the meaning of this term clear and indicates why such a term is useful in the context in which it occurs.

The ambivalence of the competition between the opposing guest parties becomes intelligible when viewed in the light of the marriage alliance. Opposing parties, in assuaging the mourners' grief, "want to dance in peace"; they say to each other, "I am holding your daughter's hand." Swanton explains this in a footnote by saying "the daughter of one Wolf man being the wife of another and vice versa" (Swanton 1908a:440, footnote B). The expression recorded by Swanton fits the structure in Diagram B. At other times in the potlatch, the opposite parties of guests compete. This may be related to the fact that in alternate generations the host lineage is more closely linked with one side, while in the next generation it is more closely linked with the other side. The deceased maintained closer ties with the lineage containing his father, wife, and son, while his successor will be more closely linked in the same way to the side containing his father, wife, and son.

Within the lineage and household, "there seems to have been a certain antagonism between the members of a maternal family, depending upon the clan affiliations of the fathers. Thus in the Finn house we find that one side of the house is occupied entirely by Ganaxtedi sons, ie. sons of Ganaxtedi fathers, the other side by Luknaxadi sons and that the greatest rivalry existed between the two groups" (Durlach 1928:55). Durlach presents two complementary terms—*akekdax*, one side, and *henax*, other party—which refer "to both sides of the house, the two branches of a maternal family" (Durlach 1928:55). This is couched in a somewhat different framework by De Laguna who, instead of emphasizing the rivalry between groups within the maternal family on the basis of clan affiliation of fathers, notes the positive bonds of sentiment uniting children whose fathers are of the same sib. "The father child tie is one which is stressed on all possible occasions. Children of the men of a sib, for example Kagwantan children, are supposed to form a particularly close and happy group, like 'brothers.' To address or to refer to a group as 'Kagwantan children' brings pleased smiles to their faces" (De Laguna 1952:10).

The tripartite division is consistent with marriage pattern, household structure, and potlatch analysis. This refutes Needham's reduction of father's sister's daughter marriage to a dual organization on ethnographic grounds. Finally, in terms of the implications for the structure of sentiment, one can understand the preference for father's sister's daughter marriage since there is a particular bond of affection between ego and his father, and ego's father has control over his sister's daughter with regard to marriage arrangements. In addition, ego's father's lineage plays a distinct role in the potlatch given by ego, and he allies himself within his own household with other sons of his father's lineage. The structure in this case reinforces the specific sentiments postulated by Homans and Schneider.

The multifunctional nature of the Tlingit potlatch was exhibited in our analysis of the potlatch described by Swanton. One of the fundamental functions of the potlatch is the distribution of blankets to all guests in return for the service of witnessing. Guests are called to bear witness to the succession to title and the acquisition of status. As noted in Chart B, clan crests and property inherited from deceased clan members are displayed; "they said 'he spent so much money to let the people see them' " (Swanton 1908a: 442). This is clearly payment for witnessing. It is said again at the final distribution of property that "it would be afterwards said of him that so many blankets 'were lost to see him' " (Swanton 1908a: 442), indicating an awareness on the part of the actors that the basic exchange is for the service of witnessing.

In contrast, among the Haida there are two basic types of potlatches, in addition to several subsidiary ones. "The *Sik!* potlatch was only made at the raising of a grave post . . . for a dead chief by the man who took his place" (Swanton 1905a:156). The other basic type of potlatch was called *Walgal,* and took place after the building of a house. Though the sponsor in these two different types of potlatches may be the same individual, the groups of guests with whom he will interact at each kind of potlatch will be different. Though both groups of guests are of the same moiety, they are of different lineages and correspond structurally to the two different parties of the opposite moiety represented at the single type of Tlingit potlatch. The *Sik!* and *Walgal* potlatches combined are equivalent to the one potlatch of the Tlingit. The three-sided structure found at a Tlingit potlatch resolves itself into two parts with donor and guests I interacting at one type of potlatch and donor and guests II interacting at the other.

The only published account of an actual *Sik!* potlatch is Swanton's. The account describes a potlatch which took place at Masset. The main activity was the raising of a grave post (*xat*) for a dead chief by his successor. The mourning ceremonies for the dead had already taken place. The two groups which interact in the *Sik!* potlatch are the lineage of the deceased, his successor being the donor-host, and the members of the opposite moiety who are of the deceased's wife's lineage. Although Swanton refers to the latter solely as members of the opposite moiety, it is apparent from other evidence that the members of the opposite moiety who are involved are those of the lineage which is most closely linked to the deceased, that of his wife-father-children (see Diagram B). Swanton notes that "when a man died, the members of his wife's clan conducted the funeral; and when his successor made a potlatch to put up the gravepost, he invited them to it" (Swanton 1905a:68). Murdock indicates that "when he dies, the women of his father's clan decorate his face with red stripes, clothe the body in ceremonial garments, and prop it up in a lifelike position" (1934a:253). Swanton, in discussing the funeral of a shaman, notes that "his father's sister made a strong mat for him, with strong cords at the corners" (Swanton 1905a:53). Noting once again the equation of wife's lineage and father's lineage, as substantiated above, one can see that the group within the opposite moiety involved in the *Sik!* potlatch (see Chart C) derives from the wife-father lineage. The wife of the donor and her lineage, who play such an important role at the *Walgal* or housebuilding potlatch, are never mentioned in the *Sik!* potlatch.

Murdock presents a generalized description of a *Sik!* potlatch that conforms to Swanton's. Murdock notes that the *Sik!* potlatch is the occasion during which the classificatory grandchildren of the deceased, who are members of his moiety, have their ears and nasal septums pierced (Murdock 1936:13). He observes that this service is performed by the *sqan* (FaSi and FaSiDa) of the donor of the potlatch. This does not seem to be consistent with all the other data on who attends the *Sik!* potlatch and who performs services. It is more likely that the *sqan* of the children are performing these services since these individuals are members of the wife-father-children lineage of the deceased (in fact, father's sister to the children would be the deceased's daughter). (See Diagram B.)

Chart C. A *Sik!* Potlatch of the Haida

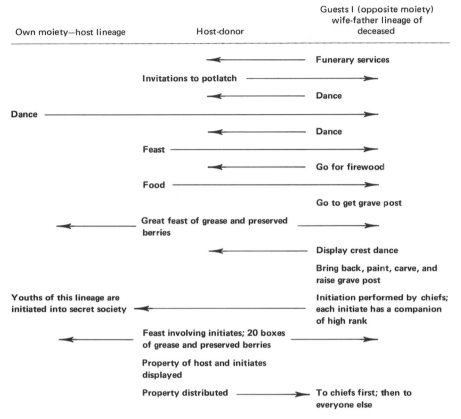

Source: Swanton 1905: 176–80.

The housebuilding or *Walgal* potlatch, by far the more important type, is described at some length by both Murdock and Swanton. It is apparent that the central roles here are played by the lineage of the donor and that of the donor's wife. So important is the wife's lineage in the *Walgal* potlatch that Murdock considers her the actual host at the potlatch. However, in terms of our own analysis, it is the husband who should be considered host and donor. We concur with Swanton in this. We will here analyze the

Walgal potlatch that occurred at Skidegate, as described to Swanton by an informant recalling the sequence of events (see Chart D).

In Murdock's description of a *Walgal* potlatch there are two important points which appear inconsistent with Swanton's. The most important of these is Murdock's conclusion that the wife is to be considered the donor of the potlatch. The large contributions of the wife's group, her prominent role in the distribution of property, and the assistance rendered by some of her clansmen at the distribution led Murdock to conclude that the actual donor was the wife and not the husband. We feel that this is incorrect. If Murdock were correct that the wife was the actual donor of the potlatch, she would be acting as a member of her natal lineage and one would expect that her brother or maternal uncle would necessarily play an important role of some kind in the potlatch. Nowhere, however, are these two individuals mentioned in the *Walgal* potlatch as described by either Murdock or Swanton. Though the Haida are matrilineal, all important power positions are in the hands of men, and it is impossible to imagine that the *Walgal* potlatch, the most important type among the Haida, and a central institution in the rank system, should be consistently given by female hosts and donors. Murdock is equivocal on who presides at the final distribution, though he indicates that his data on this point substantiate his view of the wife as donor. He notes that it is "she who superintends the actual distribution. To be sure, he [the husband] presents the 'coppers' but he merely stands by while she gives away the blankets, dishes and other articles. In Skidegate and Hydaburg, the husband presides over the distribution of blankets, but in the latter place it is specifically stated that the wife alone has the power to decide how many each recipient is to get and to correct her spouse if he makes a mistake" (Murdock 1936:12). On the other hand, he also notes that "the hostess supervised the distribution, aided by her husband, who stood by her side and called her attention to any mistakes" (Murdock 1936:11). Another point referred to by Murdock in support of his view of the wife as donor is the fact that the participants in the spirit performances are her kinsmen. In Swanton's account of the spirit performances and spirit initiation, the initiates are members of the wife's group, while the older spirit companions are members of the husband's group (Swanton 1905a: 162). Both groups participate in the spirit performance; the husband's group initiates youths belonging to the wife's group. Murdock ends by justifying his contention in terms of the fact that the native view states that all potlatches are given to the opposite moiety, and since husband's lineage built the house, wife's lineage must be the donor. As can be seen from Chart D, clans of both moieties are necessary participants in a potlatch. Native theory does not anywhere imply that distributions of property flow only from donor to the opposite moiety. Finally, Murdock himself notes in his description that "it was at this point in the proceedings, apparently, that Kingigwau [the husband] assumed his 'potlatch name'. . . . When a house chief dies, his potlatch name descends to his heir and successor; the latter assumes this honorific title, however, not at the funeral potlatch (although one informant so stated) when he comes into the position and property, but only *when he subsequently gives a housebuilding potlatch*" (1936:9; italics added). It is apparent, therefore, that Murdock contradicts himself and in this particular statement views the donor of the potlatch as being in reality the husband rather than the wife. This conforms to Swanton's presentation, which we have accepted throughout our analysis.

The second major difference between the Swanton and Murdock accounts involves the question of who builds the house. In the Murdock account, the host's clan invites members of his clan from another town to come to his town to build the house. In the Swanton account, the host has his house built by members of his clan who reside in his own village, though members of his clan from other villages are later invited to participate in the final part of the potlatch and in the tattooing of members of the wife's clan. It is possible that the differences in the accounts are due to individual

Chart D. A *Walgal* Potlatch of the Haida

Husband's lineage and related clans	Hosts husband-wife	Guests II wife's lineage
Capture slaves for host ———————▶		
	Husband hunts and fishes to acquire wealth	
	Wife gathers produce; gives to her brothers and uncles ———————▶	
	Wife gives blankets and all sorts of things to people of her lineage, called "spanking the needle" or "fighting an inferior" ———————▶	
◀———————	Husband calls in his side for tobacco to discuss assignment of work in regard to bringing in house timbers	
Help husband to accumulate property and food ———————▶		
◀———————	Feast of preserved berries and assignment of work involved in housebuilding	
Go to obtain house timbers under leadership of chiefs of lineages related to host		
◀———————	Host summons members of own group, his "friends"	
They dance into the house. Dance is called sq!a'dal, "coming in streams" ———————▶		
Timbers brought to village ———————▶		
	Host calls in "town people" for tobacco; they sing spirit song	
		Initiates perform
Spirit companions assist in initiates' performance		
◀———————	Boxes of preserved berries distributed ———————▶	
◀—————————————————————		Initiates perform and bite people
◀———————	Host recompenses members of his own group with blanket if bitten by initiates	
Each in his own seat		
◀———————	Boxes of grease distributed	
	◀———————	Property in payment for what wife had given them
◀—————————————————————		Payment of ten blankets and preserved berries to each of the inspired (spirit companions)
		They sent grease and berries through the fire to the dead members of the clan

Chart D (continued)

Husband's lineage and related clans	Hosts husband-wife	Guests II wife's lineage
		They commenced to give away property;
Spirit companions ◄───────────────		Two blankets each
Chief who started dancing ◄──────────		Five blankets
Cutters of house pole ◄─────────────		Two blankets each
		Those who gave property took new names from wife's house's list of names
Carve and raise house pole ────────►		
◄─────── Feast of grease		
Diggers of hole for house pole ◄─ 1 blanket, 5 fathoms of cloth		
Each chief ◄───────── 1 blanket and cotton cloth		
Remainder of house erected ◄───────	Invites own clan (another town) to potlatch	
"Come dancing towards town on canoes" displaying crests		
Dance ─────────────────►		
◄────────── Feast		
		Those about to be tattooed go to prospective tattooers with
Chiefs ◄─────────────────────		ten blankets and a whole role of cotton cloth
	Display of property; host shows how he obtained his property and displays his crest	
	◄────────────	FaSisSo beats drum for host
	Many blankets distributed[a]	
	Call for witnesses	
		Those who were to be tattooed dance
	Wife displays crest	
	House filled with eagle feathers (signifies peace)	
Chiefs tattoo ────────────────────►		Those to be tattooed sit in front of chiefs who do tattooing
		Those tattooed receive new names
Chiefs pierce nose, ears, lower lip ──────────────────────────────────►		
	Distribution of blankets:	
He who got house pole ◄──── 10		
Two who carved it ◄──── 10		
Four who got 4 gable planks ◄─ 6 each		
Those who got wall planks ◄── 6 each		

[a]Swanton does not note to whom these blankets were given.

Chart D (continued)

Husband's lineage and related clans	Hosts husband-wife	Guests II wife's lineage
Six stringers on roof ◄———	4 each	
Those who put up four corner posts ◄———	4 each	
Those who put up front and rear posts ◄———	4 each	
Those who put up ridge poles ◄—	2 each	
Post hole diggers ◄———	1 each	
Those who put up roof planks ◄—	8 each	
Those doing tattooing ◄———	3 each	
Chiefs in front of tattooee ◄—	10 each	
Town chief ◄———	100	
Townspeople ◄———	40, 30, 20	
Host's sister ◄———	as many as 60	
Visitors ◄———	large amount	
	Now the host could be called a house chief and be treated as such at other people's potlatches	

Source: Swanton 1905: 161–70.

variation. The *Walgal* potlatch described by Murdock offers further support for the equation of wife's lineage and father's lineage. As was noted earlier, in discussing the *Walgal* potlatch, Murdock indicates that informants "confuse father's clan and wife's clan," which according to our analysis are one and the same. Further evidence on this point is offered by Murdock when he notes that "the host explained to the assembled people that he was bestowing upon his son the name of his father, who had been cradled in a 'copper' the day after his birth. He also announced that his father St'ast the chief and last survivor of the Dogit'ane clan of Eagles, had said that his grandson and namesake should inherit from him" (Murdock 1936:10-11). The genealogy of the Eagle moiety presented by Swanton indicates that there is a close relationship between wife's lineage and father's lineage in this case. A final point of evidence is provided by Swanton in the *Walgal* potlatch described in Chart D in that father's sister's son is singled out by name as beater of the drum, indicating the active role of father's lineage at the potlatch (father's sister's son being obviously of father's lineage).

What of significance is happening at a *Walgal* potlatch? A *Walgal* potlatch necessarily involves the building of a house, and in this respect the Haida are in accord with practices among other Northwest Coast tribes where housebuilding and potlatching are intimately associated. The anomaly of the *Walgal* potlatch is that the house is built by the host's own lineage, who become the owners of the house. Among the Tsimshian and the Tlingit the house is built by lineages other than the host's. It is interesting to note that among the ambilateral peoples further south (Kwakiutl, Bella Coola), the building of a house associated with the potlatch is performed by the host's own group.

The other important activity which takes place at a *Walgal* potlatch is the initiation and tattooing of youths of the wife's lineage. Here a vital service is performed by donor's lineage in exchange for property. Both housebuilding and initiation are integral parts of the potlatch and both are involved in the rank system, but in somewhat different ways. The donor's lineage benefits by obtaining a new house which has been built by closely related lineages and the donor receives the title of house chief by virtue of the possession of this new house. The wife's lineage, which has provided much of the property, benefits by having its children tattooed and initiated. Tattooing is a major element in advancing one's rank, as Swanton points out (1905a:170). In fact, Murdock notes that the *Walgal* potlatch as a whole is a means of conferring rank on the donor's own children. He notes that "one's own potlatches count for little in comparison with those given by one's parents" (Murdock 1936: 19). This particular emphasis is not echoed in the Swanton account.

Diagram C shows the reciprocal nature of the exchanges involved in a *Walgal* potlatch. Though the wife's lineage gives away property at this potlatch, the property is given in exchange for

Diagram C. Scheme óf Exchanges at a *Walgal* Potlatch of the Haida

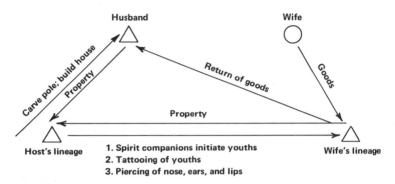

services rendered, since youths of the wife's lineage are initiated and tattooed by chiefs of the host's lineage. Goods which members of the wife's lineage give to the host are in return for goods which the wife had previously given to them. The host's lineage in turn is the greatest recipient of property since it receives from both host and his wife's lineage; the host's lineage provides services for both host and his wife's lineage. One further element of significance should be noted: the host's sons and daughters gain in prestige by their father's potlatch. Though they may reside in the host's household, they are members of the wife's matrilineage.

The *Sik!* potlatch must be performed by any successor to office. The *Walgal* potlatch is not obligatory. Though both are involved in the rank system, they relate to rank in very different ways. An aspirant to political position must marshal support from other members of his lineage, accumulate property, and distribute that property at a *Sik!* potlatch to members of the opposite moiety who are of the lineage allied to the deceased, his wife's lineage. This is the mechanism for an individual's advancement to a position of political power via potlatching. The *Walgal* potlatch, on the other hand, though much more important in terms of the amounts of property accumulated and distributed, is not obligatory. The maximum benefits derived do not accrue to the donor but rather to his

Diagram D. Relations Between Households among the Tlingit and
the Haida

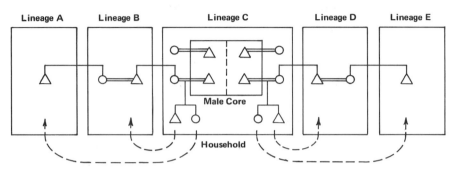

children, who are members of his wife-father's lineage. This illustrates the significance of complementary filiation in the Haida rank
system: actions of the father are of less importance to the members
of his matrilineage in terms of achievement of rank, and of very
great importance to the lineage to which he is linked by marriage.

Matrilineal descent, avunculocal residence, and preferred father's
sister's daughter marriage among the Tlingit and the Haida generate a structure which has the following characteristics. Each house
or lineage is paired with two other lineages of the opposite moiety.
The core of the household consists of a group of males related matrilineally, brought about by the shift of residence of adolescent
boys to their mothers' brothers. Within this core of males there is
a recognized division according to the matrilineages of their fathers.
The identification of father's and wife's lineage (also son's lineage)
means that the females marrying into the household are of two distinct lineages—the matrilineages of the husbands' fathers. Sons and
daughters grow up in their father's house, and in time both leave.
Daughters join the households of their husbands and sons move to
the households of their uncles. Diagram D illustrates this sche-
matically.

Women never reside in households controlled by their own matrilineages. They reside successively in the two households linked
to their own in marriage. Diagram D illustrates the chains of rela-

tionship existing between lineages. The identification of a man's son with that man's father, evidenced in the concepts of reincarnation and in the passing of names from a man's father to his son, supports the transgenerational continuity of the structure.

Neither the Tlingit nor the Haida give indication of ranking of groups as an important feature of their structure. Instead, intragroup ranking is an important feature. Though there is a rule of succession, its operation is flexible and dependent upon the ability to mobilize support. As shown, the status of an individual is to some extent dependent upon the activities of his father. By and large, rank is achieved either by the activities of the individual or as a result of the potlatching activities of his father.

Both the kinship structure and the rank structure find expression in the potlatch. The triadic organization of the Tlingit potlatch recapitulates the ordering of kin groups.[6] The "two opposites" and their symbolic competition reflect the structure of their relationship to the host. For the Haida, the two types of potlatches, the funeral (*Sik!*) and the housebuilding (*Walgal*), reflect a ceremonial separation of the interactions between a lineage and the two lineages with which it intermarries. Further, they reflect the separation between the claiming of a title at one's predecessor's death through a *Sik!* potlatch and the advancement of the status of oneself and that of one's children at a *Walgal* potlatch. The advance in rank of children by virtue of the potlatching activity of their father is distinctive of the Haida and may be advantageous for them in claiming titles in their own matrilineage. The two types of Haida potlatches may therefore be related to this unique method of social advancement which Murdock noted for the matrilineal Haida.

Among the Tlingit and the Haida, marriage is not the occasion for potlatching. Since prerogatives and privileges remain within

---

[6] As has been pointed out to us by our colleague Morton Klass, such a triadic structure requires a minimum of four groups in order for it to function. The presence of four groups combined with the three-sided marriage structure produces moieties. This will be explored theoretically in our conclusion.

the matrilineage and cannot pass from fathers to their children, marriages are not contracted with the aim of raising the rank of the children. Marriages therefore do not provide the occasion for a potlatch, since potlatches usually involve rank as a central feature. As noted above, the amount of intergroup ranking is minimal or nonexistent. This is consistent with the presence of preferential father's sister's daughter marriage and results in a structure in which affines are equals, thus providing another reason why marriage is not a potlatch.

However, affines are very much a part of the potlatch when it does occur. We have been at great pains to illustrate that the structural relations between groups of affines underlie the potlatch. The competition, if it occurs at the potlatch, is between groups which are affinally related to the host group, as in the Tlingit example.

If marriages are not the occasions for potlatches, funerals most certainly are. On these occasions, groups of affines perform critical services in return for goods. Looking at the potlatch behavior of both the Tlingit and the Haida, one can see clearly that goods, services, and women are being exchanged with two groups of affines to create a long-term cycle of exchange and alliance. Though women may not move in the same direction in every generation, it is very clear that the relationship is continued and perpetuated. For example, in the case of the Haida, a man from lineage A marries a girl from lineage B. At the death of the man from lineage A, his wife's matrilineage performs funerary services and is thereby reciprocated for its services by the dead man's lineage. Meanwhile, a girl from lineage A has married a man from lineage B, and when he dies lineage A performs funerary services and is reciprocated. Thus, in every generation, marriages and funerals are the focal points for a series of reciprocations which continue to link these lineages over time, though women reverse direction in each generation. Lévi-Strauss's focus upon the exchange of women resulted in his characterization of patrilateral cross-cousin marriage as creating short cycles. Needham's adoption of this same point of view resulted in his conclusion that generations could not be kept separate conceptually, and he therefore saw such a structure as unstable. Our point of view, which takes into account the total field of exchange and total social phenomena, encompasses, in addition to marriage, other critical occasions for exchanges, such as successions and funerals. This point of view enables one to see the manner in which exchanges provide for the stability of such a system over long periods of time.

CHAPTER IV. *THE NOOTKA*

THE PRECEDING chapters have examined three Northwest Coast societies which have matrilineal descent and a preferential marriage rule which enables us to generate elementary structures, in Lévi-Strauss's terminology. The Nootka have an ambilateral rule of descent and a marriage pattern which involves choices. These elements we have used for our structural model of Nootka society. Since choice and option are present in both group affiliation and selection of marriage partners, Nootka structure may be categorized as complex rather than elementary. The structure of Nootka society is manifest in the Nootka potlatch.

The Nootka inhabit the west coast of Vancouver Island and Cape Flattery, which lies across the Strait of Juan de Fuca, and speak a Wakashan language related to Kwakiutl. They do not refer to themselves as Nootka, and they do not constitute a single political entity, though in terms of commonality of cultural patterns and high frequency of interaction they form an identifiable unit.

The constituent social units of the Nootka represent several successively more inclusive levels of complexity. The following categories have been differentiated in the literature: the house, the local group (or band), the tribe, and the confederacy. No native terms exist to differentiate these levels of organization. It is sometimes difficult when using the textual material and the ethnographic data to know if one is dealing with a local group or with a tribe; moreover, tribe and confederacy are sometimes confused. The Nootka use geographic place names to designate local groups, and the name of one local group is used also for the entire tribe and confederacy.

The confederacy, as a social entity, is more common and more firmly established in the northern than in the central and southern parts of the Nootka area. It represents the union of several geographically contiguous tribes which share "a common village site— in this case a summer one—to which all, or most, of the people repaired for sea fishing and hunting" (Drucker 1951:220). The confederacy takes its name from one of its local groups. Where confederacies existed in the north, "there was a very real feeling of solidarity within these confederations. They were units for war as well as ceremonials. Intraconfederacy wars were very rare, almost unknown" (Drucker 1951:221). From Drucker's accounts of the histories of the various confederacies, the amalgamation of tribes into a confederacy was apparently sometimes the result of warfare (Drucker 1951:234, 240).

The tribe consists of a number of local groups who are united through the common possession of a winter village site. At the winter village, each local group has its great carved houses and named posts. These are the location for important ceremonials.

Sproat refers to the Nootka as the Ahts, since Nootka is not the term which they use to refer to themselves. Aht is the suffix denoting those people constituting a tribe, as, for example, Tsisa'ath and Muchalat. Sproat also indicates that the "tribes practise different arts, and . . . [recognize a] tribal monopoly in certain articles produced . . . [and] go a long way . . . to barter for those articles, which, if they liked, they themselves could easily produce" (Sproat 1868: 19). Since Sproat does not refer to the local group level, it is possible that this regional specialization may be at the local group rather than at the tribal level.

The tribe is composed of a number of local groups which Drucker occasionally refers to as lineages and which Boas and Sapir both call septs. The local group centers "in a family of chiefs who owned territorial rights, houses, and various other privileges. Such a group bore a name, usually that of their 'place' (a site at their fishing ground where they 'belonged'), or sometimes that of a chief; and had a tradition, firmly believed, of descent from a common ancestor" (Drucker 1951:220).

Each local group consists of one or more house groups which, in fact, occupy plank houses at the winter village and at the summer village. These houses can be as large as 40 feet by 100 feet. Every local group has at least one permanent house in the winter and summer villages. The house frames remain at the sites, while the roofing and the siding are moved with the group (Drucker 1951: 69). The house group comprises a number of nuclear families, each with its own hearth, and can number up to 35 persons.

It can be seen that the levels of organization among the Nootka parallel those found among the northern groups. However, the manner in which Nootka group membership is determined is different. Among the northern tribes—Tsimshian, Haida, and Tlingit—affiliation is determined on the basis of matrilineal descent, but among the Nootka an individual can claim membership in a group by tracing kinship in any line. The Nootka thus have ambilateral descent.[1] Demonstration of kinship is the only prerequisite to group affiliation. In order to activate a claim to membership, it is necessary for an individual to reside with a group and to participate in that group's activities for the time of his residence. As Sapir notes in a brief life history, "As far back as he can remember, Tom has been accustomed to think of himself not merely as a Ts'isha'ath, though he is primarily that by residence and immediate descent, but as a splintered participant in the traditions, in the social atmosphere, of several other Nootka tribes" (Sapir 1921:235). The text material collected by Sapir and Swadesh specifically mentions Tom residing at and moving to and from six different village locations in the course of his life, including among them Uchuklesit and Nitinat, as well as Tsisa'ath, sites (1939). Drucker also notes that residence serves to activate membership in one of a number of groups with which an individual can claim membership by virtue of kinship. He states: "With whatever group a man happened to be

---

[1] Our interpretation of descent among the Nootka differs from that of Service, who calls them patrilineal at one point (page 205) and then continues to refer to "lineages" without further stating the type of descent (Service 1958).

living, he identified himself completely. For the time being, he centered all his interests and loyalties in that group, and participated in all its activities. He tended the chief's fish traps, contributed food and property for feasts and potlatches, danced and enjoyed himself at the festivities" (Drucker 1951:279). Participation through residence with one group does not negate the possibility of actualizing membership in other groups with which one is affiliated through kinship. Sapir notes that "descent and privileges seem to descend equally in male and female lines. Thus a name may be selected from either the father's or mother's family. Also, the *eitcaen* [family history] of both father and mother's family is learned by the child" (Sapir Field Notes IV:19).

Consonant with the type of descent described above, inheritance of property, of rights, and of privileges devolves through a variety of kinship lines. Drucker notes: "A given privilege could be inherited by the eldest son, or shared by several children (all having the right to use it); it could be given to a daughter until her marriage and then bestowed on her brother; it could be given to a son-in-law, who might, as the giver specified, have sole right to it or share it with his wife's brother" (Drucker 1951:267). Sapir provides an excellent illustration of the passage of names, one of the most important of Nootka properties, when he tells how Tom successively acquired the five names which he held at different times in his life. Diagram E shows this acquisition. The five names came to Tom through the following kin lines: FaMoMo, FaMoFa, FaFaMo, FaFaFa, MoFa.

Nootka kinship terminology (Drucker 1951:276-78) may be classified as Hawaiian in type on the basis of cousin terminology. Generational terms are used for both siblings and cousins. This accords with the ambilateral descent, the multiple options of residence, and the nature of the house group. Terminological distinctions between elder and younger are applied to individuals within one's own generation. Distinctions are made between older and younger siblings and between the children of one's parent's younger sib-

Diagram E. Multiple Lines of Inheritance of Privileges among the Nootka

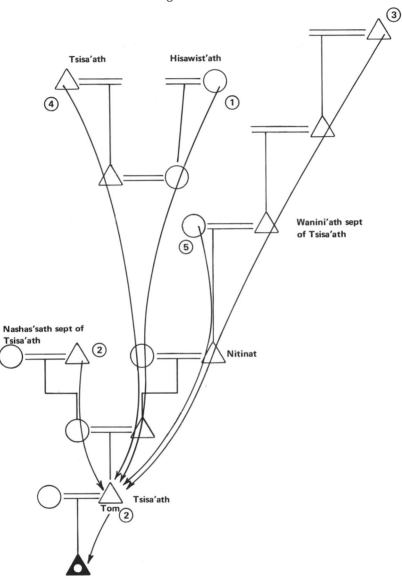

Source: Sapir 1921.

lings. Niece and nephew terms are distinct from the terms for one's own children. Descent lines are therefore not made distinct by the application of the criterion of bifurcation, but rather by distinguishing junior from senior lines.

One may ascertain the composition of the local group for a given point in time. But since individuals shift their residence from place to place for varying periods, the composition of the local group does not remain fixed or bounded. Named local groups persist through time though their membership varies.

It is therefore not possible to have a rule of lineage or clan exogamy as is found in the north. Thus, the marriage rule is framed in terms of the individual: marriage is prohibited between first and second cousins but one may marry a more remote relative, or, as Boas puts it, "cousins and second cousins are not allowed to intermarry, but there is no restriction against marriages between members of the same gens" (Boas 1891:595). Further, as Drucker notes, "mates were deliberately sought among more remote relatives" (Drucker 1951:287).

An examination of the unpublished field notes of Morris Swadesh supports these general principles.[2] From the genealogical material provided by Swadesh we have extracted information about 56 marriages in which the tribal affiliation of both the husband and the wife is known. Table 3 summarizes these data. In that table, each partner is identified by his primary group membership. The figures show that 43 percent of the marriages are between members of the same tribe and 57 percent are between members of different tribes. There is no marked tendency toward marriage either within the group or outside it. This contrasts with Swadesh's own statement that "since most tribes were made up of

[2] We have been able to relate the Swadesh field notes to life history material collected by Sapir (1921) as well as to the textual material published by Sapir and Swadesh (1939, 1955) since the same names reoccur in these accounts. This has enabled us to construct several extended genealogies with the Tsisa'ath tribe as a central focus. This, taken together with the Boas material on the Tsisa'ath (1891), has provided us with a corpus of data on several Nootka groups which can be compared with Drucker's work on the northern groups (1951).

several clans or lineages, and since the preferred form of exogamy implied marriage into an altogether different tribe, a man frequently had closer relatives in the enemy tribe than in most clans of his own" (Swadesh 1948:92).

Concerning the general structural implications of ambilateral descent, it is clear that, if the options for kin group affiliation remain open, kinship groups of exclusive membership are not present and the terms "endogamy" and "exogamy" are not relevant.

TABLE 3. *NOOTKA MARRIAGES*

Marriages within the tribe		*Marriages between tribes*	
Tsisa'ath to Tsisa'ath	19	Tsisa'ath to Hopachisat	8
Hoiat to Hoiat	3	Nitinat	5
Others	2	Ucluelet	4
	24	Hoiat	2
		Hochoktlisat	2
		Hatcaat	2
		Others	4a
		Other exogamous marriages	5
			32

Total marriages: 56

ª Including one Tsisa'ath marriage to each of the following tribes: Comox, Hesquiat, Ahousat, and Toquiat.

The partners in the 56 marriages are likely to have had the options of membership in groups other than the one with which they are identified in the genealogy.

Preference for marriage with remote relatives, together with the evidence of a high percentage of intra-tribal marriages, cuts down on the proliferation of descent lines. Ambilaterality, coupled with a preference for marriage with more remote relatives, also seems to be consonant with the weakness of a separable category of affinal relations. In the words of a Nootka informant, "O Chief. The reason I have never ceased to be related to you generation after generation is that we continue to take daughters from each other" (Sapir and Swadesh 1955:182).

It appears that marriage takes place between individuals who place themselves in different groups. For example, when Old Tom, Sapir's chief informant, whose primary identification is Tsisa'ath, marries a Tsisa'ath girl, he sends his Nitinat kinsmen to woo her. During the marriage rite Old Tom identifies himself as a Nitinat (Sapir and Swadesh 1939:137). This initial phase of the wedding rites involves contests of skill during which members of the groom's family compete in performing various feats of strength and endurance. The wedding rites involve exchanges on both sides, but both Sapir and Drucker say that the conception of bride price is used to refer to the transfer of blankets from groom's side to the bride's side. Then, or at the birth of a child, the groom is given prerogatives, privileges, and title to property by the father of the bride. "Our [groom's] marriage payment consisted of thirty blankets. [Later the father] brought the dowry gift. He enumerated dam-traps on the river for cohoe and also funnel-traps for dog salmon and tyee salmon" (Sapir and Swadesh 1939:177; see also Drucker 1951:286 ff.). Sapir also presents an example in which the highest seat in a band passed in this way: "Nanatsukwil built his house next to LaLaqok'wap's . . . and married his daughter 'nasayilim; then Nan[atsukwil] got middle seat of rear as dowry, while LaLaq-[ok'wap's] took seat on right hand side of middle" (Sapir Field Notes XV:41). This aspect of Nootka marriage, in which important privileges involving names and seats move from wife's father to daughter's husband, will be seen as important among the Kwakiutl and the Bella Coola. This is one of the ways in ambilateral societies by which the link to a daughter's child is proclaimed, enabling the child of the marriage to claim membership and prerogatives later through his mother in her group.

Consideration of rank is also involved in selection of marriage mates by the parents. Since important prerogatives regularly pass from bride's family to groom's family, it is clear that this transferal is an important consideration in the strategy of marriage arrangements. Marriage can be used to achieve social mobility for one's children. Sapir notes that an extremely high-ranking name has the meaning "Who alone parts (with his *topatis* as dowries) when suitors come for his daughters (= 'has *topatis* scattered among many tribes')" (Sapir Field Notes XI:19). In this quotation, *topatis* means privileges. It would appear that a successful strategy for a high-ranking chief with many daughters is to marry them out, thereby giving those privileges to sons-in-law. The privileges will ultimately devolve upon his grandchild who may return to his group.

Another strategy in arranging marriages involves a return marriage. "This was done to get back *topatis* that had gone away from one of lines. Desire to get *topatis* was main motive in arranging matches" (Sapir Field Notes XVII:42a). Drucker notes that "a man could not change his own rank, but he could better—or lower—that of his descendants by his marriage. Members of the higher middle class could marry into the eldest families or slightly beneath their own level without arousing disapproval. This held true for persons of any station. It was only marriages of persons widely separated in rank which carried stigma" (Drucker 1951:245). Boas also notes that "the child belongs to that sept which is considered the nobler. If, for instance, the mother is a Ts'ecaath, the father a Kuai'ath, the child will be a Ts'ecaath" (Boas 1891:595).

The chiefly position (native term *ha'wil*) comprises a clearly differentiated political position involving rights to certain territories, and the potential for command over people and for the making of decisions in their behalf. "Whatever authority a chief had derived in final analysis from the various rights he had inherited" (Drucker 1951:247). House and village sites and strategic economic resource areas such as fishing sites, hunting areas, and beaches are "regarded as the property of certain chiefs" (Drucker 1951:248). An individual has access to these resources by virtue of membership in a house group, which signifies a kinship tie with the chief of the house who is the titular owner not only of the house but also of the resources associated with his position. Public recognition of the chief's ownership is attested to in a variety of ways, among them official opening of the fishing season at a particular site and regular payment of "tribute." As Drucker points out: " 'A chief did not work'. . . . His real duties were of an executive nature. . . . The activities of his people were in his charge: he decided on the time of the seasonal movements, directed group enterprises, such as construction of large traps and weirs, planned and managed ceremonials, and had the final voice in matters of group policy" (Drucker 1951:244). Thus it can be seen that the position of chief is one of power and decision-making and also has important economic features, since the chief is the central node in a redistributive network. As Drucker notes: "The food-stuff collected in this fashion was always used to give a great feast, at which the giver announced it had been obtained as tribute . . . from that place" (Drucker 1951:251).

The owner of the house, the chief of the house group, occupies the right rear corner of the house. The chief next in rank, usually a brother or other close kinsman, occupies the opposite corner; the corners to the right and to the left of the door are similarly places of honor and are occupied by other important branches of the house group (Drucker 1951:71). Within the house, there are individuals who are referred to as *ma mutswinilim* (under the arm to) who are often closely related to the chiefs. They also form part of a larger category of individuals referred to as *maiyusta* (tenants), all those residing in the house.

House ownership is apparently synonymous with chiefly position. The group of individuals residing in the house constitute the minimal exploitative unit. During residence in the house, individuals owe allegiance to the chief; they are "his people," both "those under his arm" and those who are his "tenants." They exploit the resources which he owns and pay him tribute in various forms. He distributes to them in the form of feasts and may also grant them some of his minor privileges. This sharing in his greatness and partaking of his largess is his way of attracting people, for it is important for a chief to have manpower at his command to exploit his resources. As one of Drucker's informants notes: "That is the way with a chief. . . . If his 'tenants' are good, helping him lots (working for him, giving him wealth), then he will get a good name, he can do much (i.e., potlatching). If they are no good or don't care for him he can do nothing" (Drucker 1951:273). The people need the chief, for by their relationship to him they have access to the house, membership in the house group, and use of the stretch of beach and the fishing and berrying sites that he owns; the chief needs his people to exploit his resources, though there seem to be few activities outside of the construction of the large salmon weirs and whaling which require coordinated communal activity. As previously noted, chiefs obtain tribute from their people, but this involves a share of what each man obtains. A fascinating myth collected by George Hunt describes how Raven, chief of the Ts'awinath of the Moachat, obtained for his people the sun, which was the property of a chief of another Moachat local group. Having obtained the sun through a series of adventures, Raven refuses to return to his people and says, "I will not go to my village . . . the people shall pay me to bring light into the world" (Boas 1916:891). It is Wren who finally devises the plan which induces Raven to return; he states, "I think that if we promise our chief that whenever any of us catch fish or clams or game, we will give him one of each kind before we take ours out of the canoe (for we will treat him like a chief)—I think he ought to be pleased with this and will let us see the sun" (Boas 1916:892). Thus the present-day chief through his mythological ancestor the Raven is the provider of all things, including the sun, and claims tribute from his people.

In terms of exchange, the chief gives access to economic resource areas, gives food at feasts, makes ceremonies at which his children are initiated, and makes available ceremonial privileges that he owns. The people, in turn, give tribute, political allegiance by subordinating themselves to his political leadership, ceremonial assistance, and deference.

Unlike the situation with the peoples further north, succession to chiefly position is not open to competition. A strict rule of primogeniture exists (Sapir 1921:242, 1915:364 f.; Drucker 1951:245). In addition, the position of chief is passed on to the eldest son while the father is still alive.

Younger brothers and collateral relatives like cousins are usually invested with lesser privileges and positions. They have the option of remaining with an older brother who is the chief, leaving his house to claim rights in another house by various ambilateral lines of descent, or residing uxorilocally and claiming rights through their wives. Lastly, they have the possibility of moving off and founding a new house and attempting to attract followers. It is interesting to note that, given the principle of primogeniture and the pattern of residential options, two brothers will not be of the same rank and often may not be found in the same house (Drucker 1951:274). Clearly, Radcliffe-Brown's principle of the equivalence of brothers is not operative here.

Should a younger brother decide to remain within a house, then he has a position as a lesser chief and occupies one of the lesser corners. If his descendants remain in that house, they constitute a "junior line." The composition of the house accords with a number of the features associated with the concept of the conical clan (Kirchhoff 1959:266-67). The presence of options in choice of residence which do not depend solely upon nearness of descent provides the major point of difference. Close relatives may not be present in the household and, further, data from Drucker and Swadesh on household composition indicate the presence of individuals who may not be able to trace their exact relationship to the chief and even of individuals unrelated to the chief (Drucker 1951:286).

No substantive data on fission are provided, though Sproat notes that "subdivisions of tribes occasionally take place by the secession of restless, influential individuals, who, with their families and friends, endeavour to start new tribes under their own chiefship" (Sproat 1868:20). An analysis of Drucker's material on the several northern Nootka confederacies indicates that expansion and splitting of houses occasionally take place in the process of confederation. These actions invariably occur as a concomitant of warfare and conquest, and the role of younger brothers as war chiefs is consistently mentioned. According to Drucker, "few head chiefs ever assumed war-chief names themselves, but usually installed their younger brothers or cousins in the position" (Drucker 1951: 270). The position of war chief is hereditary and involves specific ceremonial privileges and rites. Warfare involved the extermination of the enemy and the acquisition of his territory and all of his hereditary privileges. Warfare is more important among the Nootka than among any of the other Northwest Coast peoples, all of whom engage in it. Warfare therefore provides an avenue for social mobility in that younger brothers and collateral relatives, should they decide to stay in their natal household, may use its resources in war expeditions. These, if successful, may enable them to become independent chiefs, at the head of a junior line of descent with its own house. They presumably seek to attract followers. According to the ideal picture, the new chief would be ranked junior to his brother, the head of his natal house. However, Drucker provides much evidence to indicate that his own activities and those of his successors, when successful, may bring about changes in the relative ranking of chiefs. Drucker points out the inconsistencies between the actual and the ideal picture when he notes:

According to traditions of the Kyuquot confederacy, the local group called the qwowinasath is supposed to have been given highest rank at the time the world was put in order, along with most of the important property rights. Yet in the order of precedence of the latter half of the last century, their chief ranked 20th in the list of 25 (or 27) lineage chiefs. Informants account for this by referring to traditions in which the qwowinas chiefs gave away various of their important rights, and even their potlatch "seats," to sons-in-law—they themselves must have consistently made poor matches, if this is the correct explanation. It is probable that other factors entered the picture. Personal prestige, numerical strength of the local group, conquests in war, and the like must all have had their effect (Drucker 1951:246).

Kirchhoff's model of the conical clan does not treat the question of external ranking of units. It is apparent, however, that a relationship exists between the internal ranking of house group membership and the external ranking of groups—houses, local groups, and tribes. New groups originating through the process of fission are ranked at first as junior lines and are of lesser rank. The larger ranking is not fixed and, moreover, the very ranking of houses, local groups, and tribes varies in intensity in different areas. Boas specifically provides a ranking of nine septs for the Tsisa'ath, three septs for the Hopetcisath, and eleven septs for the Tokoaath tribe (Boas 1891:584). Though Drucker, in his discussion of ceremonial seating arrangements, presents the data in terms of positions of individual chiefs, in effect each chief must be taken as representative of his household group. The household group contains the chief and a category called *mastcim*. Sapir notes the following:

Not all *Mastcim* had regular seats, but only those that were related to chiefs through younger lines of earlier chiefs. (*Mastcim* < perhaps *ma'astci* "to live at a village"; Al claims it means "one supposed to help chief in potlatches and so on." Each chief would have certain *mastcim* belonging to him and living in his house; if household got too large, 'o'atslo'i' would build new house, next to old house if there was room and take certain number of *mastcim* and slaves with him. One had to be *mastcim* to somebody; there was no unattached *mastcim* class. *Mastcim* are in main part descended from younger brothers' lines that did not carry many privileges, these being always given to oldest sons. All chiefs but head are *mastcim* to him, even his own father. There is no *mastcim* class as such. Village is merely overgrown family descended from ancestor; privileges always go to oldest sons. Those inferior in rank are merely untitled younger brothers. Chiefs address "mastcim" by relationship terms, such as "younger brother, uncle.") (Sapir Field Notes XV:50)

The fixed points in both the social structure and the ranking system are the statuses of the chiefs. Chiefs play many roles. It is the chiefs who gather the people of their household around them, through kinship or through other means; it is the chiefs who own all the property, economic resources, privileges, ceremonial seats, and houses. This structure is recapitulated in the potlatches.

Direct expression of the relative ranking of chiefs within a confederacy or tribe occurs in the arrangement of ceremonial seats at a potlatch. Each chief of a local group has a ceremonial seat in a particular location, placing him in rank order relative to the other chiefs of local groups in the confederacy. Such seats are owned individually by chiefs and are transmitted to their heirs in the same manner as other rights. Drucker provides data on seating arrangements for several confederacies. "There were differences in the number of seats used, depending on who was giving the potlatch, and whether it was a large or small affair" (Drucker 1951:263). The question of who was to be invited, chiefs from the same or from different tribes or confederacies, was also a factor in determining the number of chiefs to be seated.

The Drucker data on seating arrangements for the several tribes and confederacies illustrate the varying degrees of integration accompanying the process of confederation. For example, for the Kyuquot, one of the oldest confederacies, the seating of twenty-five chiefs in order of rank is presented. It is apparent that the chief representing each house within each local group is separately ranked. Two chiefs within the same local group (sept or lineage) may be far apart in rank; for example, the two chiefs from the local group Tacisath are ranked second and twenty-second. A similar example is offered for the chiefs of the Ehetisat confederacy. The ranked seating of fourteen chiefs, each representing a house group, is provided by Drucker (Drucker 1951:262-63). These fourteen houses represent eight local groups. Two of these local groups have four houses, while others are represented by only one. The eight local groups form two tribes which are joined together in the confederacy. An analysis of the history of this confederacy reveals that "the tatcu chiefs . . . attained highest rank in the confederacy through a marriage to the eldest daughter of a Litcyaath chief"

(Drucker 1951:227). Drucker further notes that the Litcyaath chief had attained his primacy by marriage to the daughter of the Ehetis chief. It is also interesting to note that while one of the Tatcuath chiefs is ranked in the number-one position, another chief of the same local group is ranked eleventh in the confederacy. These examples contrast with the seating given for the Hesquiat confederacy. The potlatch seating is according to the ranking of the local group; though several chiefs within a local group are ranked, when the entire confederacy meets all the chiefs of a particular local group are seated together in one group according to the rank of the local group. A graded series of chiefly ranks for the whole confederacy has not yet emerged.

In the south and central areas of the Nootka, where a lower level of political organization prevails and confederacies do not exist, this situation is reflected in the ceremonial seating and ranking. The Tsisa'ath tribe is made up of a number of local groups (septs in the terminology of Boas and Sapir). In his life history of Old Tom, a Tsisa'ath chief, Sapir states that "Tom learned in time that of all the honoured seats recognized at a feast, a certain number of contiguous seats in the rear of the house belonged to representatives of the Ts'isha'ath sept, a certain number of others at the right corner in the rear to those of another sept, and so on. Thus, the proper ranking of the septs was ever kept before the eye by the definite assignment of seats of higher and lower rank" (Sapir 1921: 243).

Historically, it would appear that autonomous local groups existed and that within these local groups chiefs of the different houses which composed the local group were ranked. When several local groups were united as a tribe, frequently after a period of active warfare when one local group emerged as the dominant group, the initial process involved a ranking of local groups each of which maintained a unity within the tribe. Examples of this are to be found among the Tsisa'ath in the south and among the Muchalat in the north. In his history of the Muchalat, Drucker recounts:

"Among the Muchalat, whom we have seen in the process of consolidation, the matcli [one local group] chiefs were never challenged in their right to the first and second places, because there
were more of those people among the survivors; the a'aminqas
chiefs, bolstered by their wild upriver kin, were next in importance. The remaining places, distributed among the small remnants
of other groups, were the ones that were squabbled over" (Drucker
1951:246). Elsewhere, in discussing the Muchalat, Drucker notes
that "it took a generation for the relative rank of the chiefs to become established. Feast seats were never integrated: the chiefs of
each local group sat by themselves, as though they were still independent units" (Drucker 1951:235).

In the formation of confederacies, a process analogous to the
amalgamation of local groups into tribes occurred. The potlatch
seating arrangement for the Moachat confederacy represents an advanced stage. Thirteen rank seats are provided, each for the chief
of a particular house. The last five of the seats are allocated to the
chiefs of one tribe, the Tlupana Arm (o'wis) people, and the first
eight to the chiefs of the Kupti tribe. For the Moachat confederacy
Drucker notes that "the tribes retained their autonomy to a greater
extent than did those of neighboring confederacies, however, for
the two series of chiefs were not integrated for a long time. In fact,
it may not have been until about the middle of the last century,
when yukwot came to be used more and more extensively as a win-
tering place, and the two tribes were invited together as a single
group to potlatches, that it became necessary to work out a seriation
of chiefs' precedence" (Drucker 1951:230-31). The Kyuquot and
Ehetisat illustrate the most advanced form of consolidation.

Actual group membership in Nootka society, given ambilateral
descent and shifting residence, refers to those people interacting in
concert at a given time. Permanency is to be found in sites of villages, houses, and fishing stations, and in the positions in the social
system in which ownership rights or title to these is vested. The
head chief of a house is in such a position. He is the focal point for

those individuals who constitute his house group. Though an individual may have claims to several seats, he holds only one at a time. The one he holds depends upon where he is residing. This point is supported by the following example from Sapir's field notes: "Jackson has no son; his oldest daughter . . . is married to ah. Indian. Their girl cannot sit with Jackson in 'mukw. seat, because her people *live* with ah. and she is considered to be ah.; if Jackson's son-in-law had been living with his wife's people, his daughter would be seated next to Jackson" (Sapir Field Notes XV:45). This quotation also illustrates the fact that many women may succeed to and occupy seats in the absence of a brother, but only if they reside with their fathers after marriage. (See also Sapir Field Notes XV: 42, 42a, 43, III:165.) It is therefore clear that active participation in a household and a local group determines an individual's position in his interaction with others.

Exploitation of resources demands frequent seasonal shifts of residence for entire groups. In the wintertime, people live in winter villages. These winter villages consist of clusters of houses at a particular site, frequently on sheltered inlets, which are inhabited by one or more local groups. The winter village, as a physical site composed of house sites, as well as a social entity composed of people, persists even though the composition of the house groups as residence units may shift over time. A winter village which is composed of several houses represents what Drucker refers to as a tribe. As noted, though the Nootka do not have a set of lexical categories to distinguish house group, local group, tribe, or confederacy, each of these represents a new step in increased political complexity which brings about new problems in ordering of rank.

In some areas in the summer, larger agglomerations of people come together at the site of a summer village, usually on lower portions of inlets or on outside beaches. The summer village represents the largest grouping of people in Nootka society. Two structural units are apparent in the summer village: the house and the entire village. Tribal and local group organization is not represented in the arrangement of houses within the summer village. The structural entity corresponding to the people forming such summer villages is the confederacy. At this maximal level of political organization the eclipse of tribal and local organization is echoed by the fact that the chief of each house group has a separate rank position as represented by his ceremonial seat without regard to the rank of other chiefs in his local group, as noted above. The integrity of the house group as an entity is enhanced. Drucker further notes that house groups in this context may potlatch and feast other groups independently.

In areas where confederacies do not exist, the tribe may have a particular summer fishing station; the same may be true even of an autonomous local group.

The potlatch and the links through exchange which it reveals illustrate the dynamic interrelationship between the various aspects of the social structure: the structure of local groups, lines of descent, political leadership, significant points in the life cycle, transmission of privileges, rights, and titles between individuals, supernatural sanctions for the existing structure, and rank and mobility are all brought into play in the potlatch.

The potlatch among the Nootka has the following distinctive characteristics. Only chiefs serve as hosts of potlatches (Boas 1891: 585; Drucker 1951:182). In accord with the previous discussion of chiefs as focal points in the social structure, chiefs potlatch with the assistance of their *mastcim,* as noted above. They also share in his renown. A commoner will substitute a feast, for which a separate term is used, at important life-crisis events. When a chief potlatches, other individuals of the tribe may contribute goods or distribute goods themselves. In such cases their contributions are publically announced and they acquire esteem.

The Nootka potlatch is characterized by a minimum of competition, destruction of property, or the shaming of rivals. The competition which may be present is most often conceptualized by the Nootka in terms of competition with one's ancestor. Sapir provides only one example of competition with a rival in his extensive field material. In this example he notes: "Sometimes rivals would settle quarrel by potlatching. Once Ciwic knocked Qecqeca's father down in quarrel. Latter was too old to fight with fist. He got up and said, 'naspitap'hak' si'ya,' 'You've flopped me down, haven't you?' oh'winik!in Hawilmis 'niLak' 'let's use our wealth in fighting.' Next spring he gave his potlatch, which Ciwic could not reciprocate, and thus he was downed" (Sapir Field Notes XII:49). This is in contrast to the northern matrilineal groups where competitive eating and dancing occur. Nowhere in the Nootka potlatches described by Drucker, Sapir, and Swadesh does this kind of competitive behavior appear. Nor is the symbolic rivalry so characteristic of the Kwakiutl present here, with the exception of one very minor reference in a footnote where Sapir and Swadesh note: "Alex Thomas claims that an invited tribe often feels humiliated when looking on at a dance that surpasses what they have done themselves" (Sapir and Swadesh 1939:229). Competition is minor in the symbolic content of the potlatch, as affirmed by Drucker when he states: "Property destruction was not practiced nor was there competitive potlatching" (Drucker 1951:383).

The Nootka always potlatched to their relatives. According to native interpretation, the potlatch has the purpose of passing a privilege from the host and donor of the potlatch to another individual, frequently a child, in whose honor the potlatch is given and who is in a sense therefore an heir. Those invited as guests perform the service of public witnessing of the privilege, its past history, and its passage to a new holder. Various points in the life cycle provide occasions for potlatches. The more important a chief, the more privileges, titles, and prerogatives he possesses, the more potlatches he gives, and the more heirs he may distribute prerogatives to. According to Drucker:

Every important step along life's road, including the life crises, called for a public announcement and festivities. Of course, the extent to which this was done varied with the person's rank. A chief's life was punctuated by an infinity of public celebrations: feasts, potlatches, and Shamans' Dances, each time with the assumption of a new name to signalize his new status, from the time his mother's pregnancy became known until his heir gave a memorial potlatch to remove the tabu on the last-used name a few years after his death (Drucker 1951:118).

Of these various occasions, the most important for a chief is the first menstruation and the accompanying puberty rites of his eldest daughter.

Sapir's life history of Old Tom, a Tsisa'ath chief of a southern Nootka group, gives the potlatching career of an important chief. The text material includes extensive detail in the informant's own words on the potlatches. The following is a synopsis of Tom's potlatching career:

1. Potlatch for FaBrDaSo to wash away the taint of the child's low-ranking father
2. Wolf ritual
3. On the occasion of Tom's marriage ("bridal purchase")
4. Puberty potlatch for Tom's younger sister
5. Birth of his first child
6. Property distribution after Tom's slave ran away
7. Potlatch to Uclulet (the first property distribution for Tom involving non-Tsisa'ath; his son Douglas receives his first name)
8. Potlatch to Ahousat and Comox (Douglas receives a new name)
9. Puberty potlatch of his eldest daughter (analyzed more fully in Chart E): this was the most important of Old Tom's potlatches and involved twelve tribes
10. Potlatch to Kyuquot (he gives a name to his daughter)
11. Potlatch to Hesquiat
12. Wolf ritual for Tom's unborn grandchild

The time factor is important in the analysis of Tom's potlatching career. The first eight potlatches took place within a relatively short space of time. Then, after Tom's eldest daughter was born, he began to accumulate property and wealth and began to build a house in preparation for the potlatch he planned for her puberty rite. The birth of Tom's eldest son is marked by a potlatch, but it is a relatively minor one. In contrast, the puberty potlatch of his daughter, which he begins planning at her birth, is on a much greater scale. The potlatch and the accompanying Wolf ritual for Tom's unborn grandchild are secondary in importance and mark the end of his potlatching career. Potlatch number five, the occasion of the birth of his eldest son, is not as important as Tom's puberty potlatch for his daughter given sometime later.

The two potlatches analyzed here—Tom's potlatch for his daughter's puberty rite collected by Sapir (Chart E), and the potlatch in honor of a young son by an Ehetisat chief from Drucker material (Chart F)—are the most detailed and extensive in the Nootkan ethnographic literature and serve well to illustrate the manner in which the potlatch may be used to illuminate the dynamics of the social structure.

There are important differences between the southern Nootkan groups with which Chart E deals and the northern Nootkan tribes. Sapir notes: "In inviting another tribe, among more northern tribes, chief would often send his people around from house to house in village to collect quota of fish or other goods as contribution towards feast. In dealing with other tribes, chief is representative of his tribe. Ts!ic Indians do not think much of this method, however, as it is no great credit to chief; . . . nor do they seem to consider custom of returning potlatch money with interest as practiced among Kwakiutl Indians, as reflecting credit upon one who potlatches (among Ts!ic Indians potlatching makes one poor, not rich; witness Tom, who was once very rich and now, by potlatching, has become poor)" (Sapir Field Notes XI:18). The difference between the northern and southern groups reflects the difference in political complexity. Tom potlatches with the support of his immediate household but not as a representative of his tribe, while in the potlatch in Chart F the Ehetisat chief does potlatch as a repre-

Chart E. A Nootka Potlatch for a Daughter's Puberty Rite

A. ACCUMULATION OF PROPERTY AND BUILDING OF HOUSE

Tom begins to accumulate property immediately upon the birth of his daughter though the potlatch is not to be held for at least twelve years. As part of this potlatch, he intends to build a house and hence begins to plan this Nootka-style house and to accumulate large beams. The construction of the outer frame of the house proceeds with the help of the Uchucklesit (Hochoktlisath) and the Hopachisat. Both groups are closely related to Tom and assist him in putting up the heavy beams. Before the completion of the house, Tom's daughter begins to menstruate. With $2,000 in twenty-dollar gold pieces, Tom canoes to Victoria to bargain for the blankets which he will distribute.

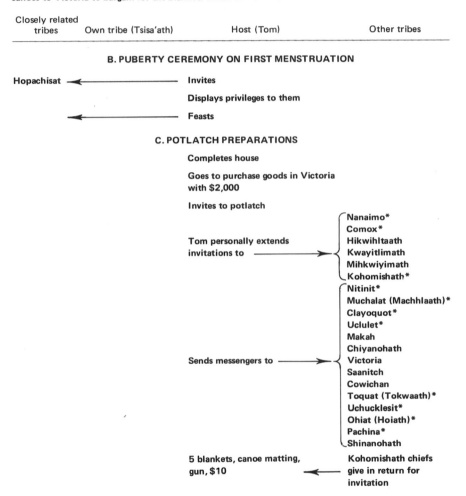

Closely related tribes	Own tribe (Tsisa'ath)	Host (Tom)	Other tribes

B. PUBERTY CEREMONY ON FIRST MENSTRUATION

Hopachisat ◄——————— Invites

Displays privileges to them

◄——————— Feasts

C. POTLATCH PREPARATIONS

Completes house

Goes to purchase goods in Victoria with $2,000

Invites to potlatch

Tom personally extends invitations to ——————►
Nanaimo*
Comox*
Hikwihltaath
Kwayitlimath
Mihkwiyimath
Kohomishath*

Sends messengers to ——————►
Nitinit*
Muchalat (Machhlaath)*
Clayoquot*
Uclulet*
Makah
Chiyanohath
Victoria
Saanitch
Cowichan
Toquat (Tokwaath)*
Uchucklesit*
Ohiat (Hoiath)*
Pachina*
Shinanohath

5 blankets, canoe matting, gun, $10 ◄—— Kohomishath chiefs give in return for invitation

D. ARRIVAL OF GUESTS

Sings Uchucklesit song

*These chiefs responded to Tom's invitation.

Closely related tribes	Own tribe (Tsisa'ath)	Host (Tom)	Other tribes
Women of Uchucklesit and Hopachisat dance	**Women dance**		
		Sings 2d Uchucklesit song	
←—————————	←—————————	Distributes tea and tells all to keep cups (to 1,800 guests)	—————————→
←—————————	←—————————	Crackers also distributed	—————————→
		"Then I potlatched to ten score people, I distributed ten score blankets. I saw that the chiefs of the tribes were abashed, for they had never done that; I had put the chiefs of all the tribes below [me]" (Sapir and Swadesh 1939: 157)	
		Sings a Tsisa'ath song to a Uchucklesit dance	
		Sings two Tsisa'ath "wealth-display" songs	
		Sings another Tsisa'ath "wealth-display" song, noting, "My wealth, it is looking for the one who is, like it, wealthy" (its equal) (Sapir and Swadesh 1939: 159)	
		Sings a Hisawistath "wealth-display" song (Tom's father's MoMoMo group). "By no one am I equalled" (Sapir and Swadesh 1939: 159)	
		Distributes one pot each —————→ 10 chiefs	
		Distributes 2 blankets to each (ten score in all) —————→ Senior chiefs	
		Sings Uchucklesit song	
		Display of privileges in the form of tableau (origin myth of Tsisa'ath)	

[Guessing game in which all including Tsisa'ath and Hopachisat take part]

		Displays topatii for girls' puberty rite. Involves a contest	
		Gives 5 blankets —————→	An Ohiat named "Chicken" who wins contest
		Displays a Tsisa'ath whale topatii and gives its origin myth involving his ancestor	

Chart E (continued)

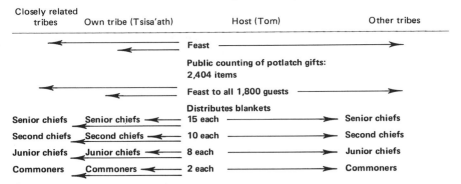

Sources: Sapir and Swadesh, "Tom Gives Various Potlatches," Nootka Texts, pp. 139–72; Sapir, "The
    Life of a Nootka Indian," Queen's Quarterly, XXVIII, No. 4 (1921), 360, 362; and the genea-
    logical information on Tom from Swadesh's and from Sapir's field notes.

sentative of his tribe. The potlatch in Chart F took place as part of
a Shaman's Dance Ritual, which is also known as the Wolf Ritual.
The informant was the sister of the potlatch giver, who was the
highest chief of the Ehetisat confederacy. The potlatch was in
honor of his young son.

In these two potlatches, dynamic features of the Nootka social
structure may be discerned. The major actors in the potlatch are
the host and giver of the potlatch, the individuals in whose honor
the potlatch is being given, the groups closely related to the host
who contribute goods and services, and the guests who have been
invited to witness the public display and transfer of privileges.
Chiefs of high rank were the hosts. In Tom's case, wealth was accumulated by Tom without assistance. Even in the building of his
house, he got assistance only to raise the beams. Though all the
Tsisa'ath shared in the reflected glory of the potlatch, it was Tom
who recounted the legends of his ancestors, displayed his privileges
from various lines, distributed his wealth, and earned the great
esteem bestowed upon the giver of a potlatch; in the final distribution he even distributed to his own tribe, as though its members
were equivalent to invited guests. In the potlatch described by
Drucker, the Ehetisat chief MH, who is the giver, is offered assist-

Chart F. A Nootka Potlatch for a Chief's Son

Closely related tribes	Other chiefs of host tribe	Host tribe (Ehetisat)	Host	Guests

A. INVITATIONS AND PREPARATIONS

Issues invitations  **Kyuquot**

Gives gifts "for canoe" (money plus objects: $145)— "Some to take back to chief, some for inviters"

Feast
"He told them he wanted them to assist him by singing and dancing only, he did not want any financial aid." Sister's husband says, "Let us help him a little, giving him money for the preliminary potlatches. If the chief wants to give the main potlatch alone, we shall let him do so" (Drucker 1951: 417, 418)

Tribesmen give $600 ⟶

B. ARRIVAL OF GUESTS

Displays crest and dances

Kyuquot display crests and dance

Host's sister displays supernatural crystal and throws it ⟶

Chief ceremonially returns it

Gives small gift for witnessing display of supernatural crystal ⟶ **10 leading Kyuquot chiefs**

Several chiefs of host tribe ⟵ **Give a few dollars to each**

"Beach Owner" invites to feast ⟶ **Kyuquot**

94

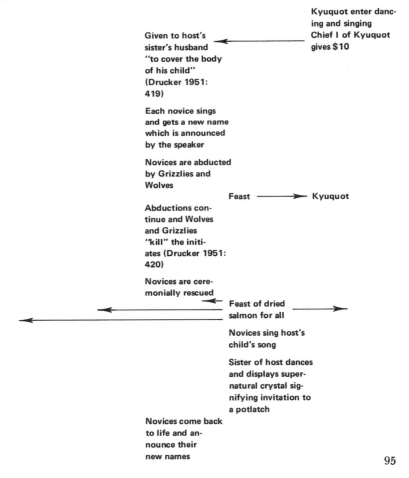

Closely related tribes	Other chiefs of host tribe	Host tribe (Ehetisat)	Host	Guests
	Displays dance			
	Distributes $140 ◄────────────			$1 or 50¢ to each Kyuquot man
	Another chief in "Beach Owner's" house feasts ──────────►			Kyuquot

C. WOLF RITUAL

[Host's son is snatched by "wolves." Chief and his father's brother are mauled by the people "for not taking care of the young chief" (Drucker 1951: 419). Other initiates are then seized; "some people might refuse (on some pretext or other) if they did not have enough money to give away" (ibid.). Twenty-three initiates (novices) were taken.]

				Kyuquot enter dancing and singing
		Given to host's sister's husband ◄──────── "to cover the body of his child" (Drucker 1951: 419)		Chief I of Kyuquot gives $10
		Each novice sings and gets a new name which is announced by the speaker		
		Novices are abducted by Grizzlies and Wolves		
			Feast ──────►	Kyuquot
		Abductions continue and Wolves and Grizzlies "kill" the initiates (Drucker 1951: 420)		
		Novices are ceremonially rescued		
◄────────	◄────────		Feast of dried salmon for all ──────►	
		Novices sing host's child's song		
		Sister of host dances and displays supernatural crystal signifying invitation to a potlatch		
		Novices come back to life and announce their new names		

95

Closely related tribes	Other chiefs of host tribe	Host tribe (Ehetisat)	Host	Guests
Nuchatlet aid Ehetisat in imitating dances ———————⟶		Dance groups perform dances and distribute gifts that they themselves furnish ———————⟶		Each giver gave to individual guests as he or she wished, but all had to get something
		Young women give gifts ———————⟶		Kyuquot women
		Old women give dishpans ———————⟶		Kyuquot women
		Old men give guns, blankets, money ———————⟶		Older male guests
		Middle-aged men give cloth ———————⟶		Middle-aged men
		Young men give shirts ———————⟶		Young male guests
			Has crane dance privilege displayed and ancestral myth recounted	
			Gives $2 each for "looking at the privilege" ⟶	4 leading chiefs
			Gives money and articles of value ⟶ in return for gifts to the inviting party (different objects than those originally given)	All Kyuquot chiefs who had given to inviting party
				Chief I recounts kin relationship to host tribe
				Dance and distribution by Kyuquot chiefs and their followers
			Chief ⟵———	Kyuquot Chief I gives blanket
			Chief's sister ⟵—	shawl
Nuchatlet ⟵—————————————————				money: $1 to men 50¢ to women
Nuchatlet ⟵—————————————————			⟵———	Younger brother of Kyuquot Chief I dances and throws double handful of silver dollars and half dollars four times
			Chief ⟵———	Kyuquot Chief II gives canoe
Nuchatlet ⟵—————————————————			⟵———	$1 or 50¢ to each male

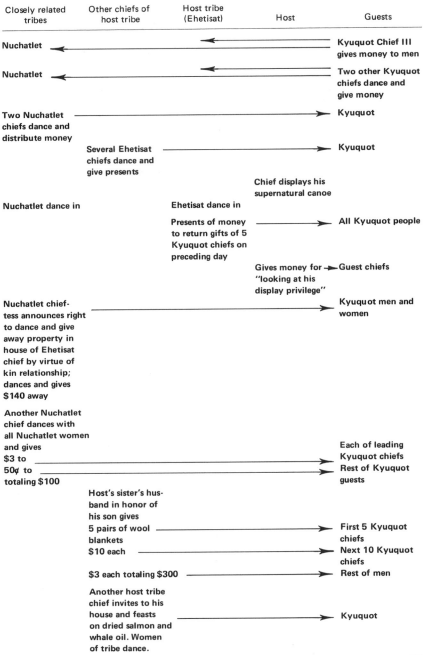

Closely related tribes	Other chiefs of host tribe	Host tribe (Ehetisat)	Host	Guests
Nuchatlet ←		←		Kyuquot Chief III gives money to men
Nuchatlet ←		←		Two other Kyuquot chiefs dance and give money
Two Nuchatlet chiefs dance and distribute money →				Kyuquot
	Several Ehetisat chiefs dance and give presents →			Kyuquot
			Chief displays his supernatural canoe	
Nuchatlet dance in		Ehetisat dance in		
		Presents of money to return gifts of 5 Kyuquot chiefs on preceding day →		All Kyuquot people
			Gives money for → "looking at his display privilege"	Guest chiefs
Nuchatlet chieftess announces right to dance and give away property in house of Ehetisat chief by virtue of kin relationship; dances and gives $140 away →				Kyuquot men and women
Another Nuchatlet chief dances with all Nuchatlet women and gives $3 to → 50¢ to → totaling $100				Each of leading Kyuquot chiefs / Rest of Kyuquot guests
	Host's sister's husband in honor of his son gives 5 pairs of wool blankets → $10 each → $3 each totaling $300 →			First 5 Kyuquot chiefs / Next 10 Kyuquot chiefs / Rest of men
	Another host tribe chief invites to his house and feasts on dried salmon and whale oil. Women of tribe dance. →			Kyuquot

Closely related tribes	Other chiefs of host tribe	Host tribe (Ehetisat)	Host	Guests
	Chief distributes:			
	shotgun ⟶			First Kyuquot chief
	pair of wool blankets ⟶ each			Next 3 Kyuquot chiefs
	canoe ⟶			Fifth Kyuquot chief
	$130 ⟶			Guests
	cloth and dishes ⟶			Female guests
		Novices ⟵	Feast of steamed ⟶ clams, dried fish, boiled fish, boiled potatoes, salmon eggs, and tea	Kyuquot
	Speeches emphasiz- ing kinship to Kyuquot			
	One chief displays a marriage test priv- ilege in honor of his novice daughter. Sings his property- giving song. Gives 2 canoes, 3 render- ing kettles, 3 pairs of woolen blankets, $120 ⟶			All Kyuquot
	Two other chiefs dance and give away money ⟶			All Kyuquot
		Novices ritually bathe, marking end of Wolf ritual and freeing of novices from restrictions at New Moon		
Chief of Queen's Cove group (close- ly associated with hosts) gives feast ⟶				Kyuquot
		Kelp Cod women's ⟶ dance group dance and give presents at feast of chief of Queen's Cove. Also at Queen's Cove feast, Butterfly women's dance group dance and give away silk scarves ⟶		Kyuquot women
				Kyuquot women

D. POTLATCH PROPER

	Classificatory nephew of chief holds pot- latch in honor of his son in house of host			

Closely related tribes	Other chiefs of host tribe	Host tribe (Ehetisat)	Host	Guests
		Kelp Cod women dance at potlatch of chief's classificatory nephew. Give sticks representing sacks of potatoes and food delicacies ——————————→		Kyuquot
	Classificatory nephew of chief displays privileges, using three dancers whom he pays. Displays privileges obtained by him in spirit quest. Dances given for future use ——————————————→			Kyuquot
	Gives away $115:			
	$5 each ———————————————————→			Kyuquot Chiefs I and II
	rest ————————————————————→			Kyuquot guests
	His wife gives away cloth and dishes ————————→			Kyuquot women
				Kyuquot chief through his speaker says, "We shall be glad to use the dances . . . because we Kyuquot are closely related to your house" (Drucker 1951: 428)
	Feast and giving of "going-away gifts" by brother-in-law of host			
		Each house group in turn dances and presents gifts including blankets, clothing, dishes, food, mats ——————→		Friends among the guests
			Invites guests to main potlatch	
				Kyuquot chiefs called and seated by rank for first time in ritual. Rest of Kyuquot called, men seated at one side, women on other
			Sings property song	
			Gives $40 ——→	Kyuquot Chief I

Chart F (continued)

Closely related tribes	Other chiefs of host tribe	Host tribe (Ehetisat)	Host	Guests
			Gives $30 ——⟶	Kyuquot Chief II
			$10 each —⟶	Other 10 seated Kyuquot chiefs
			$5 ——⟶	Kyuquot men
			$2.50 ——⟶	Kyuquot women
			Host's wife and —⟶ sister give house- hold articles	Kyuquot women
			Sings property song again	
			Distributes $80, —⟶ $1 to each as far as it goes	Kyuquot men
			Makes speech at the potlatch in honor of his child and sister's child: "They had bought so many wives from each other that they were just like one tribe" (Drucker 1951: 429)	
				Kyuquot Chief I reaffirms kin ties

Source: Drucker 1951: 417–29.

ance by fellow tribesmen but he declines it. Nevertheless, his tribesmen contribute to the potlatch. Other Ehetisat distribute in their own names at various points in his ceremony and thereby gain esteem for themselves. However, the goods they distribute are not considered part of MH's potlatch distribution. Close kinsmen of MH and all the Ehetisat assist in the singing and dancing and entertain the Kyuquot guests in their houses. It was MH, the Ehetisat chief, who, as giver of the potlatch, announced the potlatch and brought it to a final climax with his great distribution.

During the course of the potlatch ceremony, the host displays a number of his privileges. In Tom's case, the privileges come from a number of his lines. He uses a Hisawistath wealth display song from his father's mother's mother's mother; he uses four Uchuckle-sit privileges derived from his mother's mother; and he uses several Tsisa'ath wealth songs derived from his mother's father, his father's mother's father's father; and another from his father's father's mother. As Sapir notes: "At last analysis rank is not a permanent status which is expressed in a number of absolutely fixed ways, but is rather the resultant standing attained by the inheritance of a considerable number of theoretically independent privileges which do, indeed, tend in most cases to be associated in certain ways, but may nevertheless be independently transmitted from generation to generation" (Sapir 1915:362). Throughout the potlatch, the giver is the central figure rather than the person being honored.

The individual, or individuals, in whose honor the potlatch is given are usually children. The potlatch serves to transfer privileges, prerogatives, and other rights from the host to the child. Inheritance and succession to title occur during the lifetime of the previous holder. By this means, children inherit titles long before they themselves become adult and begin to potlatch. When they first potlatch, they assume the roles of a chief and thereby enhance their own rank and status. This is because status and enhanced rank accrue to the potlatch giver rather than to the individual being honored and to whom titles, etc., are being transferred, despite the fact that it is the life crisis of the person being honored, and not that of the potlatch giver, which provides the occasion for the potlach. This is exemplified in both of the potlatches described: a girl's first menstruation, and initiation into a secret society involving the ritual killing of the novice and his renaming. Tom's potlatch career also supports this point; most of his potlatch occasions are other people's life crises, and his final potlatch is in honor of his unborn grandson being carried by his pregnant daughter-in-law.

The guests invited to the potlatch provide the service of witnessing. There is no clear-cut category of "opposites" to whom

groups or individuals potlatch. No moieties, no wife-giving and
wife-taking groups, and no clear-cut category of affines exist. One is
always potlatching to one's relatives. In MH's potlatch, he very
frequently reiterates the kinship between the Ehetisat and the
Kyuquot, stressing that they are relatives because "they had bought
so many wives from each other that they were just like one tribe"
(Drucker 1951:429). Given ambilateral descent and the multiple
lines of inheritance, the quotation signifies both consanguineal
descent and affinality. The minimization of competition in potlatches relates to the fact that one potlatches to those whom one
recognizes as relatives. The absence of a clearly delimited group,
separate from one's own, from whom one regularly takes wives is
in agreement with the absence of competing groups which potlatch.
Yet, though competition may be minimal in Nootka potlatches,
one still finds statements such as Tom's: "I saw that the chiefs of
the tribes were abashed, for they had never done that; I had put
the chiefs of all the tribes below (me)" (Sapir and Swadesh 1939:
157). During the process of enhancement, it is inevitable that some
competition is engendered as a concomitant of the potlatch in
general. However, Nootka potlatching does not seem to be aimed
at provoking, embarrassing, or shaming one's guest. Guests who
were invited, as kin, "were expected to know something of his [the
host's] ancestry and the truth of his claims" (Drucker 1951:386).
"When a chief feted another tribe, it was not because he wanted to
make a show of his privileges to just anyone, but because he wanted
to show them to his kinsmen" (Drucker 1951:274). The kinship
affiliation of guests relates directly to the ambilaterality. The many
privileges from multiple descent lines which the host displays require an audience of witnesses who represent the various descent
lines to which he is related and to which he is publicly calling
attention. Every privilege that is displayed (mask, dance, song, dish,
etc.) requires a statement of its origin myth, the way in which it
was transmitted to its first human holder, and the line of descent
to its present holder. Only closely related local groups are invited

to a small potlatch. The more important a chief, the more numerous are his privileges and the grander is his potlatch. The circle of guests will come from far and wide, from other tribes and even from other confederacies, and will represent the wider circle of kin in which he operates by virtue of his greatness. In such circumstances, people from descent lines most closely related to him servé as semi-hosts, as is illustrated in both potlatches. Old Tom uses Uckucklesit and Hopachisat, as well as Tsisa'ath dancers; and the Nuchatlet in consort with the Ehetisat display privileges at MH's potlatch.

Closely related kin, in their roles as subsidiary hosts, feast the guests in their own houses. They also claim the right to give subsidiary property distributions at another's potlatch by virtue of their close relation to the host. In the MH potlatch, the Ehetisat Beach Owner and another chief in the Beach Owner's house both give feasts. Nuchatlet chiefs in the same potlatch also display privileges and distribute property; in particular, the Nuchatlet chieftess claims this right on the basis of her kinship to the host. Other Ehetisat chiefs display privileges and give property away in honor of their children, thereby accruing esteem to themselves.

Drucker, in his analysis, has placed emphasis upon ceremonial seating and the order of precedence in that seating. It is interesting to note, however, that even among the Ehetisat, who are of the northern Nootka group, seating of chiefs in their ceremonial order of precedence occurs only at the very end of the potlatch ceremonies just prior to the final and greatest distribution of goods. Drucker notes that there is a prohibition against the graded seating of chiefs until the Shamans' Dance proper has ended (Drucker 1951:387). At most of the distributions, the first and second chiefs are singled out and given larger amounts. At Tom's potlatch three divisions of chiefs are taken into account in the distribution of property, but no mention is made of ceremonial seating.

Another interesting feature of MH's potlatch is the dance group performances. The groups are organized on the basis of age and sex criteria (Drucker 1951:399). Differences of rank and lines of descent are not relevant in the formation of these groups. Yet they distribute property to their counterparts among the guests, the characteristic activity of a potlatch.

As is so characteristic among the Northwest Coast groups, the potlatch among the Nootka frequently involves the building of a new house. Tom plans to have the potlatch at his daughter's puberty rite coincide with the completion of a new house which he began to plan as soon as he knew that a daughter had been born. For twelve years, Tom proceeded with the building of his house, which was to conform with the dimensions of the ancient Tsisa'ath house. The house as an entity is a symbolic manifestation of the people forming the house group. Its carved posts and painted decorations symbolize the ancestors of the chief, its owner, and those of that particular descent line. Tom's building of a new house may have had one of several different meanings. His aspirations for social mobility would, he may have thought, be furthered by his ownership of a large Nootka-style house. It might also have represented the budding off and the formation of a new house group, or his old house may have been in disrepair. In each case, a potlatch would have been necessary to consecrate the new house, to witness the importance of its chief through his display of privileges and through the membership of the group gathered around him in the house. According to Sproat: "There are always feasts and distributions when a new house is built" (Sproat 1868:59).

Among the Nootka, the potlatch is the occasion for dramatizing rites and privileges and for enunciating the ambilateral lines of descent associated with the privileges, as well as for transferring formally such rites and privileges to the new holder. Analytically, the potlatch may be seen as the dynamic manifestation of the ambilateral social structure.

The final life crisis, death, is also the occasion for a potlatch. Treatment of the corpse and burial are carried out by relatives, members of one's own tribe. A number of recurrent features of the funerary complex of the Northwest Coast reoccur among the Nootka but in an attenuated form. Memorial poles are not set up, though a crest may be left as a marker at the grave of an important chief. Valuables of various types may also be left there. The heir makes a mourning feast which is followed by a "Throwing Away" potlatch at which time the dead chief's last-held name and some of his prerogatives are "put away" for a set period of time. The taboo is formally removed at a subsequent potlatch some years later. There is a relationship between death, potlatching, and succession. However, among the Nootka, where succession in large part has occurred through the transfer of privileges during the lifetime of the individual, the significance of the memorial potlatch as a demonstration of the validation of claim to office is much less important and less formalized than among the Haida, Tlingit, and Tsimshian. The destruction of an important chief's private property occurs. Sapir specifically states that "in the old days the whole house might be burned down, and tales are told how the mourning survivors moved off to another spot to build them a new house" (Sapir 1921: 366). Drucker, on the other hand, notes "that the big multifamily houses were never burned even when the chief died" (Drucker 1951:150).

The direct relationship between the potlatch and social mobility, such as was found among the northern matrilineal groups, does not exist among the Nootka. In the northern groups, succession to political office involved competition among several candidates for office. The ability to accumulate property and followers and to potlatch first marked the successful candidate. Among the Nootka, primogeniture and the passing on of titles and chiefly prerogatives to young children at potlatches given during the course of the incumbent chief's lifetime eliminate competitive potlatching of rivals and that type of social mobility within the group. Local groups and tribes are ordered hierarchically. This ranking is flexible and, as seen above, shifts in rank, especially in the northern tribes, have occurred through time. The ideal order of precedence, in which the descendants of elder brothers rank higher than the descendants of younger brothers, has been overturned. These shifts seem to have been due to conquest by war rather than the result of pot-latching activity. Changes in the system of rank are the result primarily of marriage—which is a potlatch—and warfare.

CHAPTER V. *THE BELLA COOLA*

THE BELLA COOLA inhabit the lower Bella Coola River, the Kimsquit River, and the South Bentwick Arm in British Columbia. Ambilateral in descent, the Bella Coola exhibit a structure which, in its general features, is similar to that of the Nootka. They are in some ways the simplest of the societies considered here. They speak a dialect of the Salishan family. According to Boas, their language is quite similar to the language of the Coast Salish dialects of Oregon, Washington, and British Columbia, from which they are separated by Kwakiutl and Athabascan speakers (Boas 1898:26).

The term Bella Coola is a variant of a Kwakiutl word (Boas 1898:26). The Bella Coola have no term for themselves. Their unity is based upon common language, common ceremonial and mythical structure, and common cultural heritage rather than upon any kind of political organization. McIlwraith noted forty-five distinct villages, of which he wrote: "Each village was practically an independent political unit . . . indeed, bloodshed between towns of the Bella Coola valley itself was not uncommon" (McIlwraith 1948 I:17).

In Bella Coola mythology, each village was settled by "First Settlers," the descendants of which are said to form the ancestral family or *minmints* which still occupy the village. The prerogatives of *minmints* membership are land and names. The names are embodied in an origin myth. An ancestral family—that is, a village—is associated with an area which is itself internally diverse, including hunting grounds, collecting grounds, and areas of the river which are used for fishing. "Practically a man hunts only in the grounds of those ancestral families in whose origin myths he has names, though theoretically, he is entitled to hunt on any hunting-ground of any ancestral family of which he is a member whether or not he holds a duly validated name from its origin myth. It is not necessary to confirm the right to property as with a name, though a validated ancestral name is the usual mark of a man's right to that area of the ancestral family to which that designation belongs" (McIlwraith 1948 I:132). Since, however, only a limited number of traps may be placed at any one salmon weir, "the system of ownership prevailing . . . was that *individuals,* not groups, had rights to certain sections of the weir which were willable like other personal property. In most cases this right was transmitted with a name, marking the section of weir, which had to be duly validated by presents" (McIlwraith 1948 I:136).

McIlwraith states that "every Bella Coola has at least one name embodied in an ancient myth" (1948 I:167). It must be kept in mind that these are myths and on no account may they be accepted as history. The myths function as a justification for the social structure and are used at rituals and ceremonials precisely for this purpose. There are myths or *smaiusta* which are said to embody the names of the First Settlers of each village; and there are also legends or *simsma* which are differentiated from the former by the fact that they have no ritual significance. The names of the First Settlers are prestigious and the men who hold these names and have validated them are recognized as being men of influence and thus of high rank. The names embody prerogatives such as totem designs, dance ceremonials, and songs. These names are transferred from one individual to another. The basic mode of transmission is by inheritance, which must follow kin lines. As will be discussed below, the Bella Coola trace descent ambilaterally. Therefore, names may be acquired from mother's or father's kinsmen. Either or both may bestow names upon a child, signifying his right to membership in the respective kin group. Names may be transferred to a son-in-law but must then descend to the children of the marriage. If there are no children, a conflict may arise. The name may be returned by a "return marriage" which serves to bring the name back to the original kin unit. A name may also be lent to a non-kinsman for a financial consideration. It may not be passed on by him to his descendants and must ultimately be returned.

As noted above, ancestral names and prerogatives associated with them derive from myths called *smaiusta*. McIlwraith notes: "Two myths may give different people as the first occupants of a certain village, nor does such contradiction trouble the Bella Coola. Each man, convinced of the authenticity of his own family account, is quite willing to believe that the one belonging to someone else is equally correct" (1948 I:294). The implication of this is that there may be several ancestral myths associated with a single village. McIlwraith comments that it seems quite likely that legends or *simsma* have in the past been turned into *smaiusta* (1948 I:293). Through this mechanism, new *smaiusta,* or ancestral myths, are created which give legitimacy to the claim of a family that they are descended from "First Settlers." Thus several families, unrelated, may claim descent from mythical ancestors whom they consider to be the "First Settlers" of a village; as McIlwraith notes, the inconsistency of more than one set of "First Settlers" in a village is not seen as a conflict. The fundamental flexibility of the Bella Coola ranking system, which will be discussed below, is demonstrated by the lack of rigidity in their approach to ancestor myths, which are their ideological justification for existing social structure.

McIlwraith indicates an identity between an ancestral family and a particular village. A village consists of a number of houses and their constituent households. The heads of these households trace their relationship back to ancestors whom they consider to be the "First Settlers" of the village, though the household heads may in fact not be related to one another. Relationship back to the "First Settlers" may be traced ambilaterally, and usufruct rights in the property of the village are based upon this reckoning.

Residence with wife's *minmints* is a possibility and in such a case a man as the husband of a *minmints* member has access to strategic resources, though he would not be a member of the *minmints* by

descent. The children of such a man claim full rights of membership in the *minmints* through their mother (McIlwraith 1948 I:
132). The Bella Coola *minmints* is characterized by a singular absence of group solidarity. McIlwraith notes that members are not
responsible for one another's activity and that the *minmints* does
not act as a revenge unit. In contrast to the Kwakiutl, the *minmints*
does not potlatch as a unit.

A village consisted physically of a row of houses along the shore
of the river. The number of houses ranged from three or four to
twenty or thirty. There was no definite arrangement of the houses;
a person could build wherever there was a vacant space. Though
McIlwraith tells us that the houses could contain from three to ten
families, he nowhere gives us data on actual household composition
or numbers of people involved, nor do his field notes contain material on these points. Our analysis of the material leads us to the
conclusion that the household is *the* significant unit of the social
structure operative in economic assistance and potlatching. The
following quotation from McIlwraith on household composition
supports this view:

On the other hand, a wealthy and powerful man usually has a larger
family. Not only may he have several wives, but his aged relatives, and
those of his wife, look to him for support and assistance. Such are usually welcome to live in his house; they lend what aid they can in collecting food, and it gratifies a man's pride and sense of power to be closely
surrounded by a large family. . . . The married sons of a chief usually
live in his house, and if he is very powerful, the husbands of his daughters may also reside with him (1948 I:144-45).

The origin myths indicate that, of necessity, the first settlers married outside of the village, but soon a pattern of village endogamy
was said to have been established (McIlwraith 1948 I:120). It is
very clear from both Boas's and McIlwraith's materials that the
descent rule is ambilateral. "A man belongs to the village where
his first ancestor came to earth, though he is equally a member of
other towns into which his ancestors may have married" (McIl-

wraith 1948 I:138). McIlwraith further notes that "a man may claim descent from as many as eight . . . ancestral families" (McIlwraith 1948 I:120). There is a tendency toward virilocal residence after marriage. McIlwraith notes that [the girl] "usually lives in the house of X's [the boy's] father, though economic circumstances may compel her husband to live in her home" (1948 I:399). This implies that residence is optional or bilocal, though virilocality is said to be more common.

Though an individual may claim and even validate membership in several groups, he can live in only one village at any given time. The tendency toward virilocal residence results in a corresponding tendency to affiliate with father's *minmints,* and this may give a "patrilineal" slant to what is in fact an ambilateral group.

Distance in space and time combined to effect lapses in *minmints* membership and claims to *minmints* resources and property. "As with names, there is no doubt that a man tends to lose those rights and property which are strictly his, if they are located at a distance" (McIlwraith 1948 I:131-32).

The presence of ambilateral descent and choice in group affiliation may result in a situation where two brothers reside in different villages, so that the principle of the equivalence of brothers is not applicable here. This is aptly shown in the context of McIlwraith's discussion of murder and revenge when he notes: "A man's son, brother, or father are the only persons strictly liable, and even here the common sense of the Bella Coola outweighs their theoretical laws. A murderer's brother, living in another village would not be held liable; but more distant relatives living with the offender and considered as his family are liable" (1948 I:147-48). This also supports our previous point that the household is the effective unit of social action.

Inheritance is limited to personal property and names, since access to strategic resources is by virtue of *minmints* membership. Before his death, a man usually calls his relatives together and wills his personal property in slaves, canoes, and names (McIlwraith

1948 I:127). Names do not become the property of the new owner unless there is a validation by means of a distribution of property. "If, during this period, some other member of the ancestral family should desire it [the name] for a child, or for himself, he can take possession of it by the customary distribution of presents. In doing so he would anger the legatee, but the latter cannot himself use the appellation since it is already in use" (McIlwraith 1948 I:127).

With respect to rank and chiefs, our conclusions, based on an interpretation of McIlwraith's field notes, differ somewhat from his published interpretation. In his published statement, he makes the following points. There is no fixed structure of rank among the Bella Coola. The position of a chief is more open to individual definition and initiative than among the other Northwest Coast tribes considered here. There is no fixed ranking of individuals vis-à-vis one another and no order of precedence. Names are not hierarchically ordered nor is there a fixed arrangement of seats, as among the other groups. Names are inherited, however, and they must be validated by the distribution of goods. A name and its bearer become as great as the distributions of goods which validate the name. McIlwraith gives the term *staltimx* as the equivalent of chief, one whose influence is due to success in giving potlatches. "After a fourth potlatch a man is accorded a position of eminence, and is termed a *numitl* chief. *Numitl* is an untranslatable word, with the significance of passage, an allusion to the amount of goods which have passed through his hands" (McIlwraith 1948 I:173).

In his book, McIlwraith places much greater emphasis upon achievement of rank through potlatching activities than upon ascription of rank by means of inheritance. Though there is no question that potlatching is necessary to achieve rank, it is also quite clear that one must have a legitimate claim to a chiefly name. Both are necessary conditions to attain positions of rank. In this, the Bella Coola are similar to the other potlatching societies considered here. In the absence of fixed rules of succession among the Bella Coola, there is a certain amount of competition for names and chiefly position among contending heirs. This lends a strong element of individualism to Bella Coola potlatching, an aspect of their rank system that McIlwraith has exaggerated.

In support of our contention, we cite the following information from McIlwraith's field notes: "*Tyi* [a chief, a term repeatedly used in the field notes but which does not appear in the published version] purely hereditary. None but *tyi* can be *hlym* [potlatch donor] if ancestor dies a *tyi*, my grandfather a *tyi*, but did not add to family glory nor did father. I am still *tyi* but wish to add, so announce I am to become a *hlym* . . . first ancestor is resurrected in me, his glory is added to any that I may have" (McIlwraith Field Notes, page 682). Again he notes elsewhere: "Son of *tyi* in deference to his rank would always get presents in *hlim* if he fails to give return *hlim* he loses his place as *tyi*" (McIlwraith Field Notes, page 267). Within the existing pool of names, some have more prestige than others, because they are the names of First Settlers. Even in his published work McIlwraith notes that these names are more venerated than others (1948 I:141).

A parent during his lifetime may prepare the way for a child. In both the field notes and the published work, McIlwraith notes that during the engagement and subsequent marriage great attention is paid to the future position of the child. An ancestral name is given to the child; he is treated with respect and given presents by potlatch donors until his parents potlatch in his name (McIlwraith 1948 I:383; Field Notes, page 647). McIlwraith also notes that "an old man would often step down in favor of his son, caring nothing" (Field Notes, page 665). Though there are certain resemblances to the Kwakiutl and the Nootka, particularly in the last quotation, there are two significant differences. Among the Kwakiutl and the Nootka, in contrast to the Bella Coola, there is a fixed rule of succession by primogeniture and an actual position of chief. This position is embodied in a name which is ranked with respect to other names. In the course of their lifetimes, Kwakiutl and Nootka chiefs step down and their sons assume their positions. This mechanism of

succession ensures acceptance of the choice of heir through primogeniture and eliminates competition for positions of leadership. In
contrast, among the Bella Coola, there is no fixed mode of succession and certainly no rule of primogeniture. Because of this, the
funeral is the occasion for a potlatch. A number of individuals who
are able by various descent links to claim kin connection may compete for a prestigious name. In his field notes, McIlwraith gives the
following account of the passage of a single name, possessed by the
family of his principal informant, Joshua Moody (referred to as J
in the field notes).

> Klakamut I was J's MB (mother's brother) died in Westminster
> Klakamut II came dashing over with ten pair blankets, grabbed name
>   without *hlim* (potlatch), gave fifteen years later, should have been
>   Joshua's
> Klakamut III Peter Elliot grabbed it on advice of Judas, gave *hlim*
>   four years later
> Klakamut IV Charlie Libby has now grabbed it without *hlim* (Field
>   Notes, page 273)

Chiefly *tyi* names with great prestige may be inherited by individuals who do not fulfill their obligations as the holders of great names
by potlatching. McIlwraith in his field notes indicates that "Potles
was a *numitl* (one who has potlatched four times) accordingly the
name of Potles went up in the world and his influence was great,
but his son is useless so he has gone down" (Field Notes, page 1468;
see also Field Notes, page 271). It is also possible for powerful individuals to elevate a completely new name through frequent potlatching. McIlwraith gives several examples, such as the name
"The Toilet One," a newly created name which was given great
honor at a notable potlatch (McIlwraith 1948 I:171).

   Within a household, the authority of a chief as the head of the
household was clear-cut. On this point McIlwraith states: "In small
matters, too, people gladly carry out the wishes of a chief. Work
around the house is done for him without thought of disobedience.
An old man was asked whether, when he was young, chiefs gave

many orders and acted as masters in their households. 'You bet,' the old man answered emphatically with a dry chuckle" (McIlwraith 1948 I:174).

Within the village, some chiefs were more influential than others, though this depended not upon the holding of an important name but rather on the frequency of potlatching, those having pot-latched four times assuming thereby the position of *numitl* chief. Potles was said to have been the last Bella Coola chief whose power was so great that "he was a virtual ruler, daring anything. If he requested a young man to take his food box home and the youth was slow to obey, Potles had no hesitation in killing him on the spot" (McIlwraith 1948 I:175). Thus it can be seen that, in addition to the power in his own household, a chief's power may extend over a much wider circle, the extent of which depends upon the influence of his name. This in turn depends on the degree to which he has elevated it in potlatching.

Therefore it is evident that internal ranking was present within the household as well as within the village, though the system of ranking was a flexible one, subject to individual manipulation. With regard to the ranking of *minmints* or villages, there is no evidence of a hierarchy in which villages were externally ranked.

Both Boas and McIlwraith comment on the distinctiveness of the Bella Coola preference for endogamous marriages. Boas claimed that this was unique for the Northwest Coast. However, if one examines the marriage rule carefully, its similarity to that of the Nootka is evident. Marriage is prohibited with sister, aunt, niece, or any first cousin, though marriage with the last is said to have occurred. McIlwraith notes:

Having eliminated those girls who are too closely related, or who are unsuited on account of the poverty of their parents, the father and mother can concentrate on others of about the same age as their son. The most desirable is a member of the ancestral family of one of the parents. . . . Indeed some ancestral families are so "stingy," (to use the Bella Coola expression), that for generations they have habitually married endogamously. . . . The most common marriages are between the grandchildren and great-grandchildren of first cousins, or between the child and grandchild of a first cousin when of suitable age (1948 I:375).

The structural implications of this type of marriage rule in the presence of ambilateral descent provide a mechanism of a pumplike nature, in Lévi-Strauss's terms, whereby relatives who become successively more remote in succeeding generations are then transformed into affines and their children are thereby brought back into the system. If consistently followed, this serves to cut down drastically the number of options for affiliations of offspring. The Bella Coola view is that this serves to keep prerogatives within the family.

Our analysis of Bella Coola marriage, which rests upon the genealogical materials contained in McIlwraith's field notes, leads us to question whether the concept of endogamy is appropriate for the Bella Coola. McIlwraith collected several interrelated genealogies from his principal informant, Joshua Moody. The genealogies and associated material in the field notes have enabled us to identify a certain proportion of the individuals in the genealogies with regard to *minmints* membership. Of the fifteen marriages where the *minmints* membership of both partners is given, we find only two where both husband and wife were identified as being members of the same *minmints*. Because of the manner in which McIlwraith collected the genealogies, he does not seem to have been aware of the fact that his informant had married his second cousin (mother's mother's brother's daughter's daughter). From the genealogical materials and the field notes, it is clear that Joshua had names from eight different *minmints*. His wife, Annie, had names from three *minmints*. Though there is an overlap of *minmints* identification, the primary *minmints* of each is different. Joshua's marriage accords with the Bella Coola ideal of second-cousin marriage. However, this marriage and the other marriages discussed are certainly in no sense endogamous. Given ambilateral descent, second-cousin marriage renews kin relations between households after those links have grown weak with time. It is interesting to note that the genealogies do not go further back than the grandparental generation, and include the grandparents and their siblings and the latter's descendants. On the basis of this, we speculate that eight is the maximum number of affiliations that can be remembered, which is in fact what McIlwraith notes (see quotation on p. 111). Collateral relatives linked above that generation are marriageable and may be transformed into affines.

The Bella Coola marriage rule therefore contains both a prohibition of marriage with close relatives, including first cousin, and a preference for marriage with second cousin. However, this is one of several possible marriage strategies involving individuals beyond the circle of prohibition. The second-cousin marriage strategy involves renewing ties, of which an alternatively named form is referred to by McIlwraith as "return marriage," when privileges which have left the family through marriage are returned by marriage at a later time. Another alternative is exchange marriage in which girls are exchanged by families in order to avoid a later return marriage. This is sister exchange. McIlwraith notes that still another strategy has become fashionable in recent years. Some Bella Coola families have sought wives from foreign tribes in order to obtain the new prerogatives which were brought as dowers by these wives.

Thus, in their marriage system the Bella Coola exhibit a complex rather than an elementary structure, one made up of several options which embody significantly different goals. The strategy which any particular individual follows depends upon his own rank, the size of his group, the privileges which his group possesses, whether he has sons and daughters, and how many he has of each. Since the marriage strategies may involve families of different rank, marriage is an integral aspect of social mobility. Therefore one might expect that marriage among the Bella Coola would be a potlatch. In fact, it is. In line with the above, it is clear that Bella Coola marriage represents an important means of obtaining or keeping prerogatives. It is a ceremonial bond between two families with the main emphasis on either the conservation of, or the opportunity to obtain, prerogatives and wealth. The presence of what is called ceremonial marriage supports this point. An infant girl may be betrothed to an influential chief to display the wealth of the bride's family and increase the prestige of the bride. The repurchase before puberty marks the severance of the relationship. If a daughter is not available, and "if a man wishes to ally himself by marriage to a famous chief . . . he can perform the marriage rite with a 'bride' consisting of his finger, leg, hand, or other part of the body" (McIlwraith 1948 I:425).

The Bella Coola conceptualization of marriage manifest in the above ceremonials clearly emphasizes the exchange of goods, the connection between the families, and the rise in rank of either family, rather than any conception of sexual access and procreation. The latter aspect is obviously totally missing when the "bride" is another man, a hand, a foot, or a dog. Bella Coola individuals initiate such a relationship, which they view as constituting marriage, and carry out all the appropriate transactions so involved, in order to raise status and rank. This particular kind of marriage thus serves to illuminate one of the most important goals of ordinary bisexual marriage.

The ritual of engagement and marriage, the relationship between the families of the bride and groom, and the exchanges of goods and prerogatives clearly indicate that marriage has all the attributes of a potlatch even though McIlwraith does not refer to it in this way in the published text. In describing an idealized marriage, McIlwraith notes: "The relatives included in the 'family' of either X [the boy] or Y [the girl] are not always the same; uncles, aunts, grandparents, may or may not take part in the giving and receiving of presents, the parents alone always do so. Sometimes distant relatives take a leading part in the arrangements, either in hope of receiving valuable gifts, or of obtaining social influence by lavish giving" (McIlwraith 1948 I:380). This illustrates that marriage is the affair of a household, involving, as it does, the various members of that household. The potlatch, too, involves the members of a household. The possibility of obtaining social influence by giving is also characteristic of a potlatch. Further, in keeping with the character of a potlatch, the more lavish the giving on all sides the more importance the event assumes, and the more the prestige for the participants.

Initially, and during the period of the engagement, presents and an ancestral name pass from the father of the groom to that of the bride. This name cannot be passed on in the bride's family. It should go to future children which the bride bears or be returned via "return marriage" to the groom's family at a later time. During the marriage proper, an ancestral name is given by the bride's father to the groom for use by his children. Valuable presents which are called "weapons of war" are given by the groom's family to the bride's family. "These gifts are called 'weapons of war,' since the assumption is that X [the groom] is acting like a warrior in taking something of value from Y's family" (McIlwraith 1948 I: 392). Presents are given in return by the bride's family. "They are said to be 'bed covering.' . . . The greater their value the greater her prestige" (McIlwraith 1948 I:396). These presents, which constitute the "bed covering" plus other goods which are received at that point from the bride's relatives, are then redistributed by the groom's relatives to their fellow villagers at a potlatch to establish the groom's potlatching seat.

At some future time, the bride's family repurchases her by the payment of goods to her husband. A woman who has been repurchased many times is accorded the title of *yetsalt*, which is equivalent to female chief. The goods of the repurchase are subsequently used by the husband at a potlatch. The repurchase of the bride therefore is an integral part of the potlatch, as will be seen to be the case also among the Kwakiutl.

As among other Northwest Coast societies, the Bella Coola potlatch was a focal ceremonial institution which combined the sacred and the profane in a series of highly dramatic performances. Unfortunately, in contrast to the data on the other societies examined here, where actual potlatches of real individuals were described, McIlwraith provides only an ideal statement of what a potlatch ought to be like. This takes the form of "when a man X gives a potlatch," making it impossible to identify donor, family, participants, and guests and their relationship to one another. The potlatch described contains the following central features, though McIlwraith indicates that they may not all have been included in every potlatch: wife repurchase; strengthening of the name and seat of the potlatch donor; establishment of a name and seat for sons, daughters, or other relatives of the donor; giving of a first name to children of the donor or his relatives; initiation into the sacred *sisaok* society, the Bella Coola version of the secret society; a memorial for the dead relatives of the donor who return during the dramatic ritualization; and the destruction and rebuilding of the house of the donor. There is a structural consistency in the occurrence of these events at a single occasion and the accompanying distributions of property marking that occasion. The unifying theme is rank. The various events enumerated above involve succession to the position of rank of the deceased, elevation of that position, competition between individuals of rank, the strategy of marriage choices in relation to rank, and the strategy of social advancement for one's children. It is the giving of goods to guests who witness and attest to these occurrences which provides the mechanism for the validation of the achievement of rank.

From another point of view, a series of life crises are celebrated: birth, initiation, marriage, maturity, and death. A man has died and his spirit must be laid to rest. This is accomplished at the potlatch by his successor, who attains maturity in so doing; this maturity is symbolized by the creation of a new house for him. Marriage demands repurchase of the wife, and the flow of property from wife's family to the donor at the time of the potlatch is a crucial element in his ability to distribute. This flow is essential to maintain and reaffirm the position of the wife in her natal family and to ensure the claims to position in her family of the children of the marriage. Younger people go through initiatory rites which acquaint them with the supernatural. Children and newborn infants are given names at this time which serve to mark their position in their kin groups and place them on the first rung of the rank ladder. All of these life crises involving different individuals bound to one another by both consanguinity and affinity find expression during the course of a single potlatch.

Chart G constitutes a schematized picture of the ideal potlatch which McIlwraith describes (1948 I:187-243). As was noted among other Northwest Coast societies, potlatching does not involve single individuals but is an affair concerning a kin group. The significant kin unit among the Bella Coola is the household and not the *minmints*. McIlwraith affirms this in his field notes when he notes that "if Joshua should give a *hlim* [potlatch] his wide family would not help, his wife's immediate family would help, and also his son" (Field Notes, page 644). We have therefore considered the donor and his family to be a single entity with regard to the activities of the potlatch.

It is clear from the previous discussion and from Chart G that the potlatch is crucial in the rank system of the Bella Coola, involving as it does both succession to, and elevation of, people in rank positions. These points clearly support our theoretical premises regarding rank. However, the method of presentation utilized by McIlwraith makes it impossible to ascertain the validity of our premise that one potlatches to one's affines. Clearly affines are present at the potlatch and involved in its activities. The repurchase of the wife by her natal family provides the donor with an important component of the goods which he will distribute in a fashion identical to that to be described for the Kwakiutl. Rivalry between foreign chiefs is present, though not a central part of the potlatch. Destruction of property occurs within the context of rivalry. Property is also destroyed in memory of the donor's ancestors. In the

Wife's family	Donor (D) and his family	Other fellow villagers	"Foreign" guests	Comments
Gives donor financial support	Amasses property			Preparation for potlatch
Announces prerogatives to be given husband later	←	Help to destroy D's house walls		Announcing potlatch; destruction of house is a time of license
	Chooses and announces workmen for rebuilding			
	Food distributed ——→			
	Sisaok initiates confined			Initiation into secret society—children of D, BrChild, SiChild, or Wi relatives
	Food distributed ——→			
	Validation of Sisaok names			
	Goods distributed ➤Influential villagers get more			More influential recipients will repay later
	Invitations extended ————————————————————→			
			Guests arrive; dance	
	To chiefs ← { Distribute presents			Called "eagle downness," signifying good will
	To D ← ———————————— {			
				POTLATCH PROPER
	Special foods ————————————————→			1ST DAY: chiefs get more
	Sisaok names announced			
	Food distributed ————————————→			2D DAY
Repurchase of wife				
Goods and food ——→				Distribution is to validate the names bestowed on donor
Names and prerogatives ——→				
	Repayment of old debts ——→			
	Return of deceased ancestor			
	Masked figure dances			
	D destroys copper			Copper has "made bone for the dead"—copper is now valueless
	Gifts termed "eagle down" distributed ————————→			Validate the crest Displayed—not returnable
	Large presents of ————————→ food		Chiefs who have shown D generosity	3D DAY

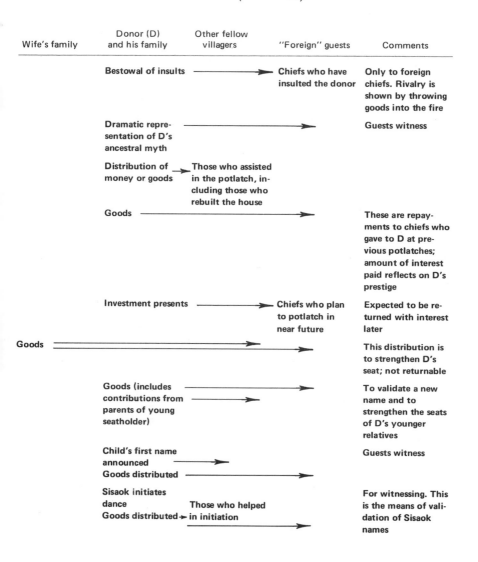

Wife's family	Donor (D) and his family	Other fellow villagers	"Foreign" guests	Comments
	Bestowal of insults ⟶		Chiefs who have insulted the donor	Only to foreign chiefs. Rivalry is shown by throwing goods into the fire
	Dramatic representation of D's ancestral myth ⟶			Guests witness
	Distribution of money or goods ⟶	Those who assisted in the potlatch, including those who rebuilt the house		
	Goods ⟶			These are repayments to chiefs who gave to D at previous potlatches; amount of interest paid reflects on D's prestige
	Investment presents ⟶		Chiefs who plan to potlatch in near future	Expected to be returned with interest later
Goods ⟹				This distribution is to strengthen D's seat; not returnable
	Goods (includes contributions from parents of young seatholder) ⟶			To validate a new name and to strengthen the seats of D's younger relatives
	Child's first name announced ⟶			Guests witness
	Goods distributed ⟶			
	Sisaok initiates dance			For witnessing. This is the means of validation of Sisaok names
	Goods distributed ⟶	Those who helped in initiation ⟶		

Source: McIlwraith 1948 I: 187–243.

latter case, a copper is thrown into the fire, thereby rendering it valueless. Another recurrent feature of potlatching throughout the Northwest Coast area, the building of a new house or the symbolic destruction of part of an old one in order to rebuild, is also present among the Bella Coola. The manner in which the old house is destroyed is highly dramatic. A number of young men rush in with a battering ram and a mock battle ensues with those inside the house. As they are ejected from the house, the battering ram is used to knock down both the front and the rear of the house. From McIlwraith's description, it is clear that the family of the donor's wife is present at this preliminary event and is most likely involved in the sham battle. It would seem that sides are involved and a symbolic conflict between the sides ensues. This is reminiscent of the symbolic features of warfare involved in the marriage rite itself.

Warfare among the Bella Coola is highly ritualized and is not designed to annihilate one's foes and take over their territory. In this, the Bella Coola resemble the Kwakiutl and contrast with the Nootka. McIlwraith notes: "Nevertheless, war was secondary in importance to ceremonial rites. During the winter, peace reigned and members of hostile tribes were even received as guests at some dances. At potlatches they might be subjected to insult, later to be avenged in the same manner or by active hostility, but seldom was actual violence offered either to envoys or guests" (McIlwraith 1948 II:338). The relationship between potlatch and warfare is quite clearly spelled out in McIlwraith's description of the war between Potles, the great Bella Coola chief, and Tcibisa, his Kitkatla counterpart. A lengthy and vicious war is brought to a close by an enormous potlatch. "The ceremony that took place that night in the house of Potles is said to have been the most spectacular ever witnessed in Bella Coola" (McIlwraith 1948 II:359). Tcibisa and the Kitkatla remained with the Bella Coola until spring. Mauss has referred to the feast which turns into a massacre (Mauss 1954: 80). The Bella Coola example presents a massacre which turns into a feast.

The association of house, kin group which occupies the house, and the potlatch as the mechanism by which a new head succeeds to the position of head of household is apparent. McIlwraith notes that the return of the ancestor in the form of his crest is the most important aspect of the potlatch (1948 I:220); it is distinctive of Bella Coola potlatches as compared to potlatches elsewhere on the Northwest Coast.

McIlwraith makes a distinction between what he calls the memorial potlatch and an ordinary potlatch, using the term *skwanat* for the former and *lim* for the latter. However, he indicates further: "At the present time, a memorial potlatch is almost identical with an ordinary potlatch in practice. The same rites are often carried out at both. . . . In fact, it may be said that the chief difference between the two is in the minds of the donor and his guests" (McIlwraith 1948 I:459). It is clear that the same analytical elements which we have considered as central to the "ordinary" potlatch are present in the memorial potlatch. McIlwraith notes: "A memorial potlatch is considered a fitting tribute of respect to a chief, and if none of his near relatives should hold one, they would brand themselves as unmindful of the fame of their dead kinsman" (1948 I: 473). It is important to note that though this quotation seems to indicate that it is the fame of the dead chief which demands the potlatch, in effect the burden of accumulating goods, and the glory from their distribution, devolve on the deceased's heir since "so much wealth is required that it can be carried out by chiefs alone" (McIlwraith 1948 I:458). In his field notes, McIlwraith indicates: "When a *staltimx* (chief) lost his relatives he might wait for several years before attempting a *skwanat* (memorial potlatch)" (McIlwraith Field Notes, page 643). Given the absence of a fixed rule of succession, it is clear that some large-scale ceremony must occur, which is widely witnessed, preferably by foreigners, in order to acknowledge publicly the accession of a close relative to the position of head of household formerly held by the deceased. This occurs at a memorial potlatch.

It is apparent that social mobility is an integral part of the Bella Coola conceptualization of rank, and that the potlatch is the primary means of advancing oneself and one's position. Social mobility is achieved by the skillful manipulation of the two components which form the basis of the achievement of rank: claims to names and their associated prerogatives, and validation of the claim through potlatching. Names vary in significance and receive their power from the sacredness of the myth within which they are contained. However, as noted above, ordinary stories may be raised to the status of ancestral myths, thereby elevating ordinary names to the level of esteemed ancestral names. This is one of the standard mechanisms of social mobility whereby an individual skilled in goods accumulation can turn an ordinary name with little prestige into an ancestral name with great prestige. Of course, any name may be made great by potlatching and thereby validating and elevating it.

In his field notes, McIlwraith presents an account of another means of raising one's status:

One of common herd wishes to become *tyi* (chief) but he has no *tyi* ancestors. He persuades a *tyi* girl to marry him, if he is of good character, no objections. At marriage, the bridegroom gives potlatch (small one). Strong as he is he cannot reach the desired potlatch, she draws it within his range. Wife's father helps. For four or five years he saves like mad, wife's family also, to give big potlatch. If meanwhile a male child is born, the potlatch is carried on, and old *tyi* man's name is given to father. Passed on to son. Immaterial whether child is born. Husband hunts and brings wood for wife's father, till latter is compelled to help him to *tyiship* (McIlwraith Field Notes, page 689).

This clearly indicates that a man without any claim through kinship to a *tyi* position can aspire to such a position. The strategy used in this case was to marry a woman with such a claim by virtue of her position as daughter of a *tyi*. The strategic advantage for the bride's father, who is a chief, is to have grandchildren to claim who will carry on his line. Such a marriage is likely to have occurred in the absence of a son and often resulted in uxorilocal residence. It is apparent also from the above quotation that, as previously noted, marriage is a potlatch. Another point to be noted is the passage of a name from father-in-law to son-in-law, a potential source of conflict if no children are born from the marriage until the groom's family returns the name by a "return marriage."

The strategy of social mobility is exhibited in a physical sense by the movement of individuals into the households of individuals becoming more important and rising in social prestige. McIlwraith notes: "Not only does the family thus appear constantly to be attracting to itself members of the ancestral family of either parent, but these relatives themselves are deeply interested in the affairs of the family" (1948 I:48). Such dependents share in the prestige and the largess received by the head of the household. In return, they assist him in accumulating property when he is planning to potlatch. Being a member of such a household makes it possible to gain and validate ancestral names for one's children, initiate them into the *sisaok* society, and even claim succession to the position of head of household when the present head dies.

The following configuration of our potlatch model is characteristic of the Bella Coola: Though external ranking is absent, internal ranking is present and of supreme importance. In the absence of a fixed rule of succession, funerals are potlatches; since affines are of unequal rank, marriage too is a potlatch. Thus, potlatches are central to the validation of rank, an integral part of a marriage, necessary for recognition of succession, and finally the only means to achieve social mobility.

CHAPTER VI. *THE KWAKIUTL*

THE KWAKIUTL have been the subject of more ethnographic research and analysis than almost any other society. Yet, "despite Boas' 'five-foot shelf' of monographs on the Kwakiutl, this tribe falls into the quartile of those whose social structure and related practices are least adequately described" (Murdock 1949:xiv, footnote 5). Professor Murdock's judgment may be attributed not to Franz Boas's deficiencies in the collection of data but rather to Boas's reluctance to seek out the underlying principles of social organization. The structure underlying Kwakiutl culture did not emerge of itself from the data as Boas anticipated it would, in line with his theoretical assumption that gathering great amounts of ethnographic material in the form of texts would inevitably lead to this result. The emergence in recent years of the concept of ambilateral descent permits an analysis of greater depth to be made of Kwakiutl society. Such an analysis has greater significance when set within a comparative areal framework including other Northwest Coast tribes. A treatment of Northwest Coast variations in social organization can best be understood within a theoretical framework which emphasizes the system of exchange so characteristic of this area—the potlatch. In this manner, variations in the form of the potlatch can be related to variations in social structure, including marriage patterns, rank, and succession.

The northern end of Vancouver Island and the adjacent coastal areas are the aboriginal homeland of the Kwakiutl, a people speaking a language of the Wakashan family. The Kwakiutl branch of the Waskashan family is divided into three groups: Heiltsuk (Bella Bella), Haisla, and Kwakiutl. The Kwakiutl, the people studied by Boas, will be our main concern. Boas delineates three dialect groupings among the Kwakiutl; however, the largest cohesive social unit is the tribe. In his final statement on Kwakiutl social organization, Boas lists twenty tribes (1966:38-40). These tribes form the foci for systematic interaction involving marriages, potlatches, and shared conceptions of rank on an intertribal level. Members of a tribe also share a winter village.

Some tribes are subdivided into septs or subtribes, though this occurs in only two of the twenty tribes, the Kwagul of Fort Rupert and the Leqwildax, the tribe listed last by Boas, which may be a catch-all category. Though the sept is not referred to as a territorially delimited entity, it does form a unit of action in some social contexts. The five septs of the Kwagul frequently act independently of one another and potlatch to one another. Within the wider tribal context, all of the septs of the Kwagul act in concert in opposition to other tribes.

Tribes without septs are directly subdivided into numayms (*nememot*), the Kwakiutl term which Boas uses for descent groups. The five septs of the Kwagul are also subdivided into numayms, twenty-two in all.

The minimal social unit is the house. A numaym may occupy one or more houses. The house referred to in this context is usually the one located in the winter village (Dawson 1888:64). Thus a man may consider himself a member of the Number One Maamtagila house, of the Maamtagila numaym, of the Guetela sept, of the Kwagul tribe (living at Fort Rupert).

The spatial distribution of population varies through the seasons. During the winter, those units which constitute a tribe gather at the winter village, "where the most substantial houses are found." During the summer, these units go "scattering to various fishing places and other resorts" (Dawson 1888:64). For example, Dawson notes that the Kwatsino tribe

inhabit Forward Inlet, Quatsino Sound, but also resort to the west coast of Vancouver Island to the north of the Sound for halibut-fishing, where they have rough temporary huts at several places. Their principal or winter village, named Owiyekumi, is on the east side of Forward Inlet, opposite Robson Island, and occupies the low neck of a small peninsula, with a good beach for canoe-landing at each side, and bounded by a low cliff inland. They have also a second little village, of ruder construction, named Tenaate . . . on the north shore of the upper part of Forward Inlet. . . . This may be classed as a "summer village," but is rather an "autumn village," in which they reside when the dogtooth salmon is running up the small streams in its vicinity (Dawson 1888:68).

Since fishing grounds are the property of individual numayms (Boas 1921:1347), one may presume that the several huts in a particular location used for halibut-fishing are occupied by members of the same numaym.

Boas only indirectly presents data related to household composition. The houses in the winter village, as described by Boas, are square, "the sides of which are from 40 to 60 feet long" (Boas 1897: 367). "The house is inhabited by several families, each of whom has a fireplace of its own. The corners belonging to each family are divided off from the main room by a rough framework of poles" (Boas 1897:369). "The place of honor is the middle rear of the house, then the right side, next the left, and finally the door-side. The bedrooms which stand on the embankments are arranged accordingly, the owner having the middle room in the rear" (Boas 1909:416). Dawson gives essentially the same description (1888:75). From material provided by George Hunt (located in the American Philosophical Library archive) on the population of Fort Rupert in the 1920s, the mean house size for sixteen houses is 7.3 individuals; the range is from one to a maximum size of fifteen. Dawson provides figures for 1885 which concur closely (Dawson 1888:65). In Dawson's time, there were twenty-five houses and the mean house size from his figures is 6.8. Here again it seems likely that there was a wide range in actual size of household. Though Boas does not specifically indicate that the individuals within a house are related to one another, it would appear that to reside in a house one would have to claim a kinship tie. Ford's life history of Charley

Nowell, a Kwakiutl, includes details on the composition of Nowell's household, substantiating this point on the kin composition of the household. Charley's house includes the following people: his mother, his father, his two elder brothers, one elder brother's wife, his elder brother's wife's mother, his mother's sister's husband, and four mother's sister's children—a total of twelve people. In his final summation on the social organization of the Kwakiutl, Boas's sole reference to household group is as follows: "The numayma consist of families embracing essentially household groups and the nearest relatives of those who married into the household group" (Boas 1966:48).

The concept of descent among the Kwakiutl has been the subject of much controversy and misunderstanding. Boas, himself, in the course of his work vacillated on this point. In attempting to clarify this concept, we begin with a consideration of the ways in which individuals may affiliate with groups (in this case with the nu-maym). The primary means of affiliation is through selection of options available by virtue of ambilateral descent. On this point, Boas is most explicit in one of his earliest publications when he notes that "the child does not belong by birth to the gens of his father or mother, but may be made a member of any gens [nu-maym] to which his father, mother, grandparents, or great-grand-parents belonged. . . . The child becomes member of a gens by being given a name belonging to that gens. On this occasion property must be distributed among the members of the gens according to the rank of the name. By taking a name belonging to another gens, to which one of his ancestors belonged, a man may become at the same time a member of that gens. Thus chiefs are sometimes members of many gentes, and even of several tribes. One Kwakiutl chief, for instance, belongs to six gentes" (Boas 1891:609). Though in Boas's later publications on the Kwakiutl he reiterates the above statement in much the same fashion (Boas 1920:115, 119; 1966:51), he confounds his readers by immediately contradicting the state-ment on a succeeding page, claiming that "it is clear that the concept of patrilineal descent pervades this system" (Boas 1966:52).[1] Boas's difficulty arises from the fact that he confuses the distinctions between descent, succession, and inheritance. Our analysis of the Hunt data and the Boas data, including the life histories (Boas 1925:112-357) and the family histories (1921), confirms the basic ambilateral nature of the structure which has already been noted by Davenport (1959) and Hazard (1960). But numaym membership may also be obtained by the acquisition of a seat within the numaym. A number of examples are provided of instances where individuals who heretofore are unrelated to the numaym are given seats as gifts or obtain names in the numaym by killing the previous owner (Boas 1925:83 ff.; Boas and Hunt 1905:33). In this sense, therefore, membership in a numaym may be brought about by factors unrelated to descent. Though a large proportion of the members of the numaym affiliate by virtue of descent, the numaym is in its composition more than simply a descent group.

Property among the Kwakiutl includes hunting lands, fishing sites, berrying grounds, and other exploitative resource areas, houses, masks, feast dishes, coppers, names, crests, dances, privileges to perform certain ritual acts, and other tangible as well as intangible items. The transfer of property may occur while the holder is still alive, as the account of a Kwakiutl chief to be considered below will demonstrate. While a child is still young, his parents begin to bestow various names and privileges upon him in the course of potlatches made in his honor. This extends to the point where a father relinquishes his own great name and the concomitant privileges attached to it including his ranked seat, saying that henceforth he, the father, will be ranked last in the numaym (Boas 1921:1349, 1351). As Boas notes:

Awaxalagilis told all the chiefs of the tribes that not he, himself, had invited them, but his prince, Laqwagila . . . "and also my seat at the

---

[1] Others in addition to Boas have had difficulty in characterizing Kwakiutl descent. For example, Mauss refers to "the modified matrilineal clan of the Kwakiutl" (1925 [1954]:33) and Belshaw as recently as 1965 states that "the numaym is essentially a patrilineal descent group" (1965:22).

head of all the eagles, as I stand at the head of the tribes. Now it will go to my prince, Laqwagila, and this house, and what is in it, the red cedar bark (he meant the cannibal dance and the other dances; therefore he named the red cedar bark), and my chief's position. All these will go to Laqwagila, and this copper, about which you all know, chiefs, this Lesaxelayo which is worth nine thousand blankets, and fifty canoes, and six thousand button blankets, and two hundred and sixty silver bracelets, and twenty gold-backed bracelets, and more than seventy gold earrings, and forty sewing machines, and twenty-five phonographs, and fifty masks. These will go to my prince Laqwagila. Now he will give these poor things to you, tribes. You will give property to me in the last seat of my numaym, the Maamtagila." Thus said Awaxalagilis (Boas 1921:1351).

In addition to illustrating the way in which property devolves from a father to a son during the father's lifetime, the above paragraph also contains a long list of what constitutes property. Inheritance is one form of transfer of property. It may take place at a potlatch, but this event is also the occasion for another type of property transfer in which guests from other tribes receive what are referred to as "poor things," or "trifles" (Boas 1925:343). One cannot tell solely from the nature of the object what kind of transfer is involved nor the type of relationship between recipient and giver. For example, coppers may be given as inheritance from a father to a son, as illustrated above, or may be transferred as a marriage gift from son-in-law to father-in-law. Coppers may also go as a marriage repayment from father-in-law to son-in-law, and may go to a rival in another numaym in the course of a potlatch. Primary emphasis upon the goods exchanged does not serve to illuminate the exchange relationship. The crucial nature of that relationship between numayms is masked by the use of the term "trifles" to refer to goods exchanged between them. These goods are, in fact, just the opposite of trifles.

Consonant with the Kwakiutl ambilaterality, property associated with the myths and ancestry of particular numayms may be transmitted along multiple lines through males or females. But an important distinction is made between such ancestral property and property transmitted from a father-in-law to a son-in-law. As Boas notes:

I will say again that all these are not given away in marriage to the son-in-law of the chief, namely, the family history, privileges, and the names, and the house, and what is in it. The only privileges which are given away in marriage are those obtained in marriage, and the names, and the house obtained in marriage, and what is in it, and it goes to him who marries the daughter of the owner of what I talked about; for the privileges given in marriage are those obtained by marriage; the privileges, and the house, and what is in it; and they go to him who marries the princess (Boas 1921:1358).

As noted above in the discussion of numaym composition, names, which constitute a kind of property, may also be transmitted to unrelated individuals. Coppers represent a special kind of property since they may be given to an heir, to a son-in-law as part of the repurchase of the bride, or to totally unrelated individuals (Boas 1921:1351, 1114; 1925:95). Coppers may also be sold, but only to individuals who are considered rivals (Boas 1897:345).

If the ancestral privileges and property have not been transmitted to heirs during the lifetime of the holder, such property will devolve after death to an heir designated by the dying holder (Boas 1925:73 ff.). Personal effects of the deceased are burned after his death, though such useful items as canoes, if not manufactured by the deceased's own hand, may be passed on to his heir (Boas 1921: 709, 1330).

A final distinction must be made between communally held property and individually owned property. The members of a particular numaym hold title to such economic resource areas as fishing grounds, berrying grounds, hunting grounds, and beach areas (Boas 1921:1345 ff.). Unlike the Nootka, where title to this type of property is held by individual chiefs and may be passed as dowry with a daughter, ownership among the Kwakiutl is held by the entire numaym rather than by the chief alone, and there is no evidence to support alienation of such property out of the numaym.

In contrast to the complexity surrounding the transmission of property, the rule of succession to ranked position and its associated name is explicit; the position always passes by primogeniture to the first-born, regardless of sex. In the absence of a child, the position will pass to the next younger sibling regardless of sex and then to the offspring of that sibling. Individuals of the senior line, though younger or female, always take precedence over individuals in junior lines. The important structural implications of this rule warrant several citations from the data. In Hunt's words: "And when the head chief of a numaym has no son, and his child is a girl, she takes the place of her father as head chief; and when the head chief has no child, and the younger brother of the head chief (among the brothers of the man) has a child, even if she is a girl, then the head chief among the brothers takes the eldest one of the children of his younger brother, and places him or her in his seat as head chief of the numaym" (Boas 1921:824). Another equally clear statement from Hunt on this point indicates that

this office of giving away property never goes to a younger brother; it is only the eldest child that takes the office of giving away property to all the different tribes. Even if a girl is the eldest one of the children of the one whose office is to give away property, she takes it although she is a woman. Often the younger brother of the eldest sister tries to take away the office of giving away property from his elder sister, but all the chiefs do not agree because it never goes to the next one to the eldest. The only time the office of giving away property is given to the younger brother is when the eldest one dies, then it cannot be denied him. The time when this is done is when the eldest one does not live long enough to have a child before he dies. When the one whose office is this, to give away property, never had a child, he adopts the eldest one among the children of his nearest relative, a nobleman (Boas 1925:91; see also Boas 1921:1087, 1107; 1920:116; 1966:52).

Such a rule of succession is in complete accord with previous statements concerning ambilateral affiliation to groups and ambilateral transmission of property.

The office of chief is conceptualized by the Kwakiutl as a cere-

monial position in the potlatch, actually a seat. Hunt notes: ". . . for
it is a sign among the Indians that he is a chief, the one who has
the office of giving away property among the tribes" (Boas 1925:
99). From information on the transmission of property, it is clear
that chiefs are the owners of houses. The extensive data on indus-
tries presented by Hunt indicate that economic resources are usually exploited by single individuals. Included are hunting bear and
mountain goat, and most forms of fishing and shellfish gathering
(Boas 1909; 1921). Porpoise and sea otter hunters appear to have
hunted in small informal groups (Boas 1909:506). Only the building of large salmon weirs, presumably, involved communal labor.
However, the data indicate that when chiefs built houses they utilized the labor not only of their own numaym but also of individuals
from related numayms (Boas 1921:1338 ff.). A portion of every type
of catch was presented to the chiefs of the numaym (Boas 1921:
1333). Hunters of seal usually gave all but one animal to their
chiefs since seal meat was not preserved and only the chief could
make the feast in which the seal meat was utilized (Boas 1921:
1333). In the course of potlatch activities, the chief acted as the
representative of his entire numaym vis-à-vis other chiefs representing their numayms (Boas 1921:1340-44). This is the most explicit example of the chief acting in his executive capacity on
behalf of the numaym.

Rank operates on the three levels of groups delineated above.
With regard to intra-numaym rank, Boas notes in his last statement
on the subject that one may "consider the numayma as consisting
of a certain number of positions to each of which belongs a name, a
'seat' or 'standing place,' that means rank, and privileges. Their
number is limited, and they form a ranked nobility" (Boas 1966:
50). These positions or seats are serially ranked. The Hunt manuscript material presents the order of seats for all the Kwagul numayms. The list for the Laalaxsendayo numaym of the Gwetela
sept contains fifty-three individually named seats, of which the first
eighteen apparently represent one category; seats nineteen to

thirty-six are described as being held by old men who have given up their seats to their sons; and seats thirty-seven to fifty-three are listed as "common man." These three categories are also recapitulated in the lists for the other numayms. The distinction between the first two categories relates to the difference between those who hold high rank now and those who have held it in the past. Since the total number of seats for twenty-one Kwagul numayms, as presented by George Hunt, adds up to the staggering figure of seven hundred and ninety-four positions, it seems most likely that at no single time were all of these seats in actual use. Population estimates from Codere (1950) and from Dawson (1888) indicate that it is extremely unlikely that there were ever enough people to fill all the seats among the Kwagul, as presented by Hunt. In our opinion, the list rather represents an ideal conceptualization in the minds of informants of positions, potential seats as well as those actualized and validated by potlatching. The rank order, if gathered from several informants, would probably vary and be subject to dispute. Further, it is apparent from the Hunt-Boas correspondence that the recording of the Mamaleleqala rank order of seats (Boas 1897:339-40) gave permanence in the act of recording to something which had been flexible when it existed as a set of cognitive concepts. Hunt notes that the recorded rank list was used in disputes by the Mamaleleqala themselves (Hunt-Boas correspondence).

Kwakiutl ideology conceptualizes the numaym as a descent group with an eponymous ancestor who came down from the sky at a particular place (Boas 1921:802 ff.), though the material is equivocal on this point (see Boas 1935:43-44). The presence of ambilateral descent, primogeniture, and options regarding numaym affiliation has several consequences. Individuals may be members of, and hold seats in, more than one numaym. Numayms in their active membership contain fewer than all the individuals potentially eligible by descent for membership since an individual must inherit a name and distribute goods to assume his position in a

numaym. Individuals activate options for numaym membership on
the basis of rank, selecting the higher-ranking numaym. In accordance with the strict rule of primogeniture, the oldest child succeeds
to the highest position of either parent. As Boas notes: "Hence
when a father and mother are of equally high rank, the first-born
child may be assigned to one numaym, the following to another
numaym. . . . The inference from the general point of view of the
modern Indian is that the younger lines had names of inferior rank
and formed the lower classes" (Boas 1940:360-61). By implication
from the above, one would expect that two siblings would have
their primary affiliation in different numayms. By virtue of the
primogeniture rule and the presence of rank differences, rivalry is a
structural concomitant of the relations between younger and older
siblings. In societies with unilineal descent groups, rivalry is toned
down between siblings, who, by the rule of descent, usually remain
members of the same group despite the rule of primogeniture. In
societies with ambilateral descent groups, like the Kwakiutl, the
rivalry between siblings of either sex resulting from primogeniture
may find institutional expression in the potlatch rivalry between
numayms, since siblings are frequently members of different numayms. When siblings belong to two different numayms, their
mother's and their father's, this rivalry between numayms in the
sibling generation is a recapitulation of the rivalry in the previous
generation, since marriage relations parallel potlatch rivalry (see
below). If siblings are in the same numaym, then their rivalry is
not overtly expressed. As Hunt notes: "This is the reason why it is
said that the younger brother often bewitches his elder brother,
that he may die quickly, because the younger brother wishes to
take the seat of his elder brother after he dies" (Boas 1921:1358). A
younger brother who decides to remain with his older brother after
the latter succeeds to the title of chief "often . . . was his warrior,
and, at the same time, the head warrior. . . . He never accumulated
stores of provisions. Therefore, notwithstanding the property that
he acquired by plunder, he could not maintain a family. Many war-

riors never married" (Boas 1966:106; see also Boas 1935:43; 1910: 477).

Kwakiutl warfare had several distinctive features. As Boas notes: "The reason that led to warfare was generally the murder or even accidental death of a member of a tribe" (Boas 1966:109). There are no examples in the Kwakiutl material of warfare in which an enemy tribe was exterminated and its economic resources, names, and privileges taken by the victors. In this, the Kwakiutl differ from the Nootka, where warfare is a primary means for expansion and attainment of rank. This view of Kwakiutl warfare parallels that presented by Codere. She notes:

It is impossible to discover in Kwakiutl warfare an underlying economic motivation. In a recent study of the Nootka, close neighbors of the Kwakiutl, Swadesh shows that their warfare was economically motivated in almost every case, although this motive was often obscured somewhat by pretexts that they fought for revenge. In Kwakiutl, unlike Nootka, most of the wars are not on villages but on campers or on people passing by in canoes. In most cases, plunder does not figure at all or it is of minor importance. Where the warrior does take plunder, it is specified that he does not store it or derive economic benefit from it. The economic value of the slave captured in war was so slight as to be non-existent. There is no instance in the Kwakiutl literature in which the purpose of war is to gain land or fishing rights and the Nootka kind of war which was consistent with such purposes, war which aimed at the annihilation of the group in possession of certain riches such as a fine salmon stream, was not at all characteristic of Kwakiutl (Codere 1950:105).

In our discussion of Nootka and Kwakiutl, we have delineated the important role of the younger brother in warfare. The differences in type of warfare noted above relate directly to the difference between the potentialities of the position of the younger brother in Nootka and Kwakiutl social structure. Among the Nootka, chiefs own strategic economic resource areas as individual property, and the younger brother as successful warrior may establish himself as an independent chief, given the Nootka type of warfare. Also, chiefs potlatch on their own initiative as individuals. In contrast, among the Kwakiutl, numaym solidarity overshadows individual initiative. Individual chiefs do not own strategic economic resources, but numayms do. A younger brother can therefore not achieve social mobility through individually initiated acts such as warfare. Warfare consequently does not have economic import. The younger brother is compelled to seek success through the rising fortunes of the numaym with which he affiliates, either his elder brother's or another. The potlatch among the Kwakiutl also reflects this in that it is initiated by a numaym rather than an individual.

The significance of birth order in rank is emphasized symbolically in the bestowal of names in a myth: "Their three boys were Property-Giver, the eldest one; Property-Gatherer, the middle one; and From-Whom-Property-is-received, the youngest one" (Boas 1905:375).

Up to this point, we have discussed rank as it operates within the numaym. We turn now to a consideration of how numayms are ranked. Though the numaym is conceptualized in Kwakiutl ideology as a descent group, the relationship between numayms is not usually characterized in terms of descent. "In most cases, the ancestors of the various numayma of one tribe seem to be unrelated" (Boas 1966:43). There are instances, however, where ancestors of two numayms within a particular sept of the Kwagul are considered to have been brothers. According to the Boas and the Hunt data, the numayms within a tribe or sept are ranked. Boas early noted that

the gentes differ in rank, and in festivals are placed accordingly, those highest in rank sitting in the rear of the house near the fire, the others arranged from that place towards the door, ranging according to rank. In each gens those highest in rank sit nearest the fire. The proper place of a gens is called *tloqoe*. The gens highest in rank receives its presents first. The latter are not given individually but in bundles, one for each gens (Boas 1891:609).

There are several instances where the specific rank of numayms is provided by Hunt: when the chief of the numaym Senlem invites the other numayms of the Kwagul to a feast, the head chief of each numaym, in order of rank, is called (Boas 1921:792-93); the four numayms of the Nakwakdax are seated in rank order at a marriage feast (Boas 1921:1046). The Hunt manuscript material provides the rank order of all the numayms of the septs of the Kwagul. Numayms in feasts, potlatches, and marriages act toward other numayms as units and are represented on those occasions by their head chiefs. The details of the internal ranking within the numaym on those occasions are of secondary importance. The basis of the numaym ranking system is not descent, since a common descent ideology does not unite all the numayms within a tribe. It appears to relate rather to the potlatch system.

The four septs within the Kwagul tribe are ranked. Tribes, too, are ranked. One example of tribal ranking appears in a family history collected by Hunt (Boas 1925:81 ff.). Recording the way in which the goods to be distributed in a mourning potlatch were stacked up, Hunt relates:

And the top pile of blankets will be given to the Gwetela and under them are those for the Qomoyaye, and under them those for the walas Kwagul, and under them those for the Qomkutes of the walas Kwagul, and under them those for the Nemgis, and under them those of the Lawitses, and under them those for the Madilbe, and under them those for the Denaxdax, and under them those for the Awailela, and under them those for the Qweqsotenox, and under them those for the Dzawa-deenox, and under them those for the Haxwamis, and under them those for the Gwawaenox, and nearest to the floor are those for the Gwawaenox, for they are the last to whom it is given when it is given to all the different tribes (Boas 1925:83, 85).

Thus the potlatch can be seen as the context in which the tribal ranking system is brought into play. The building of a house and marriage repurchase offer other instances of tribal ranking (Boas 1925:345).

In contrast to the over-all rank structure in which individuals are ranked within numayms, numayms within septs or tribes, and tribes among themselves, there is mention at several points of paired rivalries. This creates an apparent paradox since a hierarchically ordered structure with its basic inequality would not seem consistent with paired rivalries in which the rivals are of equal status, and yet both rank and hierarchy, rivalry and potlatching are integral, continuously stressed themes of Kwakiutl culture. The seeming paradox may be resolved by viewing the ranking of numayms and tribes not as a rigid and fixed structure but as a flexible one in which ranked position may be altered in response to challenge. The hierarchical orderings provided by the examples are orderings at particular events. They are open to challenge, to reinterpretation, and ultimately to shifting. The variation in ordering which the ethnographic material shows is due to these factors. The ordering may also differ depending on the informant in a particular numaym in a given tribe. The order of distribution at a potlatch reflects the consensus at a particular point in time. The seating and distribution arrangement at each potlatch may represent a shift from the previously accepted consensus since it incorporates the results of the most recent potlatching activities on the part of the participant numayms, who are now receiving goods and being seated in accordance with their rank relative to other recipient numayms.

The documentation on rivalries relates to the rivalry occurring between chiefs of numayms in the same tribe and that which occurs between chiefs in different tribes. As Boas notes:

The chiefs of various gentes of one tribe are, when still young, instigated by their elders to outdo each other in feats of bravery as well as in giving festivals. This spirit of rivalry is kept up throughout their lives, and they continually try to outdo each other as to who will distribute the greatest amount of property. Generally this strife is between the chiefs of two gentes; among the Nemkic, for instance, between Tlagotas, chief of the Tsetseloalakemac, and Waqanit, chief of the Sisintlae (Boas 1891:609).

Three examples of intertribal rivalries are provided. It is interesting to note that no two versions are in complete agreement.

Boas 1897:343	*Boas 1920:115*
Gwetela vs. Mamaleleqala	Gwetela vs. Mamaleleqala
Qomoyaye vs. Qweqsotenox	Qomoyaye vs. Qweqsotenox
Qomkutes vs. Nimkish or Laokoatx	Walas Kwagul vs. Nimkish
Walas Kwagul vs. Lawitses or Tsamas	Qomkutes vs. Lawitses

Boas 1925:185
Gwetela vs. Mamaleleqala
Qomoyaye vs. Nimkish
Walas Kwagul vs. Lawitses

The four Kwagul septs, considered as separate tribes in these matchings, are opposed to three or four neighboring tribes with whom they regularly interact, intermarry, and potlatch. The four Kwagul septs are ranked (with minor variations) and the four other tribes facing them are also ranked (with variations). The pairing of specific groups, that is, who is opposed to the Nimkish, is of less importance than the opposition of the clusters. The Kwagul group regularly interacts with the Mamaleleqala, Nimkish, and Lawitses; these are the groups with whom its members intermarry most frequently; and these are the groups who serve as witnesses to Kwagul accessions to office and in religious ceremonies. These are also their great potlatch rivals.

As might be anticipated from the earlier discussion of rank and its dynamic aspect, tribes in close proximity in the rank hierarchy would necessarily be rivals of one another. Ford provides an example of the Nimkish challenge to the Mamaleleqala. They do this by giving a number of potlatches to the Fort Rupert tribes to announce their intention of moving into fifth place, displacing the Mamaleleqala. "But the Mamaleleqala met the challenge and also gave potlatches to the Fort Rupert people. The latter, sitting in judgment over the two tribes, decided that the Nimkis had not yet earned the right to change their position" (Ford 1941:20-21).[2] This

---

[2] Ford represents Kwakiutl society in the form of a linear hierarchy. Every individual and every group had a fixed position relative to and known by all. In this scheme, the Mamaleleqala were in fifth place after the four Kwagul septs. His view is not in accord with our analysis of the data. In the Boas material, the four Kwagul tribes are the rivals of the Mamaleleqala, Nimkish, and Lawitses (see above).

demonstrates the importance of paired rivalries as well as the function of witnessing and the judgment on the part of third parties regarding rank and status. It was at subsequent potlatches given by the Fort Rupert Kwagul that the resultant rank order was reflected in seating and order of distribution. The seating and order of distribution at the Nimkish and Mamaleleqala potlatches reflected the host's version of the rank order of the Kwagul septs. Sometimes this version was not accepted and a dispute resulted. It is interesting to note that the Kwagul sit in judgment with regard to Nimkish-Mamaleleqala rank order, though in a larger context they are paired rivals of the Nimkish and Mamaleleqala. As will be repeatedly demonstrated in Chapter 7, one needs one's rivals.

Just as potlatches pair opposites, so too does marriage. This is because marriage is, in effect, a potlatch. As has been consistently demonstrated throughout the Northwest Coast, one marries the people with whom one potlatches. Though Boas's lack of understanding concerning the social structure, and in particular the marriage pattern, resulted in his inability to comprehend the structural significance of the potlatch, he did recognize the similarity between marriage and potlatching, for he notes that "marriage is conducted on the basis of the potlatch" (Boas 1966:53). He again notes:

The advance in social rank arising from the potlatch features of the marriage often overshadows entirely the primary object of a marriage, namely, the establishment of a family. Instead of this, the transfer of names and privileges becomes the primary consideration, and fictitious marriages are performed, the sole object of which is the transfer of names, privileges, and property previously described (Boas 1966:55).

Boas does not make clear here that the property which is being transferred by such fictitious marriages is limited solely to the kinds of property which are transmitted through affines. Codere has also noted the essential similarity between potlatching and marriage. If one checks the Boas family history materials which she used, one discovers that many of the potlatches which she records in her Table 16 and Table 17 are not labeled potlatches at all in the text material, but are property distributions at marriages or wife repurchase payments which are distributed (Codere 1950:90-93).

The symbolism surrounding marriage is the same as that involving warfare. For example:

According to the expressions used by the Kwakiutl, a wife is "obtained in war" (*winanem*) from a foreign tribe. The chiefs make war upon the princesses of the tribes. . . . The fiction is also maintained in the actual marriage ceremonies, which occasionally include a sham battle between the wooing party and the relatives of the bride, or in which the groom's party is subjected to tests that show that the powers of the bride's father cannot vanquish them (Boas 1966:53; see also p. 108).

It should be understood, of course, that the symbolism signifies the rivalry of opposites who interrelate to form the system, rather than any notion of extermination, which is not present in Kwakiutl warfare in any case.

The symbolism of marriage also involves the notion of spouses from different tribes. Even marriages within the same tribe or numaym, which are not uncommon, will be phrased in the same ideology. Boas notes that "the fiction that the marriage is one between two tribes or villages is maintained throughout" (Boas 1966:54). This may be interpreted as a clear statement regarding the category of affines which has structural importance throughout the course of marriage. The wife is never incorporated into her husband's numaym but retains membership in her natal numaym. The repurchase of the bride by her father clearly supports this point, since after this ceremony she is free to return to her own numaym. The seeming contradiction between marriage with close relatives and the symbolism of opposite sides in marriage is resolved when one considers that there are certain kinds of property that can only pass to affines and from affines, in particular the ceremonial dances, names, and privileges involved in the all-important Winter Dance. Since the only means of obtaining such property is from affines, one must have affines. In the case of close marriages, consanguines are symbolically turned into affines. This is most easily accomplished when close relatives are in different numayms. In marriages between individuals who are members of the same numaym, they are turned into affines when they marry. The only stipulated rule regarding marriage is that one may not marry one's mother, sister, or half sister (if mother is the same). Examples show that marriages may occur with younger brother's daughter, half sister (different mother), and first cousins, though in an early publication Boas claimed that "the gentes are not exogamous, but marriages between cousins are forbidden" (Boas 1891:610). In a detailed discussion of "endogamy," Hunt provides an extended example of a series of very close marriages with younger brother's daughter and with half sister (same father, different mothers) to which Boas in a footnote provides additional examples (Boas 1921:781-82). Boas in his 1920 article on Kwakiutl social organization offers an extended discussion of these "endogamous" marriages (Boas 1940:361-62; see also Boas 1966:50; Ford 1941:36, 56, 124). Marriage permitted with younger brother's daughter relates to the rivalry between brothers discussed above, since it is easy to place one's younger brother in the category of rival and then affine, particularly if he is affiliated with a different numaym.

Theoretically, a society with ambilateral descent groups might have a rule of descent group exogamy, compelling an individual to seek a spouse outside of the descent groups with which he is affiliated (his numaym). Even in that case, close relatives in other groups—half siblings or brother's daughter—would not be excluded by such a rule if they were not affiliated with ego's group or groups. But, in fact, the Kwakiutl do not have such a rule, though Boas repeatedly claims that "marriages in the consanguineal group are not customary" (Boas 1966:50; see also 1889:828).

The Hunt manuscript material contains a list of 840 names; "these names dated back to 1866 to show how many people use to live in Fort Rupert" (Hunt manuscript material:1514-40). The arrangement of the material indicates the marriages and the numaym affiliation of each spouse. Table 4 presents data extracted for 190 marriages. This information has enabled us to determine the frequency of marriages within groups and between groups. It is evident from the table that no clear-cut preference for endogamy or exogamy exists. As to in-marrying female spouses, 46 percent come from different tribes and 54 percent are from the same tribe, 19

TABLE 4. *TABULATION OF 190 KWAGUL MARRIAGES*

	Spouse							
	Same numaym		Same sept		Same tribe		Different tribe	Total
	No.	Percent	No.	Percent	No.	Percent	No.	Percent	
In-marrying female spouse	6	3.5	27	16	61	35	80	46	174
In-marrying male spouse	0		5	31.2	8	50	3	28.8	16
									190

percent are within the same sept within that tribe, and 3.5 percent are within the same numaym. This empirical evidence thus further demonstrates that it is impossible to make a clear-cut statement about endogamy and exogamy. The distribution of marriages confirms the absence of a definite marriage rule.

Table 5 is an analysis of marriages within the Kwagul tribe, presented by sept instead of by numaym, since, as Table 4 shows, there are only 6 intra-numaym marriages. A rather high proportion of the marriages occurring within the tribe are also within the same sept. There is a greater chance of Gwetela marrying Gwetela and

TABLE 5. *MARRIAGES WITHIN THE KWAGUL TRIBE BY SEPTS*

	Gwetela	Qomkutes	Walas Kwagul	Qomoyaye	Total
Gwetela	14 (38%)	2	3	4	23
Qomkutes	4	0	0	1	5
Walas Kwagul	14	3	8 (44%)	11	36
Qomoyaye	4	2	4	11 (39%)	21
Madilbe	1	4	3	1	9
	37	11	18	28	94

Walas Kwagul marrying Walas Kwagul than of their choosing a spouse from any of the other septs, though they all live at Fort Rupert. Geographical proximity is obviously not a factor. In all, 33 out of the 94 marriages are within the same sept.

Table 6 is an analysis of Kwagul marriages to other tribes. From the table it is apparent that of the fourteen tribes with which the four Kwagul septs intermarry, marriages with three tribes account for 60 percent of the out-marriages. These three tribes—the Mamaleleqala, Nimkish, and Lawitses—as was noted above, are the tribes which repeatedly appear as opposites at a variety of occasions, particularly potlatching, in interaction with the Kwagul. Once again, the high rate of intermarriage recapitulates the high frequency of

TABLE 6. *KWAGUL MARRIAGES TO OTHER TRIBES*

	Mamaleleqala	*Nimkish*	*Lawitses*	*Other tribes*	*Total*
Gwetela	5	6	6	15	32
Qomoyaye	3	5	5	11	24
Walas Kwagul	5	8	1	5	19
Qomkutes	4	0	2	2	8
	$\overline{17}$	$\overline{19}$	$\overline{14}$	$\overline{33}$	$\overline{83}$

interaction in rivalry and in potlatching. It should be noted that there seems to be no great tendency for a particular Kwagul sept to be linked to any one of these tribes. The Gwetela marry into each of these three tribes with equal frequency. Conversely, the Mamaleleqala, for example, intermarry with each of the four septs with equal frequency. Our interpretation of the discrepancy with regard to the paired rivalries provided in the 1897, 1920, and 1925 accounts is that the specific pairings are irrelevant and that it is the opposition of clusters of groups which is significant. This is borne out by the marriage data which we have presented.

To summarize the data on marriages within groups and between groups: roughly 50 percent of the marriages are within the tribe and 50 percent are with members of other tribes. Within the tribe, marriage within the numaym occurs, though infrequently, and there is a tendency, though not a marked one, for marriage within the same sept. Most Kwagul marriages outside the tribe are arranged with the three tribes that are close neighbors of the Kwagul —the Mamaleleqala, Nimkish, and Lawitses. The reader must keep in mind that this discussion of intra- and intergroup marriage is entirely separate from the issue of marrying close kin. One may marry a close relative who is a member of another sept or tribe; one may marry an unrelated person within the same sept.

With regard to postmarital residence there is no hard and fast rule. Boas notes: "This agrees with the custom that in by far the majority of cases the woman goes to live with her husband, as well when both belong to the same village as when they belong to different villages" (Boas 1920:368; see also Boas 1966:52). The data provided in Table 4 substantiate this point; sixteen in-marrying male spouses are included in the 190 marriages, constituting 9 percent of the total. From similar data provided by Hunt for the period around 1920, five of twenty-nine marriages (17 percent) are cases of in-marrying males. An analysis of the Gwasela family history furnishes three examples of uxorilocality out of twenty-two marriages (Boas 1921:836-1269). Thus it would appear that virilocality is the dominant mode of postmarital residence, though there is no rule to the contrary, and a shift in residence after marriage must be considered as one of the options open to a man.

Rank is a most important consideration in spouse selection. Both Boas and Ford note that ideally marriage should be between a man and a woman of equal rank (Boas 1966:53; Ford 1941:36). The Hunt manuscript material, in addition to the lists of names of people living in Fort Rupert, also furnished a list of the order of seats for the Kwagul. Putting together these two sets of materials, we were able to examine the relationship between spouse selection and rank, comparing rank position of spouses with information as to whether they were of the same sept or tribe, or of different tribes. Table 7 represents a compilation of those results. It can be seen that rank does not appear to have any relationship to whether a spouse is chosen from within one's own tribe or sept, or from a different tribe, since the figures for ranked and unranked individuals are virtually identical. If one looks at the category of marriages to different tribes in greater detail (see Table 8), an interesting point emerges. There is a higher proportion of marriages to people from the Mamaleleqala, Nimkish, and Lawitses on the part of those of higher rank. Unranked people seem to marry more randomly with other tribes. This difference is attributable to the

TABLE 7. *RANK AND MARRIAGE AMONG THE KWAGUL*

	Marriage				
	Same numaym	*Same sept*	*Same tribe*	*Different tribe*[a]	*Total*
Ranked (from 1 to 30)	5	16	34	39	94
Unranked	1	16	35	44	96
					190

a These marriages are broken down in Table 8.

fact that individuals of higher rank are more involved in rivalry and potlatching with these three groups, and, as a concomitant, they also tend to seek out spouses from these groups with greater frequency.

As to the ceremonies involved in the marriage and the way in which it is contracted, it is clear that the initiative in marriage is not in the hands of the couple involved. Boas is explicit on this point, noting that "marriages are arranged by the parents of the young couple, often without their knowledge" (Boas 1966:55; see also Ford 1941:36). This statement should be amended to indicate that spouses are chosen by one's predecessor in position, who may

TABLE 8. *RANK AND MARRIAGE BETWEEN THE KWAGUL AND OTHER TRIBES*

	Mamaleleqala, Nimkish, or Lawitses	*Other different tribes*	*Total*
Ranked (from 1 to 30)	30	9	39
Unranked	21	23	44

or may not be one's parent. This is the case for Charley Nowell, Ford's informant, who is his brother's heir. The older brother selects the girl whom Charley marries, though Charley's choice would clearly have been otherwise (Ford 1941). In a general sense, the marriage of a future chief is of concern to his entire numaym, and the members of the numaym exercise a certain degree of choice in preventing what they consider to be an undesirable match. For example, Hunt notes: "His numaym, the Senlem, wished that he should marry Ringing-Copper, the princess of Odzestalis. Yaqo-kwalagilis at once obeyed their wishes" (Boas 1921:960-61). In another family history he further notes: "Now Gayosdas was chief of the Senlem. Now his numaym wished him to marry a princess of some chief of the Kwagul, for they did not want him to marry outside; and also his younger brother, Smoke-All-Round, for they disliked what had been done by their father, whose wife would not let him come back again" (Boas 1921:977). This last quotation has further implications in that not only does it indicate numaym influence in marriage but it also reveals an important element in the strategy of marriage choices: loss or gain of new members is an important factor in spouse selection.

At this point, the major aspects of the marriage rites will be outlined only briefly, as this material will be dealt with more extensively in the course of the discussion of the potlatch career of Lasotiwalas, an important Kwakiutl chief. Marriage is a three-step procedure. The first step is the initiation of negotiations between the fathers of the prospective bride and groom, at which time the sum of the marriage payment is agreed upon. The next step is the formal wooing and the transfer of the marriage payment. This involves, in the case of an important chief, the participation of the chiefs of one's own tribe. A Gwetela-Kwagul marriage to a Mama-leleqala princess gives a vivid description of the Kwagul chiefs going to pay the marriage payment.

Then the numayms the Maamtagila and Gexsem and Kukwakum and Senlem went to pay the marriage money,—and also the Laalaxsendayo.

All the Kwagul went to pay the marriage money, because their strength is the same as that of the Mamaleleqala; for the Qomoyaye and Walas Kwagul are the first of the Kwagul tribes; and also the Qomkutes; and the Mamaleleqala stand at the head of the Nimkish, Qweqsotenox and Lawetses; and the Mamaleleqala do this when one of their chiefs goes to marry a princess of the chiefs of the Kwagul. They go and ask the help of the Nimkish and Qweqsotenox and Lawetses; and Aodzagalas did the same with the Kwagul. Then all went to pay the marriage money,—the five numayms of the Gwetela, and also the Qomoyaye, and the Walas Kwagul, and the Qomkutes (Boas 1921:968).

The various chiefs display privileges and make speeches. After the formal acceptance of the suit, the marriage payment, which is always in the form of blankets, is given to the father of the girl. The girl also takes with her household goods, food, boxes, baskets, spoons, and dishes.

The third and final step is the marriage repurchase. This takes place several years later, frequently after the birth of a child. It is referred to as the "repayment of the marriage debt." Boas notes: "This does not consist of blankets, but of 'bad things, trifles,' which include food, household goods of all kinds and particularly a copper, names, and privileges which are handed over in the 'privilege box.' The value of the goods paid at this time is far in excess of what the bride's father has received" (Boas 1966:54). Boas draws attention to the difference in value as well as in kind between the marriage gift and the marriage repayment. The accounts of the family histories indicate that the material objects which form a part of the marriage repurchase payment may sometimes be similar in content to the marriage gift, but the privileges and other intangibles which pass in the marriage repurchase never form part of the marriage gift. They are of a special sort, relating to the winter ceremonial, which can only pass to the husband's side. Ford notes that "the amount thus paid by the bride's father was many times the amount originally received by him at the wedding; he attempted to return as much as he could for by his liberality he gained prestige and honor" (Ford 1941:38). Thus, marriage represents an unequal exchange of property in which the groom and his side gain more than they give. The size of the repurchase is related to the rank of the bride's father, since he gives as much as he can. This factor, too, will be seen in its relationship to the strategy of marriage.

Obviously related to the structure of marriage are the claims of numayms over the children—a complex issue in an ambilateral society. Boas was aware of this question, and, in an early publication, notes: "Marriage among the Kwakiutl must be considered a purchase, which is conducted on the same principles as the purchase of a copper. But the object bought is not only the woman, but also the right of membership in her clan for the future children of the couple" (Boas 1897:358). This right of membership in the mother's numaym for the children of the couple follows from the repurchase payment made by the bride's father. One of the usual concomitants of the marriage repurchase is the bestowal of names by the mother's father upon the children. If one of the children is the sole heir of the mother's father, this will be signified by the bestowal of a high name by him. The possession of the name signifies membership in the mother's numaym for the child. This is graphically illustrated in the text material by the following:

As soon as the great chief Lalakotsa learned that his sister Lelendzewek had given birth to a boy, the heart of Lalakotsa was very glad, for he had found out that the newborn child of his sister was a boy. Therefore he loaded with all kinds of food a large canoe and came to give a marriage gift to his brother-in-law Emaxumewesageme. And he gave the marriage name Emaxulagilis as a name to his nephew. Then Lalakotsa told his brother-in-law Emaxumewesageme that he was going to take the child, his nephew, and that he should be ready to take the seat of Lalakotsa in his numaym Mamaleleqam. Thus he said, and the whole numaym Dzendzenxqayo agreed to what Lalakotsa said. Now he was just waiting for Emaxulagilis, his nephew, to grow up (Boas 1925:71).

This particular account illustrates several major points about Kwakiutl social structure. A childless Mamaleleqala chief claims his sister's son, through the marriage repurchase, as his heir. His payment of the marriage repurchase is the means by which he gains an heir. The child who is heir gains membership and an important name in the numaym of his mother. He grows up with the Dzendzenxqayo of the Walas Kwagul, his father's group. In this particular case, the boy's father dies and the boy succeeds him as chief. However, the mother's brother, on his deathbed, compels the Dzendzenxqayo to relinquish the boy in conformity with the agreement on the payment of the marriage repurchase for the boy's mother. The boy then becomes chief of the Mamaleleqala, though retaining the seat in his father's numaym.

The marriage repurchase also signifies the formal ending of the marriage. The wife may either remain with her husband or return to her natal numaym. With the repurchase, the formal obligations on both sides cease. The marriage payment and repurchase may occur again. Boas notes that "if the young wife continues to stay with her husband, she stays 'for nothing,' which is not dignified. A new contract has to be made in the same way as the first one, but the payments are generally much less. The whole matter seems to be a little more of a formality, although proud and rich people may make the same extravagant payments as they did in the first marriage" (Boas 1966:54). Another possibility after the marriage formally ends is for the woman to marry another man. Boas notes: "Often, after the annulment of a marriage through repayment of the marriage debt, the woman is married to another man. . . . After four marriages, her high rank is established, and it seems to be assumed that after this she should stay with her last husband" (Boas 1966:55). It would thus seem that serial polygamy is not uncommon for high-ranking men and women. This would account for the frequent discussion of half brothers and half sisters in the texts.

The details of the repurchase illuminate a number of the important features of Kwakiutl social structure. The ambilaterality of group membership exists in the form of options for affiliation.

The repurchase of the wife has as its concomitant the activation of such membership for the children in that they receive names from their maternal grandfather. They, at the same time, in all probability, also hold names in the numaym of their father. The strength of the claims on both sides is situationally determined, and the children may be latent members in several groups representing several lines of descent though they are active in only one of these numayms, the one with which they reside. At the same time, the repurchase payment reemphasizes the fact that though the wife is residing with her husband, she is there as an affine. The repurchase thus emphasizes the affinal category. Numaym membership is relatively permanent in that the wife may return to the numaym with which she is affiliated and which pays the repurchase price. The size of the repayment is a direct function of the rank of the wife's father. Lastly, the wife repurchase involves the transferal of rights and privileges utilized during the winter ceremonial, in which a separate structure and a different set of groups come into play.

Within the context of a family history, Boas details the types of privileges which form the repurchase as follows:

After they had eaten, the four speakers of Chief Qaed arose and told the tribe that Qaed was going to give the box with his privileges to his son-in-law, namely, the cannibal dance, the tamer of the cannibal-dancer, the rattle, and the rich-woman, and also the fire dance, all of which were in the box of privileges; for, indeed, they kept in the privilege-box the neckrings of red cedar-bark . . . and also the rattle of the cannibal-tamer. Then they took the privilege-box out of the bedroom (Boas 1921:1081).

Since the only way in which the winter ceremonial privileges are transmitted transgenerationally is through marriage, a man may not will these privileges to his son. If he has no daughter, a fictive marriage is performed between a man who becomes his "son-in-law" and his son; the son-in-law is thus entitled to those privileges which pass affinally. If a man is childless, the fictive marriage may be performed with a foot or other part of the body. This is called "taking hold of the foot" (Boas 1897:359; 1966:55).

As can be seen, no positive marriage rule exists for the Kwakiutl; they represent a complex structure, in Lévi-Strauss's terms. There are a number of culturally recognized strategies with regard to marriage. The goals in this game of strategic marriages are progeny to carry one's line, to continue one's numaym, and to maintain and, if possible, raise the status of one's children. The conditions of the game are how many progeny one has, how many of either sex, one's own rank, and, lastly and probably most importantly, whether the first-born is a girl or a boy. The culturally stated alternatives of strategy are: marrying inside versus marrying outside, marrying higher or lower in rank. For example, if one is a high-ranking chief with one daughter and no sons, one would probably marry the daughter either inside high or low, or outside low, in order to ensure that one has control over an heir. This would be achieved by uxorilocal residence or the payment of a very large repurchase price accompanied by the bestowal of a high name upon a child of the marriage. The marriage of a daughter of a chief may be the means by which the rank of his group is raised through the payment of an impressive repurchase price at a potlatch.

An entirely different strategy might be played by a middle-ranking man with several sons who would seek to marry his sons to high-ranking families since, with several sons, he would not need to be concerned about continuing his own line. He would attempt to maximize the prestige of high-ranking marriages and the resultant high repurchase payments coming from important affines. This last strategy is referred to by Charley Nowell, who attempts through magic to ensure that he will have all male children: "When my wife and I got married, I wanted a boy, and I made four small wedges of yew wood and bow and arrows which men would use, and put them under our bed and kept them there. I wanted all boys" (Ford 1941:156-57). In a footnote following, Ford comments:

One of the distinct advantages in having male children derives from the Kwakiutl marriage transactions. As will be seen in the following chapter, the father of a girl is required to pay out more than he receives when she marries. The father of a boy is not thus handicapped. If he has boys first, and then girls, he is in a strategic position. The returns from his sons' marriages help him in his obligations to his sons-in-law (Ford 1941:157).

A variety of terms exist for marriage which vary according to the strategy employed. Hunt describes them as follows: "For there are four ways of wooing, going downward, different from the 'obtaining of a slave,' and 'taking hold of the foot,' and 'the exchange marriage.' And all of these are different from what we are now finishing, that we call the 'great bringing out of the crest in marriage'" (Boas 1925:281). Elsewhere he notes: "This is called 'taking a wife outside'" (Boas 1921:782). These various terms for each type of marriage appear to describe the kinds of strategies outlined above.

We have deferred until now our discussion of the potlatch, since the potlatch can only be understood in its relationship to the social structure. The potlatch involves in simplest terms the amassing of property and its subsequent distribution in a ceremonial context. Though this massing and redistribution of property is obviously a central feature of the Kwakiutl economic system and has been so considered by Boas, Codere, Drucker and Heizer, Vayda, Belshaw, Piddocke, and others, the essential elements of the potlatch also intersect with other subsystems of Kwakiutl society. These include the ambilateral numaym structure and numaym interrelations; the political office of chief and succession to that office; intra- and inter-numaym rank; the structure of religious societies; beliefs regarding ancestry, supernatural spirits, and mythology; the performance arts, which are of such symbolic significance in Kwakiutl society; and, lastly, the life cycle and *rites de passage* through which all individuals must pass. The potlatch is thus a drama in which are played out the essential elements of Kwakiutl culture and society, while revealing the components of the social structure.

Potlatches may occur on the following occasions in the life cycle: at the age of ten months when the child receives its second name, its first being always the place name where it was born; at the age of ten or twelve, for a boy, when a new name—the third—is given; for a girl, at the first menstruation; at the young manhood of a boy when he receives his fourth name and may assume his father's seat, or is named heir; at initiation into a secret society; at the payment of a marriage gift; at the payment of a marriage repurchase; to wipe out an embarrassing accident or insult; on accession to the position of chief. Within the context of a single potlatch, several events in the lives of closely related individuals may be publicly celebrated; for example, a father, his heir, and the heir's sister may each mark a different event in their lives at the same potlatch. This again reinforces the multipurpose function of the potlatch.

The size of a potlatch in terms of people and range of groupings and size of distribution varies with the occasion for potlatching. The largest potlatches, involving many Kwakiutl tribes, are sponsored by great chiefs on the announcement of the heir's succession to the chiefly position. Such an occasion may be concomitantly a marriage repurchase, if the heir is a boy.

The large intertribal potlatches are presented in Kwakiutl ideology in terms of group versus group. Though much of the recent discussion concerning the Kwakiutl has centered on the rivalry of chiefs as individuals, this is a distortion. In reality, large potlatches involve interaction between groups as groups; Kwakiutl ideology conceives of the potlatch in these terms. In the following speech, a chief who intends to give a potlatch has asked his numaym to contribute goods. The men of the numaym gather their property to give to him. He then addresses them as follows:

Thank you, numaym, that you have come to this our house here, great numaym. Indeed, this is the way of my mind, great numaym. I depend on it that you will stand behind me in everything, when I contend with the chiefs of the tribes. Now, great numaym, I will tell you about what I have in mind. I want to give a potlatch to the tribes. I have five hundred blankets in my house. Now you will see whether that is enough to invite the tribes with. You will think that five hundred blankets are not enough, and you will treat me as your chief, and you will give me your property for the potlatch, great numaym, for it will not be in my name. It will be in your name, and you will become famous among the tribes, when it is said that you have given your property for a potlatch, that I may invite the tribes. Now look at your minds (Boas 1921: 1341-42).

The rivalry of the potlatch is no more and no less than the rivalry between affines. Groups linked as affines in marriage are opposed, and yet joined, in their interest. These are the groups who potlatch to one another. When the focus of the potlatch is a young boy, as is often the case, each potlatch in his honor is an event in a chain of events. At each potlatch, one of the numayms with which he can affiliate presents him with a name and then distributes to the other numayms and tribes, who bear witness to the acquisition of the new name. At a subsequent potlatch, another numaym with which the boy may affiliate will do the same, in a sense in competition with the first. Despite this competition, these numayms are concerned with the welfare of the boy and, in this sense, may join together to assist him in competition with other groups.

The clusters of numayms which we have pointed to as linked in marriage also pass winter privileges from father-in-law to son-in-law and buy and sell coppers to one another in order to raise blankets to potlatch one another. Though rivals are in opposition, it is apparent that they need each other—this is the essence of the potlatch. The career of Lasotiwalis, prince of the Qomoyaye of the Kwagul, will be used to illustrate the part that the potlatch plays in the life of a high-ranked individual. This life history is to be found in the form of text material subsumed under the category "The Acquisition of Names" (Boas 1925:112-357). It runs for 245 pages. The bulk of this material is summarized in charts H and I. Diagram F shows the relationships between the principal personae.

Chart H summarizes the fourteen events that make up the se-

Diagram F. Kinship Chart for Potlatch Charts H and I

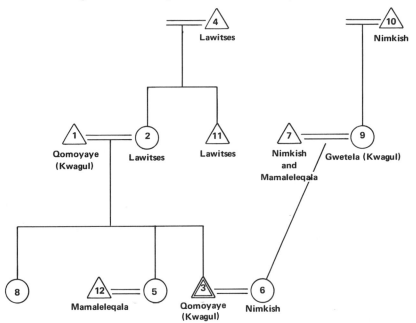

The tribal designations refer to the group referents used by these actors in the potlatches in charts H and I.

quence of potlatches and associated name acquisitions for Lasoti-walis (#3). In the first column are listed the life-crises occasions whose significance is marked either by a change in name or by a potlatch or by both. The life cycles of several individuals are inter-twined in this sequence of events. Both #1 and his son (#3) are the central participants. One of the major themes which emerges from this life history is that a number of significant events are celebrated by the same potlatch.

The importance of an occasion is reflected in the scale of the potlatch which celebrates it. The more important an event is in the life of #3, the wider the range of guests who are invited. An inspection of the sequence of events, one through eight, reveals that as #3 grows older, the occasions for a potlatch become more

Chart H. Life History and Potlatching Career of a Kwakiutl Chief

Occasion	Name	From whom name comes	Guests invited	What happens (including distribution)
1. Birth	Fort Rupert			The first name always refers to place of birth
2. Ten months of age	Wawalkin	Father?	All the Kwagul tribes	Hair scorched off and leg and arm straps placed on child; distribution of kerchiefs to men and children
3. Four days later	Megwat (Seal)		Young men of Kwagul tribes	Leg and arm straps removed; distribution of kerchiefs; receives a young man's name
4. "Painting with song" (four years later)	Satsem (Spring Salmon)		Young men of Gwetela, Walas Kwagul, and Qomkutes	All young men receive shirts and their new "paint-giving-away" names as a result of #1's distribution
5. "Spreading out"	Gixsestaliseme	Father	People who have already "spread out" Men and women with men's names From Gwetela, Walas Kwagul, and Qomkutes tribes	Name of #3 is changed to Gixsestaliseme and thenceforth he attends feasts; blankets are distributed to all; chiefs recognize him and he receives a seat and rank in the order of precedence to which his new name entitles him
6. Distribution to wipe out the shame of an accident	No name change		All men of Gwetela, Walas Kwagul, and Qomkutes tribes	Distribution of blankets by #1 to wipe out the shame of #3's canoe capsizing
7. Winter dance	Yaqoselagilis	Father	Own tribe— Qomoyaye	Marriage repurchase for the mother of #3 and #3 disappears for two months; winter dance is given by #1
8. "Giving away to his own tribe"	Yaqolaseme	Probably father	Gwetela, Walas Kwagul, Qomkutes	#3 gives out 700 blankets in #1's name, one pair to each common man and 5 pairs to chiefs of the three Kwagul tribes; #3 does the same; #5 is honored and #3 distributes for her
9. Takes chiefly name	Lasotiwalis	Father	Nimkish, Lawitses, Mamaleleqela	Copper is purchased and broken, large-scale distribution (see Chart I for details)

Occasion	Name	From whom name comes	Guests invited	What happens (including distribution)
10. Great Bringing Up the Crest Marriage	Awide	Wife's father	Twelve tribes invited by Nimkish to come to residence of #6's father	Nine great chiefs opposite in side from girl and boy display privileges in order to "move the bride"; 500 blankets given to girl's father as wedding gift; copper is immediately returned as repurchase of bride, as well as 300 blankets which are then distributed to the Kwagul tribes; Lasotiwalis promises a grease feast for the "opposite" side after the selling of the copper
11. Sale of a copper	Ewanuku (feasting name)	Father	Four Kwagul tribes go to Knight's Inlet where copper is bought by the Mamaleleqala	The copper "Sewa," the marriage repurchase gift to #3 from #7, is sold to a Mamaleqala (opposite side) chief, for 600 coal-oil tins of grease; #3 immediately makes a grease feast for all the tribes; the feast name, feast dish, and feast song were received by #3 from his father prior to the feast
12. "Sitting under his wife" (second purchase of the wife)	No new name		All the tribes	#3 collects blankets; gives 500 blankets to #7 and 500 blankets to #10; no immediate repurchase; the marriage debt, consisting of property and trifles, will be paid to #3 in the future
13. Maturity of the chief's sister	No new name		Three Kwagul tribes are invited by the Qomoyaye	Since he has no children, #3 makes #8 (younger sister) his princess; on the occasion of her first menstruation, he distributes a long list of household objects and "trifles"; these gifts are not returnable; this ceremony is rare, performed only by "The One Who Went Through Everything"

162

Chart H (continued)

Occasion	Name	From whom name comes	Guests invited	What happens (including distribution)
14. Building of a house (accompanying 2d repurchase of the wife)	No new name		A) Building the house: men from 14 numayms of the Kwagul B) 2d repurchase of #3's wife: 10 different tribes arriving in rank order	#3 assigns to chiefs of different numayms specific tasks in cutting posts, poles, and timbers; they receive blankets for this, and all are feasted; the timbers and poles are brought up to the beach, and a distribution of 400 blankets follows; adzers shape the timbers and receive blankets; all help to erect the house, blankets are distributed; chiefs of the Kwagul go to the Nimkish (where #7 and #10 are living) to invite; they then invite ten other tribes; the marriage debt is returned to #3 who redistributes it to all the tribes—Kwagul and opposites

Source: Boas 1925: 112–357.

important, and more individuals from the Kwagul tribes are invited. On the occasion of #3's assumption of the chief's name (event nine), non-Kwagul chiefs from the "opposite side," Mamaleleqala, Nimkish, and Lawitses, are invited for the first time. At the occasions after event nine, potlatches involve this wider circle. Potlatching always involves "sides" with whom exchanges occur. As the potlatching circle widens, the "sides" alter. For example, when #1 potlatches on behalf of his son to other Kwagul tribes, he represents the Yaexageme numaym of the Qomoyaye subtribe and he potlatches to the other Kwagul subtribes, all of whom live at Fort Rupert. In event nine, the circle is widened and the "sides" alter, so that when #3 potlatches his own "side" consists of all the Kwagul subtries and the "opposites" are Nimkish, Lawitses, and Mamaleleqala.

The critical service of witnessing performed by guests at potlatches is a central theme throughout. Each new name change and prerogative transferred requires an appropriate group of witness-guests; the more important the name or the prerogative transferred, the more important and the larger the group of witness-guests. During his life #3 acquires thirteen names in all. Three are winter dance names, two of which are mentioned as belonging to #3 prior to event seven. These names apparently came from his mother's side. Another name is a special feasting name (event eleven), and still another comes from his father-in-law as a privilege obtained in marriage. The remaining names come from his father, including the greatest name of all, the chief's name Lasotiwalis which is given to him at the great potlatch (event nine). The passage of this name represents the succession to the title and office of chief for #3. During the potlatch, #1 notes that he has now become his son's attendant and ranks at the bottom of his own numaym. This potlatch signifies that succession to chiefly office takes place during the lifetime of the chief (#1).

Marriage purchase and repurchase play significant roles in a number of the potlatch events. As noted earlier, marriage is a potlatch. The relationship between sides potlatching is identical to that of affines. The marriage repurchase of the mother (#2) of #3 is linked to his initiation into the winter dance and receipt of a winter dance name (event seven). The second repurchase of the mother (#2) of #3 is linked to the accession of #3 to chiefly office and title. The copper which is the repurchase gift given by #4 (#2's father) to #1 serves as the means for #3's elevation to chief. The first repurchase of the wife (#6) of #3 takes place at event ten, the occasion of the marriage itself. The sale of this repurchase gift, the copper "Sewa," forms the basis for the grease feast (event eleven). The second repurchase of the wife (#6) of #3 provides the goods used for the building of a house and accompanying potlatch (event fourteen). On this occasion, there is a distribution in honor of #3's princess, his "child" and heir (#8). There is a relationship between marriage repurchase and succession which occur at the same potlatch, as, for example, events nine and fourteen. The goods transferred through the repurchase gift are used by the recipient, the son-in-law, for a potlatch distribution or feast in honor of his heir. Boas notes in another context: "I explained before that many privileges of the clan descend only through marriage upon the son-in-law of the possessor, who, however, does not use them himself but acquires them for the use of his successor" (1897: 358-59).

Chart I summarizes the details of the great potlatch. The action in the main concerns the host (#3), the Kwagul tribes, and their opposites, the Nimkish, Lawitses, and Mamaleleqala. The Kwagul tribes act in concert on this occasion, this being exemplified by the fact that the other Kwagul chiefs are told to keep their coppers in readiness in case #3 is immediately challenged when he distributes the broken pieces. The paired rivalries which have been discussed in connection with marriage are apparent again at the feast in this potlatch. The sequence of borrowing of blankets and the return distribution reflects the ranking of the opposites. At this, a Qomoyaye potlatch, the ranking of each person, numaym, and tribe of the opposites is spelled out in the distribution. The members of the Kwagul tribes do not share in the distribution, but merely receive the empty boxes and containers at a subsequent distribution. It is interesting to note that #2, the wife of #1 and mother of #3, plays the role of tally counter. She herself is a Lawitses, of the opposite side, and she accompanies the canoes which go to invite the opposites and borrow blankets from them. Her father, #4, is the Lawitses who gives the copper which plays a central role in this event. The important role of wife as tally counter and participant at the potlatch of her husband and son is reminiscent of the central role of the wife at a Haida potlatch, and in fact the same question may be raised here as to who is giving the potlatch, since her father gives the copper, the breaking of which is the dramatic event about which the potlatch revolves. There is no question, however, that this is the potlatch of #3 and #1. The mother participates in raising the rank of her son, in analogous fashion to the Haida.

Chart I. The Great Potlatch: Takes Chiefly Name (#9)

Kwagul tribes	Host and own numaym	Other side— Nimkish, Lawitses, Mamaleleqala	Comments
	#1 buys copper from ◄——————— chief of Heldsaq; gives it to #3	Heldsaq chief	
	#3 sells copper ——► ◄———	Chief of Lawitses for 1,500 blankets	
◄———	#1 invites the other three Kwagul tribes as well as his own		"The four Kwagul tribes will act as one in the interaction with the 'other side'"
	#1 has special watch pole built which is his special privilege		
◄———	Blanket distribution for witnessing #3's name is changed to Lasotiwalis		#1 is now the attendant of his son #3
	Nine chiefs accompany #1 as his crew to invite ⇄ to potlatch	Nimkish who lend him 500 blankets	#2 goes along to count
	——————►	Mamaleleqala who lend him 600 blankets	Mamaleleqala asked for more because they ranked higher than Nim- kish and Lawitses
	——————►	Lawitses who lend him 400 blankets	
	All blankets are brought back to #1's house		
	#1, #3, #5 perform a dance		Mamaleleqala arrive
	100 blankets ——————►	Mamaleleqala for witnessing	
	Feast ——————►	Mamaleleqala	
		Mamaleleqala sing and display privileges and promise a grease feast	Nimkish and Lawitses arrive and are treated in same manner as the Mamaleleqala
	◄———————	#4, the Lawitses chief, gives the copper Dentalayu to his son- in-law #1	This copper is probably part of the marriage re- purchase from #4 to #1 for wife #2
	#1 gives copper to #3		
	◄———————	#12 chief of the Mama- leleqala makes a feast for the four Kwagul tribes; Lawitses and Nimkish are present as hosts also	Pairings at the feast; Gwe- tela sat next to Mamale- leqala, Qomoyaye sat next to Nimkish, Lawit- ses paired with Walas Kwagul and Qomkutes

166

Chart I (continued)

Kwagul tribes	Host and own numaym	Other side— Nimkish, Lawitses, Mamaleleqala	Comments
Chiefs of the Gwetela, Qomoyaye, Walas Kwagul, and Qomkutes make speeches recounting their names, the coppers they have given away, and promising feasts in return			Each of the four Kwagul chiefs gives 100 blankets in lieu of a feast
			Blankets which were borrowed earlier are tallied for return along with the 100 percent increment; last name of lowest-ranking numaym is piled first; Kwagul witness the tally
			Four chiefs of four numayms of the Kwagul, except for the Qomoyaye, mark the copper according to #1's guidance; no one knows to whom the broken pieces will be given
	#3 announces new names for #5 and #8		Indicative of the joint action of all the Kwagul tribes on this occasion is the fact that #1 calls on all to be ready with their coppers in case he should be challenged in return on the spot
	#3 gives 1st piece of copper ⟶ Mamaleleqala chief Makes speech 2d piece of copper ⟶ Nimkish chief Makes speech		Four chiefs who had marked the copper strike off the corners marked
	3d piece held in abeyance for one who had spoken badly of #3		
	#1 gives his seat and office to #3 and stands now at end of his numaym		
	Blankets are distributed ⟶ To all in all three tribes and they leave for home		
⟵ Kwagul tribes invited			
⟵ Empty boxes and baskets which held blankets distributed, also mats, dishes, spoons, paddles, all things in house			
⟵ Tribes invited, boards removed from house and distributed			#1, #3 go to live with near relatives

The last point to be noted about the great potlatch is the seeming rivalry between chiefs of the opposite sides. The form that this
accession to chieftainship takes is the breaking of a copper and the
distribution to chiefs of the opposite side. This has always been
interpreted as the epitome of challenge and rivalry. Yet our interpretation throughout has been that opposites need each other, and
serve the important function of witnessing the accession to office
of one another. A great chief needs great rivals. It is an honor,
therefore, to be selected as a rival by one acknowledged as a great
chief. When presented with the broken corner of the copper,
Waned, the chief of the Mamaleleqala, replies, "Thank you, chief
Lasotiwalis, that you do not think me too small to give this that
comes from the copper that has a name, Dentalayu. Thank you"
(1925:227). The second chief says, "Indeed, indeed, chiefs of the
tribes, is it not bad, the giving of the broken pieces of copper, just
that they give the broken pieces of copper to the real chiefs of the
tribes. This is what I mean, Chief Lasotiwalis, thank you, thank
you" (1925:229). Thus in effect, by choosing the rivals, #3 pro-
claims his own chieftainship while acknowledging that they are
real chiefs also. They therefore thank him for the honor he bestows
upon them.

As in the case of the Nootka, some of the most elaborate detail
concerning the potlatch occurs in association with winter ceremonials. Boas, in a heroic feat of participant observation, presents
his eyewitness account of the continuous winter ceremonial which
occurred at Fort Rupert from November 16 to November 27, 1895.
This is the anthropologist's richest source of direct observation;
however, the variability in the quality and in the degree of detail
makes it very difficult to analyze. People are not adequately identified in terms of their position in the social structure. Boas notes
that "at the time of the beginning of the winter ceremonial the
social system is completely changed . . . during this period the place
of the clans is taken by a number of societies, namely, the groups
of all those individuals upon whom the same or almost the same

power or secret has been bestowed by one of the spirits' (Boas 1897: 418), but this generalization is refuted by his own material. The winter ceremonial described involves the Kwakiutl, Koskimo, and Naqoaqtok. The secret (winter) societies operate within tribes, each tribe having its own variant of the secret societal structure. Boas frequently notes that the tribes are in competition, with the Kwagul ranged against the Koskimo and Naqoaqtok (Boas 1897: 579, 580, 582; 1905:485). Not only is the tribal system maintained but numaym organization is referred to as being utilized in blanket distribution as follows: "When the blankets were being brought into the house, the tally keeper of the Gopenox came in to look after the proper distribution of the blankets. He gave the names of the clans and the number of blankets which were to be given to each name in each clan" (Boas 1897:589).

As Boas himself noted, winter ceremonials play an important role as the context within which marriage repurchase takes place. Therefore we find, as expected, that marriage repurchase is an occasion for interaction between affines. "At the time of marriage the bride's father has promised to transfer his membership in one of the secret societies to one of his son-in-law's children. . . . The man who gives the dance notifies his father-in-law that he desires to have the blankets which he paid for his wife returned, and that he wants to have the box containing his father-in-law's dance" (Boas 1897:501). In the account of the winter ceremonial Boas cites numerous instances of repurchase payments which include winter ceremonial privileges, going from fathers-in-law to sons-in-law. He cites a lengthy and amusing account of how an old repurchase debt is finally repaid, in the midst of a young boy's initiation (Boas 1897:563-65). It is apparent that the winter ceremonial recapitulates the elements which have been previously cited as typical of the potlatch complex. Potlatching occurs between groups which are in an affinal relationship to one another. Winter ceremonials involve marriage repurchase, which, as has been noted earlier, is an important basis for potlatching. The sides or opposites at the winter ceremonial align themselves as potlatching rivals. Their speeches reflect this rivalry (Boas 1897:571, 576, 580, 602). The structure of the secret societies reflects the rank order within the tribe, since societies are ranked hierarchically and consist of a limited number of names. The rank between tribes is also signifi- cant in the sequence of events of the winter ceremonial. This is most evident in the following speech, made by a Kwagul chief to his own tribe at a winter ceremonial: "Oh friends! Let me ask you, chiefs and the new chiefs of my tribe, do you wish to be laughed at by your rivals? We are almost beaten by the Koskimo. We are only one potlatch ahead of them. After this pile has been distributed, we shall be only two potlatches ahead of them, instead of four as our fathers used to be. Take care, friends! Our friends the Koskimo are strong in rivaling us in distribution of property" (Boas 1905:485).

The winter ceremonial, with its secret societies, ceremonies, and extensive religious paraphernalia, thus constitutes a separate sub- system with its distinct seasonal timing and its place in the life cycle. Nevertheless, our analysis reveals that the underlying struc- ture is the same as that of the potlatch.

The foregoing examination of the Tsimshian, Haida, Tlingit, and Bella Coola revealed that funerary rites were one of the most significant occasions for the giving of a potlatch. The data support our point that funerary rites, as *rites de passage,* are the occasions for potlatching when succession to chiefly office occurs at the same time. The Kwakiutl data have shown that succession to chiefly office occurs during the lifetime of the holder of the office, and hence one would expect to find that among the Kwakiutl funerary rites are not the occasion for potlatching. Though Boas in 1889 noted that after the death of a great chief his son adopts his name at a great feast, subsequent material indicates that such is not the case. Our discussion of succession to chiefly office clearly indicates that it took place during the lifetime of the holder. A chief gives his chiefly title to his first-born during the course of a major pot- latch when his heir is still young. At that point, the former chief assumes a name which locates him lower on the rank list. This pattern was reiterated in the career of Lasotiwalis. However, Ford notes that a potlatch was given for Charley Nowell after the death of his father. The potlatch was given by Nowell's brother, who had earlier succeeded to the chiefly position during the lifetime of the father. The potlatch involved Nowell's assumption of his father's last-held name, and thus was not a funeral potlatch involving succession to chiefly office (Ford 1941:108). The substantive data appear to contradict Ford's earlier point that "the heir to the highest position formerly held by the deceased person gave a potlatch at which he proclaimed his new name and position" (Ford 1941:40).

The only extended discussion of a particular funeral is contained in "A Family History" in Boas 1925. This is an instance where a mother's brother has selected his sister's son as heir but has not yet transferred to this sister's son his name and title. (See p. 154 above.) As he lies dying he sends messengers to claim the presumptive heir. The name transferal takes place at his deathbed. But he dies before the transferal can be validated by a distribution of property. Such validation takes place after his death and involves a large potlatch to which thirteen tribes are invited. At this potlatch the succession to chiefly office is recognized, which, owing to the circumstances in this particular case, occurred after the death of the previous holder but while the successor was still a boy. It would be a misinterpretation to call this occasion a funerary potlatch.

This particular potlatch also serves to illuminate the ritual character of the rivalry. Boas notes: "Then Neqapenkem arose in his canoe and comforted Maxmewesageme [the heir], whose name was Walas Kwakilanokume [his new name], the other name of Lalakotsa [the dead chief]. . . . And each of the real chiefs of every tribe spoke comforting words" (Boas 1925:81). It is important to note that the first speaker, Neqapenkem, was the chief rival of the deceased chief in copper-breaking. This incident clearly illustrates that the view of rivals as fierce and hostile competitors is much overdrawn. The mourning of a dead rival and the comfort afforded

to his heir and successor can only mean that the death of a rival is
perceived as a loss, for one needs one's rivals. We can only conclude
that an emphasis upon antagonistic rivalry ignores the total system
and misinterprets the symbolism which characterizes Kwakiutl
potlatching.

It is clear from the previous discussion that rank is one of the
most significant variables in the system. The issue of mobility in
rank, both mobility within the numaym and mobility in the ranking of numayms, must be considered. Our examination of the material leads us to conclude that mobility within the numaym is not
the norm. The instances which we have located regarding this indicate that, though individuals may attempt to raise their status
within the numaym, no information supports the acceptance by
the chiefs of such claims. The examples all point in the opposite
direction. Codere (1957:475) uses an example from Boas (1925:97-
99) in which a commoner accumulates property and a copper, potlatches, and acts like a chief. Boas notes that "Wamis [the social
climber] was also hated by the chiefs of the Mamaleleqala, for
when one of the chiefs gave away property then Wamis also gave
away blankets, just as if he were making fun of the chief in doing
so. . . . Then Wamis became afraid of the chiefs of his tribe for
they kept on threatening to kill him" (Boas 1925:97). As a result
of this, Wamis gives up his name, his copper, and his seat to the
only true chief who was friendly to him; thenceforth he had no
seat. In another example provided by Boas, the man Wagidis, by
use of a name from his wife and a copper given to him by a chief
whom he had befriended, potlatches and tries to assume a position
of importance. Several opposite chiefs acting jointly break coppers
in challenge to Wagidis. Wagidis cannot meet the challenge and
"then Wagidis became a slave again" (Boas 1921:1116). Finally,
Ford discusses the case of an individual who attempts to usurp a
position by a claim to inheritance of a name. The outcome of this
case is that Nulis, the claimant, advances his position somewhat. In
a footnote Ford states: "Note, too, that Nulis is censured for even

the slightest deviation from the customary procedure. Any tentatives in the direction of stealing a position are immediately punished" (Ford 1941:109). These cases all indicate that, though individuals may attempt to advance their position and to move from commoner to chief, in actuality it appears to be exceedingly difficult to do this. The outcome in these cases was unsuccessful.

There are indications, however, that entire groups, numayms, and possibly even tribes may shift their rank with respect to other similar groups. We have noted above, in the context of our discussion of the winter ceremonial, the concern voiced by the Kwagul that their forebears had been four potlatches ahead of the Koskimo while they were only two ahead at the present. Ford, as quoted earlier, reports a challenge by the entire Nimkish tribe to displace the Mamaleleqala. "The Nimkis gave a number of potlatches to the Fort Rupert tribes and announced their intention of moving into fifth place. But the Mamaleleqala met the challenge and also gave potlatches to the Fort Rupert people. The latter, sitting in judgment over the two tribes, decided that the Nimkis had not yet earned the right to change their position" (Ford 1941:20-21). It would thus appear that mobility and change in rank are possible for entire groups, though the number of instances seem to indicate that they were not very frequent.

It is important to distinguish the presence of flexibility in Kwakiutl social organization and the points at which flexibility occurs, in contrast to mobility. At a number of points the Kwakiutl structure exhibits remarkable flexibility and the presence of choice. In the Kwakiutl rule of descent and in the marriage pattern the wide range of options from which choices may be made is apparent. Individuals may affiliate with a number of different numayms with which they have kinship ties and with more than one numaym at a time. The choices are made on the basis of a type of strategy involving rank of seat obtainable, rank of group involved, and its size and power. Marriages, in the absence of any definite marriage rule, are contracted on the basis of a similar sort of strategy involving own rank, affines' rank, position in birth order, etc. In fact, the exercise of marriage choices determines the numaym options open to children. The great amount of flexibility which this produces is directly related to when and in what ways potlatching occurs.

In summary, the following general points about Kwakiutl potlatching may be noted. Potlatches of varying scale mark a number of life crises, particularly of chiefs, the scale of the potlatch relating to the importance of the life crisis. Furthermore, at every important potlatch a number of people mark life crises of different kinds. Thus, the high point in a boy's potlatching career occurs when he is given a chiefly name. This same potlatch marks a *rite de passage* for the father as he moves to the bottom of the numaym upon giving up his chiefly name. The same potlatch also involves the mother of the boy and her father, since the goods with which she is repurchased by her father are used to make the potlatch. The repurchase of a wife signifies a change in the status of the mother as wife, for it means that she may now leave her husband. Her father, by the repurchase, has fulfilled an important obligation to his son-in-law and to his daughter's son. Each of these individuals has carried out a particular obligation and has moved into a new status position.

The Kwakiutl material illustrates our general principle that potlatching occurs between affines. Marriage establishes or reestablishes affinal relations between groups who are linked to one another as potlatching opposites. The giving of property follows the same lines as the giving of women, for, as was said before, marriage is a potlatch. Marriage and its attendant ceremonials, including the repurchase, provide the only occasion for the transferal of the privileges associated with the winter ceremonial, particularly the names associated with membership in secret societies.

The potlatch may be seen from a totally different analytical perspective. Kwakiutl potlatches illustrate the way in which general variables intersect in Kwakiutl social structure. The particular form of succession to chiefly office among the Kwakiutl, where the rule of succession is according to primogeniture, occurs at a potlatch during the lifetime of the holder. This pattern of succession is directly related to the ambilateral descent group structure among the Kwakiutl. Given the flexibility in modes of affiliation and the multiplicity of numaym affiliations, primogeniture and this mode of succession provide a means of stability. The type of marriage structure described above is strategic in nature and is seen as complex rather than elementary, in Lévi-Strauss's terms. It is consistent with the ambilateral descent system and with the complexity of ranking. The sequence of marriage payment and repurchase is the mechanism by which women are retained by their natal numaym. The repurchase goods are the material utilized to make the potlatch at which the heir accedes to the chiefly position.

The last major variable is the system of rank. Both internal and external ranking of groups are present. However, while internal ranking is fixed and therefore funerals are not potlatches, external ranking is flexible. Marriages of individuals in different groups or within the same group involve people different in rank. Therefore our general hypothesis that, given the unequal rank of affines, marriage is a potlatch is borne out by the Kwakiutl material. Affines are characterized by the Kwakiutl as being "opposites" who compete with one another. All Kwakiutl potlatching directly involves the flexible rank system of groups.

The particular configuration of the Kwakiutl potlatch therefore represents the Kwakiutl permutation of these key variables: the structure of descent groups, marriage structure, succession to chiefly title, and rank.

CHAPTER VII. *THE STRUCTURE REVEALED BY THE POTLATCH*

WE HAVE JOURNEYED back in time to resurrect events the like of which will never occur again. The potlatches of great chiefs, the rituals, and the distributions have been recalled to mind but seen in perspective different from that of the original ethnographic accounts.

The potlatch on the Northwest Coast has interested several generations of anthropologists because it seemed to defy explanation. It appeared to bear witness to human characteristics which were considered perverse. What made people destroy goods in order to shame a rival? What made them expend in such excess that they were left totally without material resources? What kind of a social structure demanded that an individual reduce himself in order to proclaim his greatness? The answers offered by earlier analysts who focused upon these features—with particular reference to the Kwakiutl, since the body of literature collected by Boas so greatly exceeded the data on other Northwest Coast societies—took the following form. By far the most famous was Benedict's answer, which emphasized rivalry, competition, and destruction of property. She noted: "In Kwakiutl institutions, such rivalry reaches a final absurdity in equating investment with wholesale destruction of goods. They contest for superiority chiefly in accumulation of goods, but often also, and without a consciousness of the contrast, in breaking in pieces their highest units of value, their coppers, and making bonfires of their house planks, their blankets and canoes" (Benedict 1934 [1959]:215). Benedict's conclusion was that Kwakiutl behavior reflects a megalomaniac or paranoid personality type (Benedict 1959:223). To Benedict, the paradox was that those most fully endowed with this personality type were the leaders of the society. Benedict also saw the potlatch as an example of conspicuous consumption. The point was reiterated by Herskovits as well, who considered the Kwakiutl an excellent example of Veblen's principle (1952: Chapter 21). The underlying assumption of these theories was that the environment of the Northwest Coast was characterized by a superabundance which enabled accumulation of goods in great amounts whose only use was in conspicuous display.

Barnett's work on the nature of the potlatch has been accepted as the most reasonable interpretation by ethnographers who have worked in the Northwest Coast in the past three decades. It has thus become a standard work on the subject. Taking a comparative point of view, Barnett recognizes that guests at a potlatch receive gifts as payment for the important service of witnessing the validation of a title which signifies the accession of an individual to the position of chief. He minimizes the rivalry aspect and competition and emphasizes instead the reciprocal nature of potlatching. The enduring quality of Barnett's analysis is attested to by the fact that Drucker and Heizer in 1967 utilized his framework for their re-analysis of the southern Kwakiutl (1967). They consider his conceptualizations to represent "the essence of the potlatch among all the Northwest Coast groups observing the custom" (Drucker and Heizer 1967:9).

Within the past decade, several ecologically oriented theorists studied the potlatch, explaining it as part of a self-regulating system (Suttles 1960; Vayda 1961; Piddocke 1965). Taking the environment as the determining variable, they propose that the potlatch is a mechanism to equalize variations in food supply and productivity for particular social entities within an area. Two propositions underlie this ecological approach. The first is that the environment was not characterized by general superabundance but that scarcity and even starvation occurred in different places at different times; thus the redistribution of the potlatch provided a necessary counter to scarcity. The second proposition, which follows from this, is that potlatch behavior is not irrational but is intelligible only in terms of the ecology.

These theories concerning the potlatch draw upon a variety of sources including psychology, ecology, economics, and social organization. Each of them makes interesting observations but none offers an adequate explanation, for they fail to provide an analysis of the various forms of social structure in the area and to relate them to the potlatch and its variations.

The giving aspect of the potlatch has been stressed by all of the above theorists but they have not adequately considered the questions "To whom do you give? Is the recipient of your goods, to whom you give in order to raise your status, any person in particular, or will any person do?" Barnett's idea that the guests at potlatches are witnesses paid for the service of attesting to the fame of the host is useful, but he never pursues the question of who those witnesses are and where they fit in the social structure (Barnett 1938a:26). This question is critical, for unless the relationship of donor to recipients is explicit the dynamics of the potlatch cannot be understood. The recipient at one potlatch will be the giver at another; this interconnection must be accounted for. Furthermore, the giver at a potlatch usually represents a group whose composition must be made clear. Similarly, the receiver represents a group whose composition is relevant. Hundreds, even thousands, of people may be present at a potlatch, each enacting a certain role and standing in defined relationship to the central figures, if not to all the others present. These are the personae whom we have dealt with in our analysis. Their relationship to one another is a manifestation of the social structure.

Upon what occasions do potlatches occur and with what frequency? The ecologists touch upon this question. Their answer to it leads them in a totally different direction from our own. Their focus upon the supply of resources in local groups results in the hypothesis that potlatching will occur when one group has a superabundance of resources while others have an undersupply. We find our answer to the question "When do potlatches occur?" in the dynamics of the social structure. The accumulation of resources is obviously important in order to potlatch. However, potlatches occur at critical junctures. These are occasions at which occupants of positions in the social structure are replaced, or when rearrangements of individuals in particular positions in the structure occur. Frequency of potlatching in one Northwest Coast society as compared to another relates to the characteristics of the social structure and to the number of critical times at which rearrangements such as birth, marriage, succession, and death take place.

What gets distributed and in what amounts is also important. It is insufficient simply to say "valuables." The various categories of things distributed have different symbolic meaning. Each kind of object which is distributed defines a particular kind of relationship and has a special significance with regard to it. The ubiquitous element is food, which is distributed at every potlatch. Eating, with all its inherent dangers, since it takes place in the presence of rivals and enemies, is obligatory at potlatches. Some foods are designated as special, such as "rich foods" and foods for chiefs. Foods served at potlatches are always cooked. Mauss and Lévi-Strauss have discussed the significance of food and commensality in bridging gaps between groups of men. The standard items distributed in large amounts are money and blankets, both post-contact items, probably successors of animal-skin blankets. These items could be stored and formed a kind of medium of exchange, since they could be transferred innumerable times. Coppers represent another item of value which seems to have quite different meanings in terms of the ways in which it may be disposed of in the different tribes. All known coppers seem to be post-contact items. There is an interesting identification of salmon and coppers in the mythology, but the significance of this identification remains to be explored. The last items to be distributed are the wooden bowls and ladles and finally the wooden planks of the house. After the food is consumed, the dishes are given to those who ate from them. After the potlatch ends the host gives away the planks of his house and is said to have "gone all the way." The host is then left with nothing but his great prestige and renown to clothe him.

These questions about the potlatch and their answers lead directly to the realization that the potlatch can be better understood by relating it to the social structure. Potlatching involves groups related as affines and concerns either accession to a position of rank or the manipulation of rank. These two essential features are played out in the potlatch in all the Northwest Coast societies, and find common expression in one symbolic mode, that of rivalry. Rivals vie for rank and rivalry is an intrinsic element in relations between affines. The theme of rivalry in the potlatch is given full play in the writings of Mauss. He sees rivalry inherent in the oppositions which characterize social systems. The rivalry of the potlatch does not tear the system apart but is the symbolic language by which oppositions in it are expressed.

MATRILINEAL SOCIETIES
ON THE NORTHWEST COAST

For the three matrilineal societies of the Northwest Coast, the interactions at the potlatch reveal two aspects of the social structure: the internal composition of the matrikin group and the relationships between such groups which are joined in marriage. On the basis of differences in potlatch and structure, the matrilineal examples can be arranged in two categories, the first of which consists of the Tsimshian.

The Tsimshian potlatch is a ceremonial which in essence involves two sides—the host group and the group to which it gives wives. The latter lineage, the guests, receives gifts, performs services involved in initiation, and is honored with the appellation "father's lineage." During the potlatch, father's lineage is especially honored and it is clear that it occupies a high position in relation to ego's lineage and other invited guests. Ego's lineage never appears as father's lineage at a potlatch where the former is the host. Ego's lineage is, in turn, father's lineage to a third and different lineage. Ego's lineage acts as guest when this third lineage makes a potlatch and honors its father's lineage. The essence of the Tsimshian potlatch, therefore, is to honor one's father's lineage. Father's lineage is always guest and son's lineage always host. For its participants the potlatch conceptually serves to separate wife-givers from wife-takers. It also serves to delineate the hierarchy, since wife-takers are placed in an honored position by wife-givers. Taunting and challenge express the opposed nature of the relationship. The order of taunting expresses the elevated rank of father's lineage, for its members are taunted first.

From this perspective the Tsimshian potlatch makes sense in relation to the social structure generated by the Tsimshian preferential rule of marriage with mother's brother's daughter. Ethnographers' reports on the Tsimshian are quite definite on the point that such a preferential marriage rule is present. It is clearly not stated as a prescription but as a preference. We have adopted the view first put forth by Lounsbury (1962:1310) that only a small percentage of strategic marriages in each generation, particularly among chiefs, is necessary to perpetuate the system of alliances created and maintained by marriages. Lévi-Strauss's own view is quite close to this position (1969:xxxiv). The Tsimshian have a matrilineal rule of descent, hence titles and privileges pass from mother's brother to sister's son and remain within the matrilineal kin group. Affines are unequal in rank, and rank may be maximized by strategic marriages since marriage is structurally similar to a potlatch.

In relation to the internal structure of the descent group, the potlatch plays an important role in the succession to and acquisition of chiefly position, which occurs after the death of the previous holder. The funerary potlatch is a necessary public proclamation of the succession to a power position. Since there is no hard and fast rule of succession or primogeniture, the succession to a position or a name may not be clear. Several claimants within the matrilineage may compete for the position and attempt to accumulate the property to potlatch and thereby validate the name and position. Backed by his matrilineage, the one who succeeds will proclaim his new position at a potlatch by distributing goods to people outside his matrilineage. Thus, the matrilineage has passed a critical juncture which was potentially divisive and has reasserted its solidarity by uniting behind the host, its new chief. Those who come to witness the accession are first and foremost another lineage, the one which stands in the position of "father's lineage." Hence, the singular service of witnessing, essential in all potlatches, is always performed among the Tsimshian by a group which stands in a special relationship to the host group. This is a relationship which is explicable only in terms of the marriage rule.

The association of matrilineal descent and matrilateral cross-cousin marriage is worthy of some discussion. Lévi-Strauss made the primary argument that the kind of descent rule operative in a particular society was irrelevant to the operation of the structure generated by a rule of matrilateral cross-cousin marriage. Homans and Schneider have argued that the descent system is a determinant of the locus of jural authority. They see both the structure of sentiment and the locus of jural authority as the determinants of the type of cross-cousin marriage. They proceed to demonstrate a statistical relationship between patrilineal descent and matrilateral cross-cousin marriage and between matrilineal descent and patrilateral cross-cousin marriage. The Tsimshian, who were not included in their sample, do not conform to their predictions.

Among the Tsimshian, matrilineal descent, matrilateral cross-cousin marriage, and avunculocality occur together. Homans and Schneider account for the four matrilineal-matrilateral exceptions to their hypothesis by reference to uxorilocal residence and the locus of jural authority, which in these cases is said to reside in the boy's father. (The Garo, one of the exceptions, in fact may not conform to this theory; see Burling 1958.) The Tsimshian, who are not uxorilocal, exemplify what Homans and Schneider have referred to as the Trobriand-Haida complex in that "ego typically goes to live with his mother's brother before marriage and brings his wife to stay with him there: marriage is virilocal" (Homans and Schneider 1955:47). However, unlike the Trobrianders and the Haida, they have mother's brother's daughter marriage. The Tsimshian thus do not conform to the emendation of Homans and Schneider's special hypothesis and remain an exception to their interpretation.

The Tsimshian illustrate the "structure of sentiment" hypothesized by Homans and Schneider for a matrilineal society. Yet, though the relationship between a boy and his father is most intimate, he does not marry his father's sister's daughter. Either the "structure of sentiment" is not a determining factor in the case of the Tsimshian, or it operates but is overridden by a more powerful determinant. That determinant may be the difference in their system of ranking. According to the "structure of sentiment" argument, the appropriate marriage would be with father's sister's daughter, but since she is of higher rank than her would-be spouse, such marriage would be inconsistent with the structural characteristic that father's lineage is always of higher rank.

Although the Tsimshian are an exception to the Homans and Schneider theory, they pose no special problem to the alliance theorists, who are not concerned with differences in descent. They conform to the model of matrilateral cross-cousin marriage; in fact, they exhibit what, for alliance theorists, is a critical variable—hierarchy and group ranking. The structure of mother's brother's daughter marriage creates a distinction among father's lineage, ego's lineage, and son's lineage. Among the Tsimshian, differences in status are not merely symbolic but are real differences in rank and in political power. These differences are expressed most clearly during a potlatch, with its interaction between donor's lineage and father's lineage, as well as other lineages. In the potlatch and at various other points in the life cycle, father's lineage is seen as providing services at critical stages in the life cycle, for which its members are compensated with goods. To the father's lineage this constitutes an honor and its higher status is thus publicly acclaimed. Ego's son honors ego in the same manner and the hierarchy is thus maintained and expressed.

Within the household, mother's brother's daughter marriage produces a structure in which a core of matrilineally related males live as owners of the house and of all the titles associated with that house. Their spouses are all of the same matrilineage, are lower in rank, and were born in that house, since they are the daughters of the houseowners. The composition is such that only one move by adolescent boys from their fathers' houses to those of their maternal uncles is required in this system. A boy moves to his mother's brother's house, where he is given a woman, born in that house, as a wife. The boy who is of the matrilineage of the houseowner may succeed to that title. He is thus of higher rank than his wife and her lineage. The children which she bears, however, are obviously of her lineage and thus of lower rank than their father. Even the fathering of the children may be seen as one of the many services provided by the father's lineage for which its members are recompensed in goods.

For Lévi-Strauss, hierarchy has a symbolic meaning. Leach has been interested in the economic and political correlates of rank as well as in their symbolic forms of expression. He has repeatedly emphasized that the directional movement of women does not relate to the hierarchy: wife-givers may be higher or lower than wife-receivers. He has, however, utilized as his examples only societies with patrilineal descent systems. The structure of matrilineal societies is such that, given mother's brother's daughter marriage and avunculocality, women must move upward. As Alan Coult has pointed out, with matrilineality and mother's brother's daughter marriage, avunculocality and matrilocality are by definition the same form of residence (1966). If women were to marry downward, then the core of males owning the house would be lower in rank than their in-marrying spouses and their sons who would inhabit the house until adolescence. Although this is logically possible, it is difficult to see how such a condition might continue to operate. Thus, in a matrilineal system such as the Tsimshian, women must move upward to make hypergamous marriages.

In the second category of matrilineal examples are the Tlingit and the Haida. The Tlingit potlatch, which always occurs in connection with death rites, involves three "sides." Though the Tlingit have a moiety structure so that guests are of the moiety opposite to that of the host, the guests are always aligned into two groupings, one on either side of the house. They represent two different lineages, often from different towns, one from the town of the host (lineage A) and the other from a "foreign town" (lineage B). The two groups are members of the moiety opposite to the moiety of the host but also represent opposites to one another. Thus a seemingly two-sided structure (that of moieties) sits in an arrangement representing a three-sided structure at the potlatch. Within the moiety opposite to the host, one side, lineage A, builds the house and the other side, lineage B, provides service with regard to secondary burial and the erection of a memorial. The ritual of the potlatch reveals that both competition and common identity characterize the relationship between the two "opposites" of the guest moiety. They compete in eating contests and dancing, almost coming to blows with one another. A crucial point noted by Swanton, superb ethnographer that he was, was that the two opposites of the guest moiety danced together, one saying to the other, "I am holding your daughter's hand." Swanton explains that this is done because these two groups exchange daughters with one another. This, in a patrilineal society, would be easy to comprehend; however, in the case of the Tlingit, where the rule of descent is matrilineal, it seems to create a paradox rather than lead to an explanation. The paradox is not real when one considers that the Tlingit have a rule of preferential marriage with father's sister's daughter. The structure generated by such a marriage rule explains the align-

ment of groups interacting at a Tlingit potlatch. Swanton's remarkable insight forshadows Lane's discussion of the Ambryn marriage system (B. Lane 1961). A father's sister's daughter marriage
rule necessitates relationship with two other lineages as wife-givers
and wife-takers alternatively.

The Haida have two major types of potlatch, the funeral potlatch
and the housebuilding potlatch. In contrast to the Tlingit, where
ego's lineage simultaneously interacts with the two other lineages
to which it is linked in marriage, among the Haida the funeral
potlatch involves interaction with one of these lineages and the
housebuilding potlatch involves interaction with the other. The
critical juncture caused by the death of a chief is the occasion for a
potlatch at which the funeral obsequies are observed and the succession of an heir to the new position is publicly validated. The
guest lineage involved performs various services including the
carving and erection of a memorial totem pole. This guest lineage
is linked to the host lineage in marriage, being the lineage of the
deceased's wife, son, and father. This lineage serves as witness to
the accession to chiefly position of the new chief, the sister's son of
the deceased chief, who is a member of the generation below that
of the deceased. Thus, the lineage tied in marriage to the old chief,
performing funerary service at his death, is the lineage which
serves the important function of witness to the accession of the new
chief. As guests its members mourn the passage of the old chief and
hail the succession of the new chief, a sign of their continuing relationship with his lineage, despite the fact that their kin connection
to the new chief is not close.

The funeral potlatch marks the beginning of the career of a new
chief and the housebuilding potlatch marks its apogee. At this latter
potlatch the lineage of the chief's wife is intimately involved. At
the funeral potlatch, the new chief's wife and her lineage do not
play a part in the major activities. At the housebuilding potlatch,
the current chief's wife and her lineage play central roles while the
lineage of the previous chief's wife is not mentioned. The house

which is built in connection with this potlatch is a sign of the chief's greatness. Another important function performed at the potlatch is the tattooing, ear and nose piercing, and initiation of the children of the chief—members of his wife's lineage. Thus the funeral and housebuilding potlatches conceptually keep apart the two lineages that are linked in marriage to the host lineage. This contrasts with the single potlatch where the two affinal lineages are both present at the same time but are separated in the seating arrangements.

Since funerals and housebuildings are the only occasions at which major potlatches occur, it can be seen that marriage is not a potlatch for either society. The unilineal composition of the descent groups and the unilineal pattern of inheritance preclude the passage of important rights and privileges by marriage, which is the reason why marriage is not a potlatch. Groups are not ranked among the Tlingit and the Haida and therefore affines are equal in rank. This also is related to the fact that marriage is not a potlatch. The absence of group ranking is a characteristic of a structure generated by the presence of a preferential father's sister's daughter marriage rule.

The Tlingit and Haida potlatches reveal the type of social structure generated by a preference for father's sister's daughter marriage. The nature of these potlatches becomes quite clear when one examines them in relation to the structure generated by such a marriage pattern. Examination of the Tlingit and Haida potlatches reveals the operation of father's sister's daughter structure in a way in which formal analysis can never hope to do (see Needham 1958; Coult and Hammel 1963; B. Lane 1961), primarily because formal analysts have dealt only with the exchange of women in the narrow definition of alliance theory.

Lévi-Strauss, in his work on asymmetric marriage systems, was concerned with the way in which the exchange of women formed the basis of alliances. In comparing matrilateral and patrilateral cross-cousin marriage systems, he concluded that the former provided a better vehicle of integration than the latter since the positions of wife-giver and wife-receiver in the former remained the same in succeeding generations (Lévi-Strauss 1969 [1949]:443).

If, then, in the final analysis, marriage with the father's sister's daughter is less frequent than that with the mother's brother's daughter, it is because the latter not only permits but favors a better integration of the group, where as the former never succeeds in creating anything but a precarious edifice made of juxtaposed materials, subject to no general plan, and its discrete texture is exposed to the same fragility as each of the little local structures of which ultimately it is composed (Lévi-Strauss 1969 [1949]:448-49).

In an even stronger attack on the efficacy of father's sister's daughter marriage he notes:

For all these formulas express the same truth in various forms: a human group need only proclaim the law of marriage with the mother's brother's daughter for a vast cycle of reciprocity between all generations and lineages to be organized, as harmonious and ineluctable as any physical or biological law, whereas marriage with the father's sister's daughter forces the interruption and reversal of collaborations from generation to generation and from lineage to lineage. In one case, the over-all cycle of reciprocity is co-extensive with the group itself both in time and in space, subsisting and developing with it. In the other case, the multiple cycles which are continually created fracture and distort the unity of the group. They fracture this unity because there are as many cycles as there are lineages, and they distort it because the direction of the cycles must be reversed with each generation. (Lévi-Strauss 1969 [1949]:450).

The weight of evidence on the Haida and the Tlingit presented above serves as ample evidence that Lévi-Strauss, in his statement that "it [father's sister's daughter marriage] represents the Cheap-Jack in the scale of marriage transactions" (Lévi-Strauss 1969 [1949]:449), has underestimated the structural possibilities inherent in such marriage. The Haida and the Tlingit stood stoutly alongside their supposedly better integrated (by matrilateral cross-cousin marriage) neighbors, the Tsimshian, as living proof that Lévi-Strauss was wrong.

The ethnographic evidence on the Haida and the Tlingit provides a picture not of "a multitude of small, closed systems" (Lévi-Strauss 1969 [1949]:445) but rather of long chains of marriage alliances composed of many links which continue over time. Lévi-Strauss's emphasis on the exchange of women results in his picture of father's sister's daughter marriage with the return marriage in the second generation; "the transaction is, as it were, terminated" (Lévi-Strauss 1969 [1949]:444). He then concludes that such a marriage preference cannot generate an over-all structure (it is "subject to no general plan": see above). Our emphasis on the potlatch and total exchange in considering the Haida and the Tlingit has indeed revealed a general plan. Lévi-Strauss submits that father's sister's daughter marriage fractures and distorts the unity of the group. By the unity of the group he refers to the integration of society. Our analysis of Tlingit and Haida societies has revealed that the structure generated by father's sister's daughter marriage can provide the basis for continuing alliances which link many kin groups. The potlatch and its concomitant exchanges operate according to the same structural principles, and serve as an integrative mechanism between lineages connected in marriage.

The discontinuity which Lévi-Strauss focuses upon is a result of his emphasis only on the exchange of a woman for a woman. A broader focus upon total exchange makes it clear that a whole variety of prestations move back and forth between the various groups. A woman moves to another lineage (A), has children; when her husband dies her lineage (B) performs burial service and is recompensed with goods. Her husband's sister's daughter moves to her lineage (B); when the husband's sister's daughter's husband dies then burial service is performed by a member of lineage A. In such a system of total exchange, involving goods, services, and women, who can say that the woman returned in the next generation completes the exchange? The small closed circles which Lévi-Strauss saw are a product of formal analysis in which one element out of many has been singled out as causal.

The deficiencies which Lévi-Strauss saw in father's sister's daughter marriage were elaborated upon by Needham in several works, to the point where Needham ruled such a system out of existence. In the course of his interpretation of Lévi-Strauss's writings Needham created a new technical concept for the investigation of alliance. This concept—that of prescribed marriage rules—constitutes the statement of an ideal. Lévi-Strauss, himself, has moved to a position where he states: "I feel somewhat embarrassed to confess that I fail to grasp its significance [the distinction between 'prescriptive' and 'preferential' marriage systems] and fear that it may give rise to many a theoretical difficulty" (Lévi-Strauss 1965:17; see also Preface to 1969:xxx-xxxv). In reports about the Tlingit and the Haida, one finds clear-cut statements that an individual ought to marry his father's sister's daughter, although there is no statistical evidence to indicate the percentages of such marriages. Both Haida and Tlingit say it is possible to marry mother's brother's daughter, so the other marriage is not ruled out. Nevertheless, we agree with Lévi-Strauss and Lounsbury that even a low statistical incidence of a marriage type, given a statement of a marriage rule, may serve to generate a structure (Lévi-Strauss 1969 [1949]:xxxiv; Lounsbury 1962:1310). Leach cites the Powell material on the low incidence of father's sister's daughter marriage among the Trobriand Islanders and for this reason he presents the structure of Trobriand Island society not in terms of a marriage rule but in terms of other elements (Leach 1958:137-39).

This line of argument is not fruitful. The line of reasoning should be to find out if one can derive a structure from the marriage rule. In our analysis of the Haida and Tlingit potlatches and households we have found confirmation of such a structure.

Needham's rejection of the possibility of patrilateral cross-cousin marriage systems is based upon several points. The first is that there are no extant systems of patrilateral cross-cousin marriage based upon his definition of prescriptive marriage rules. This objection may now be disregarded. Needham's conclusion concerning the impossibility of patrilateral cross-cousin marriage generating a stable system hinges on the problem of the separation of generations. "In short, it does not appear that there is any way of securing the clear and congruent division of all participant descent groups into conventional generations which is essential to the system" (Needham 1962:112). This problem arises because he focuses solely upon exchange of women and must separate the generations in order to know in which direction the women are moving. If one begins instead with succession to title, the means of resolving the problem are presented. A sister's son succeeds to his mother's brother's position and title on the death of the latter. Successive generations of chiefs take their wives from alternate sides representing different lineages. The deceased is linked as a close affine to his father-wife lineage, while his successor, his sister's son, is linked as a close affine to a lineage different from that which was joined in marriage to the deceased. In the third generation, the successor to title is joined as a close affine to the same lineage as that of his grandfather, and he is in fact identified with his grandfather. Women thus move in different directions in each passing generation. Continuity and integration are provided by the sequence of potlatches, for which the occasion is the succession of a new chief to high office, and marriages. In Needham's model, in contrast, marriages are the only critical occasion. In a continuing sequence of exchanges between two lineages linked in alliance, generations are kept separate by succession. Though women reverse direction, many other kinds of exchanges continue to take place between the two lineages.

Implicit in the above discussion is the role played by avunculocal residence among the Haida and the Tlingit, which serves to unite a core of matrilineally related males in every household. This form of residence and the accompanying mode of succession to sister's son form a coherent structure. In light of this, it is interesting to note the following point from Needham:

But according to Homans and Schneider a patrilateral system should on the contrary be matrilineal. Now if such a system could exist, and if their theory were right, consider the factor of marital residence. A matrilineal-patrilocal system would probably not be viable, and the least to be said about a patrilocal rule of residence is that it would entail serious difficulties as a working arrangement. A matrilocal rule, on the other hand, would entail the kinds of disruptive tension which we have seen among the Belu. Whatever the rule of residence, therefore, Homans and Schneider's premise that a patrilateral system will be matrilineal means that it is even less likely to be a solidary arrangement (Needham 1962:117).

The obvious omission is avunculocality; with this mode of residence the logic of the system is clear. (R. Lane has made this point also, 1962.) It is avunculocality and the rule of succession to clearly defined titles which serve to keep the generations apart. The core of matrilineally related males who succeed one another come alternately from different natal families, since sister's son is never part of his mother's brother's natal family. The manner in which these elements combine in the Tlingit and the Haida lead us to suggest that here lies the structural basis of the logical association of father's sister's daughter marriage with avunculocality and matrilineal descent. Needham, in accordance with the premises of alliance theory that matrilineal and patrilineal descent are interchangeable, chose to examine the logical structure of patrilateral cross-cousin marriage solely within the context of patrilineal descent systems.

Needham's rationale for so doing is presented in a footnote: "Homans and Schneider maintain that this form of marriage is associated with matrilineal descent, but a patrilineal representation serves equally well here and is conventionally commoner. In any case, as the analysis proceeds it will be seen that it makes no difference which rule of descent one chooses to postulate" (Needham 1958:207, footnote 29). However, it is interesting to note that, of the eleven societies which he discusses in detail in his article, only four are patrilineal, six are matrilineal, and one has double descent.

While it is possible to diagram a structure generated by father's sister's daughter marriage with patrilocal residence and patrilineal descent, the clusterings of relatives in the two linked lineages and the crucial relationships to those lineages are with and through females. Though possible, this is a less likely type of structure to maintain itself.

Needham mentions total prestations in his work:

It is not only women, remember, whose communication or exchange is effected by the system, but a whole complex of prestations in which women are just one item; and it has to be supposed that in a patrilateral system—i.e., a system of prescriptive alliance parallel in all typical respects to the matrilateral, save for the different prescription— this entire scheme of prestations would have to be reversed in each succeeding conventional generation (Needham 1962:112).

In his point about reversal of prestations in succeeding generations Needham permits his focus upon women to structure his vision of total prestations. If one examines the picture of total prestations, as we have in our analysis of the Haida and the Tlingit, one sees immediately an enormous complex of goods, services, and women moving back and forth between groups in every generation. The underlying structure defining the interrelationships between groups is the triadic structure of patrilateral cross-cousin marriage.

The last important point made by Needham in his argument is that patrilateral cross-cousin marriage reduces to a form of dual organization in which father's sister's daughter and mother's brother's daughter are the same individual. This initially seemed a tempting interpretation for the Haida and the Tlingit, since both have moieties. Our analysis, however, has revealed a triadic structure in the marriage alliances, the structure of households, and particularly the potlatch. The narrower triadic structure requires at least four parts in order to operate, and these form the basis of the moiety structure. The groups exchanging women are not the moieties, but lineages within one of the two moieties. Thus the three-part structure seems to us to be the more basic structure.

Another related issue is the question of asymmetry and reciprocity. In an attempt to handle what she assumed to be an implicit assumption of inequality in asymmetric marriage systems, Lane proposed a model consisting of four matrilineal groups practicing patrilateral cross-cousin marriage (1961). She notes that, from one point of view, such a system may be seen as characterizing direct exchange because the daughters of men of one group are exchanged for the daughters of men of the other group (B. Lane 1961:54). The Tlingit are aware of this as a perspective of their system, for during the potlatch men of the same moiety but "opposite sides" recognize that they are in effect exchanging daughters with one another.

In summary, our matrilineal examples are composed of exogamous and clearly defined social units, which are matrilineal and avunculocal. They potlatch to their affines, those affines being defined by the particular marriage rule in each system. The affines perform the service of witnessing. The potlatch is a confirmation of the structure developed on the basis of the marriage rule. The correlations of group rank differences and matrilateral cross-cousin marriage and absence of group rank differences and patrilateral cross-cousin marriage have been noted by several theorists. The material supports these correlations in that the Tsimshian exhibit a complex ranking of groups in relation to one another while the Haida and the Tlingit do not. All three of the matrilineal examples show flexibility in rank within groups. Since succession is subject to competition, funerals are always the occasion for potlatching. The Tlingit and the Haida do not exhibit intergroup rank difference, hence mobility between groups is not relevant. Further, affines are equal in rank, and this is why marriage is not a potlatch. With regard to the Tsimshian, groups are ranked but data on the degree of mobility in the ranking of groups are fragmentary. Shifts in rank for groups did occur, according to Barbeau (1917), but the means by which they took place is not clear. It is apparent that marriage is a potlatch, since affines are unequal in rank.

AMBILATERAL SOCIETIES[1]

Ambilateral descent, in contrast to matrilineal descent, produces a system characterized by options. Thus, the answers to the ques-

[1] We have used the term "ambilateral descent," the usage suggested by Firth (1963). A number of theorists have concerned themselves with clarification of the characteristics of this type of social structure, among them Goodenough (1955), Firth (1957), Davenport (1959), and Murdock (1949, 1960). We have found the distinctions made by Firth to be the most useful to us and have therefore adopted his terminology.

tions "Who does one potlatch to? Who is present?" become more complex. If one follows the principle of "one potlatches to one's affines," who one's affines are, in an ambilateral society, is a question not easily answered.

The matrilineal societies of the Northwest Coast formed two subtypes. We have found that our three ambilateral societies do not lend themselves to such a categorization. An effective method of comparing the ambilateral societies is in terms of the way in which the significant variables operate within them. Throughout the area, donors potlatch as members of particular kin groups. Among the Kwakiutl, though individuals may hold names from more than one kin group, at a potlatch they usually identify with only one group and display the prerogatives which they own as a result of membership in that group. Among the Nootka, on the other hand, though the donor is identified as a member of a particular kin group when he potlatches, he may display prerogatives which he owns as a result of membership in other kin groups. The Bella Coola resemble the Kwakiutl in the operation of this variable. In all of these societies, by virtue of the structural characteristics of ambilateral descent, individuals may identify with more than one kin group. Among the Nootka, in contrast to the Bella Coola and the Kwakiutl, individuals are more mobile geographically, and in a lifetime will reside with several groups. Membership is retained in all such groups, though individuals identify with the group with which they are residing at the time. The maintenance of several active affiliations among the Nootka is reflected in the potlatch by the display of prerogatives from several groups.

As to the question of when potlatches occur, we have noted that they occur at critical junctures, which are points when replacement or reordering of the social structure takes place. Among the Kwakiutl and the Nootka, potlatches are frequent, occurring at the many occasions of initiation that mark the developmental cycle of an individual. Frequent acquisitions and changes of name rather than the acquisition of a single chiefly name are characteristic of these societies, representing the reinforcement of an individual's ties to more than one group. The Bella Coola show the same tendency but to a lesser degree.

Succession among the Kwakiutl and the Nootka does not occur at the death of the holder of the position but rather proceeds through a number of stages marked by the acquisition of greater and greater names and privileges until finally the highest chiefly title is turned over to an adolescent boy or young man while the father or previous holder is in his prime. This form of succession parallels the increasing incorporation of the youth into a kin group. Since the critical juncture is not at a death, there are no funeral potlatches. Both Nootka and Kwakiutl have primogeniture. In these ambilateral societies, this means that the oldest child, be it a boy or a girl, succeeds to the title but not necessarily to the power and authority of the office. With the Kwakiutl in particular, Boas is quite specific on this point. It follows that in a society where there are rank differences, individuals should succeed to a position in the mother's group if she is of higher rank than the father or has no brothers. This in fact frequently occurs. The presence of primogeniture removes the possibility of competition for succession, which in the matrilineal societies occurred in connection with funeral potlatches. For the Bella Coola, however, there is no primogeniture, nor any clear-cut succession to title. Competition may occur and funerals are the occasion for a potlatch. This competition concerns position as the head of a household. Potlatching activity occurs on occasions other than funerals and even after an individual has succeeded to the position of head of a household.

Marriage is of singular significance in its relationship to the potlatch among ambilateral societies, both as a means of defining the relationship between groups who potlatch and as an important occasion for a potlatch. We have maintained that one potlatches with one's affines. In ambilateral societies, since the exclusive identification of individuals with a single kin group does not occur, the question of who one's affines are is complex. Among the Kwakiutl, where identification with one kin group is relatively fixed, affines

are more clearly defined as the "opposites" with whom one potlatches and whom one marries. Groups can never stand perpetually
in the position of wife-givers and wife-takers because individuals
can and do claim rights through mother and father. Marriage rules
which set up categories of wife-givers and wife-takers, such as those
found for the matrilineal examples, are not found in the ambilateral societies. In their place, a different form of marriage rule is
present which recognizes that marriages between individuals who
stand as consanguineal kin to one another frequently will take
place. If groups with ambilateral descent intermarry with one another continually over a long time, then individuals are marrying
relatives. The marriage rule if present, as in the case of the Nootka
and the Bella Coola, is phrased in terms of prohibited marriage
within two degrees of relationship and preferences for marriage to
relatives within several degrees beyond that point.

Though the structure of the affinal category in ambilateral societies differs from that in the matrilineal examples, the path of
exchange of prestations represented by the potlatch is simultaneously the one traversed by women in marriage. Affines are separated and at the same time bound by the sequences of exchanges.
No rule of exogamy can define these affines, but group membership
does. It should be kept in mind that though one may be marrying
a close relative, a cross- or parallel cousin in the case of the Kwakiutl, this relative may nonetheless be a member of another group.
The important factor is identity as a member of another group.
This factor is of such importance that among the Nootka a chief,
who is marrying a girl from the group with which he is primarily
identified, utilizes an alternative membership for the purpose of
the marriage.

One of the structural characteristics of ambilateral societies is
that people maintain identity with and membership in their natal
groups throughout life. A woman does not assume membership in
or identify with her husband's group. This characteristic is expressed in institutional form by the practice of wife repurchase

by the woman's natal group, a practice that is a structural necessity in order to ensure the right of inheritance of children in the mother's group. She must maintain membership in order for them to make claims through her. Her natal kin group, through the repurchase payment, fulfill their obligations and thus reiterate her membership and the membership of her children in their group.

Marriage in ambilateral societies is the occasion for a potlatch because it represents a critical juncture for the membership of both groups of affines. The continued claims over a daughter are in jeopardy, the future kin group memberships of the children to be born come into question, and selection must be made among the options for the future residence of the couple. Just as marriage involves a potlatch, so does repurchase. The goods in the repurchase are used by the husband's kin group in a potlatch. The repurchase is part of a potlatch, the purpose of which is usually to raise the children of the marriage to high position.

There is no limit to the kinds or the number of prerogatives which children can claim through their mother. There is another category of prerogatives, among the Kwakiutl, which husbands obtain from the wife's kin group—the ones associated with the marriage repurchase. Fictitious marriages in all three societies suggest that marriages are contracted with such gains in mind. This kind of maximization involves what we have called the marriage strategy, which is concerned with consideration of gains for parents and gains for children. Since marriage in ambilateral societies is characterized by such strategy, they would fit into Lévi-Strauss's category of complex structures. Societies with complex structures, according to Lévi-Strauss, may not be examined utilizing mechanical models, since, in his view, the elements of such models cannot be characterized in terms of a simple rule, but rather in terms of frequencies. We feel, nevertheless, that our analysis has demonstrated that a model of ambilateral societies may be constructed utilizing structural variables relating to this mode of descent and to the rule of succession, rather than to a marriage rule.

The presence of primogeniture among the Kwakiutl and the Nootka has the effect of ensuring succession to title and reducing social mobility within the group. Rank within the group is very important but relatively fixed with regard to titles. Potlatching has no effect in raising the rank of individuals. Among the Bella Coola, this is not the case. Individuals may raise their status and positions within the group are open to competition. Social mobility for the Nootka and the Kwakiutl is accomplished in another way, one that is completely consistent with the high number of options open to an individual in a society with ambilateral descent. Though individuals may not rise to high position with one group, they may choose another descent line, or live with wife's group in which the options make it more possible to move up. Social mobility is thus brought about by the freedom to choose one's affiliation. An important difference between the Kwakiutl and the Nootka is that, among the latter, the younger brother who assumes the position of war chief may use it to raise his status. Through vigorous and successful warfare he may establish himself as the chief of a new group. His ability to obtain prerogatives by conquest and to obtain goods to potlatch will establish the rank of his newly formed group vis-à-vis other groups. Thus warfare is also a mechanism by which groups shift in their social rank with reference to one another. Among the Kwakiutl, in contrast, warfare is conducted quite differently and does not result in acquisition of territory.[2]

Ranking of groups is present among the Nootka and the Kwakiutl but not among the Bella Coola. These rankings are subject to change. The relative rank of groups is one of the variables involved in the choice of groups with which ego can affiliate. In the potlatch, groups vie with one another and claims to relative rank and changes in rank between groups occur. Among the Nootka,

[2] Drucker and Heizer claim that warfare among the Kwakiutl was for territorial acquisition. They cite only two examples to support their point and their evidence is not convincing when compared with the striking number of examples cited by Drucker for the Nootka (Drucker and Heizer 1967; Drucker 1951).

though the shift in rank may be a result of warfare, the new rank must be validated at a potlatch. Among the Kwakiutl, claims to advancement of group status are made by potlatching, not by warfare. Recognition of these claims must occur at a potlatch given by another group in the same manner as among the Nootka.

CHAPTER VIII. *CONCLUSIONS: THE MODEL OF THE POTLATCH TYPE OF SOCIETY*

IN THIS CHAPTER, we will delineate, in abstract terms, the characteristics of our potlatch model. We therefore shift our level of analysis from the specific cultural manifestations of our model to the model itself. Just as Mauss isolated a type of exchange which he characterized as the potlatch type of exchange and analyzed its manifestations in Melanesia and elsewhere, we have isolated what we call a potlatch type of society, using the Northwest Coast as the basis of our analysis. Mauss's emphasis was upon the potlatch type of exchange, but our emphasis is upon a series of social structural variables which we have related to this kind of exchange.

Ranking is present in the social structure of many societies. In some of them, though rank may be achieved by an individual, it cannot be transmitted to the next generation. In others, rank is automatically transmitted to the next generation through inheritance, without the necessity of large-scale distributions. In societies of the potlatch type, rank is present; it is inherited, but succession to a position of rank must be validated by a ceremony at which a large-scale distribution of goods is made to guests by their host—a potlatch. Their acceptance of the gifts and their witnessing of the ceremony constitute acknowledgment of the succession. If no distribution, or an inadequate one, is made, the claimant to a position will suffer loss of prestige or even total disavowal of his claims. Continued larger distributions in the future may further elevate his position. Such opportunity for denial of inheritance and for further distributions to establish or enhance it justifies characterizing the rank system as flexible.

Individuals potlatch in order to validate their own position, and also as representatives of groups. Thus a constant interplay between the internal structure of the group and the relationship of the group to other groups is present.

Given these defining features of our model, we can deal with variables whose particular manifestation, strength, or importance in any of the six societies examined here may differ from their manifestation, strength, or importance in another society. Each society represents a clustering of particular expressions of the variables; the nature of the expression of one is functionally related, in a mathematical sense, to the expression of others.

Within groups there is always internal ranking. Political offices embodying authority are institutionalized into rank positions which involve succession, that is, they are inherited. Beyond these leadership positions, the extent to which ranking of other names and their affiliated positions occurs varies in the several cases. The mode of inheritance of position determines whether or not internal ranking is flexible. Succession to position during the lifetime of the incumbent, accompanied by potlatching, will drastically reduce or eliminate competition for position and hence flexibility. Succession by primogeniture will usually eliminate competition whether it occurs at the death of the previous holder or during his lifetime. Primogeniture and succession during the lifetime of the holder, occurring together, serve effectively to eliminate both flexibility and competition. This constellation of features is found more consistently in societies with ambilateral descent where flexibilities in affiliation are compensated for by stability in succession. Potlatching, the concomitant of succession, is therefore more frequent in ambilateral societies where there is primogeniture and succession to position occurs during the lifetime of the holder of the position. These conditions serve increasingly to compel acceptance of the juvenile successor to the title.

Where there is no fixity in the rule of succession, claimants to position are forced to demonstrate their political abilities in lining up support. Since the means of asserting one's claim is through potlatching, the successful claimant must transform his political support into the wherewithal to potlatch and validate his succession to position. Therefore the ability to distribute widely represents in effect the ability to secure political support. The competition, though it may begin during the lifetime of the holder of a position, does not reach a climax until the death of the holder, at which time rival claimants must utilize what they have amassed to conduct the funeral potlatch of the deceased holder of the title. In societies where these conditions prevail, therefore, funerals are the occasions for potlatches.

Our model also provides a more precise view of the redistributive system, previously noted as operative in this context (see Drucker 1939). The usual conceptualization of a redistributive system is that goods move up from followers to chief of a group, these goods being redistributed by the chief at large feasts and potlatches. Our analysis has shown the model to be more complex. The chief of a group decides to give a potlatch. He requests assistance in the form of goods from the members of his group. He amasses these goods and distributes them to chiefs of other groups at the potlatch. These chiefs return to their homes and hold feasts at which they distribute what they have received at the potlatch to their followers. Conversely, when the first chief goes as a guest to the potlatch of another chief, he will make a feast and distribute what he has received to his followers on his return. The redistributive process in this case involves relations between, as well as within, groups.

Distinct from the internal composition of the group and the operation of rank within the group is the operation of external group relations and ranking. Internal rank is always present though not always flexible. External ranking may or may not be present. But where present, it is flexible—groups may shift in rank. Shifts in rank are brought about by warfare or by potlatching or by a combination of the two, since they are related. The nature of the external relationships between groups, whether or not rank is present, relates to the type of marriage system. One of the major features of the potlatch model is that one potlatches to one's affines. The marriage rule in a society in effect defines the category of one's affines. Thus, the marriage rule will delineate which groups stand in relation to one another and potlatch to one another. For example, in a potlatch type of society with a preference for father's sister's daughter marriage, external ranking of groups is not present. The exchanges in this type of society seem to preclude the possibility of the maintenance of rank differences between affinal groups, because what they exchange is equivalent. On the other hand, in a society with a preferential rule of marriage with mother's brother's daughter where women move only in one direction in exchange for goods of another type, there exists the possibility of rank differences between groups. In societies of the potlatch type where rank is a defining characteristic, such a marriage rule impels rank differences between groups, as one would expect.

In societies with unilineal descent systems, the existence of preferential marriage rules enables one to generate structures consisting of groups in wife-giving wife-taking relationships with one another. In societies with ambilateral descent, such marriage rules are not present; instead, complicated fictions are used to delineate groups which exchange women. The affinal categories thereby defined are still those who potlatch to one another. Other rules, such as the rule of succession can be used to generate the structure.

In keeping with the emphasis upon individual choice in ambilateral societies, marriage also involves individual choice and selection. In this, the ambilateral societies of the potlatch type differ from the matrilineal societies of the potlatch type. In the presence of rank differences between groups and individuals, people will select marriage partners utilizing a marriage strategy which has as its goal the maximization of their own and their future children's position. The husband obtains limited prerogatives as a result of the marriage. Every marriage sets up, in addition, different options and choices for each of the children of the marriage. In these ambilateral societies, since marriage is intimately associated with flexibility in rank, it is necessarily the occasion for a potlatch.

In the potlatch type of society, the pivotal variable is the particular kind of rank system which has been described. Critical junctures occur when the rank system is rearranged. These critical junctures are the occasions for potlatches. In a society with unilineal descent and no fixity of rule of succession the funeral will be a critical juncture in terms of succession and rearrangement of rank; hence funerals will be potlatches. Likewise, in ambilateral societies where succession and rearrangement of rank occur during the lifetime of the holder of position, the critical junctures will be the points at which he turns over prerogatives. A series of potlatches held during the lifetime of the holder will occur on the occasion of *rites de passage* for individuals, but it is structurally of much greater significance to point out that some of those same potlatches also mark *rites de passage* for the social structure. At such critical junctures, potlatches serve to reaffirm the new arrangement of the structure.

Critical junctures are also occasions at which the flexibility in the structure comes into play. Therefore, potlatches concurrent with critical junctures provide the opportunity for individuals to improve their position. A number of symbolic themes reiterate the meaning and significance of critical junctures in the social structure of societies of the potlatch type. It has been shown that important potlatches usually involved the tearing down of an old house and the building of a new home. This symbolic act of renewal is performed concurrently with critical junctures central to the social structure. The new house is the physical manifestation of the group living under its roof; the renewal of the house represents the renewal of the group. Each house is unique, since its elaborately carved columns and beams and its painted crests can be used only by the kin group which dwells within. These carvings and decorations relate to myths and ideas about the ancestors of the occupants. At every potlatch, when prerogatives are displayed, there is a retelling of the origin myth of the prerogatives. The retelling stresses continuity with the past and the relationship of the group to ancient times.

Another important symbolic component is that of rivalry. Rivalry in the potlatch is no more or less than the rivalry of groups joined in marriage. When marriage is a potlatch it is always couched in the symbolic terms of warfare and rivalry. Sham battles are often necessary to carry off the bride. This warfare is obviously not real but only symbolic, and now the groups are joined to one another and potlatch with one another. They exchange gifts and perform services for one another. While they are bound in an alliance, symbolically this is expressed by a state of perpetual war. This is the irony and the paradox of the term "alliance" which Mauss alludes to. When individuals arrive at a potlatch they come prepared for symbolic rivalry and competition, though they have been invited to a feast. On the other hand, an important concomitant is the use of eagle down, a symbol of peace. Rivalry and peace are both important symbolic features of the potlatch; each necessarily implies its opposite. Thus the potlatch not only contains these oppositions and contradictions but is at the same time the means of their resolution.

The concept of critical juncture in the social structure can be seen as, in effect, a *rite de passage* for the society. Potlatches are therefore *rites de passage* not only for individuals but for a society as well. This becomes clear only through the use of a structural approach to the potlatch.

We have shown that the potlatch ceremony is an integral part of a distinctive type of social system whose general characteristics we have delineated. Though Barnett, long a student of the Northwest Coast and the potlatch, and others have expressed doubt that the potlatch could be identified as an institution outside of and apart from the cultures of the Northwest Coast of America, we feel that our analysis of the potlatch in its social structural context now enables us to identify this structural type elsewhere in the world. Mauss, in his analysis, moved from a consideration of the potlatch type of exchange in Melanesia to an examination of it on the Northwest Coast of America. We hope to repay him for his insights by returning in the future along the path which he followed, to examine societies in Melanesia and Polynesia in the light of our potlatch model.

BIBLIOGRAPHY

THEORETICAL

Barth, Frederick. 1966. Models of Social Organization. Royal Anthropological Institute, Occasional Paper, No. 23.

Berting, J., and H. Philipsen. 1960. Solidarity, Stratification, and Sentiments: The Unilateral Cross-Cousin Marriage According to the Theories of Lévi-Strauss, Leach, and Homans and Schneider. *Bijdragen tot de Taal-, Land-, en Volkenkunde* 116:55-80.

—— 1962. The Unilateral Cross-Cousin Marriage: A Reply to Needham. *Bijdragen tot de Taal-, Land-, en Volkenkunde* 118:155-59.

Blau, Peter. 1964. Exchange and Power in Social Life. New York, John Wiley.

Burling, Robbins. 1958. Garo Avuncular Authority and Matrilateral Cross-Cousin Marriage. *American Anthropology* 60:743-49.

Coult, Alan D. 1962. The Determinants of Differential Cross-Cousin Marriage. *Man* 62, No. 47, pp. 34-37.

—— 1966. The Structuring of Structure. *American Anthropologist* 68:438-43.

Coult, A. D., and E. A. Hammel. 1963. A Corrected Model for Patrilateral Cross-Cousin Marriage. *Southwestern Journal of Anthropology* 19:287-96.

Davenport, William. 1959. Nonunilinear Descent and Descent Groups. *American Anthropologist* 61:557-72.

Dumont, L. 1961. Descent, Filiation and Affinity. *Man* 61, No. 11, pp. 24-25.

Durkheim, Emile. 1893 (1933). The Division of Labor in Society. Ed. and tr. George Simpson. New York, Macmillan. (Reissued in 1947, Glencoe, Ill., The Free Press.)

Eggan, Fred. 1954. Social Anthropology and the Method of Controlled Comparison. *American Anthropologist* 56:743-63.

Firth, Raymond. 1951. Elements of Social Organization. London, Watts and Co.

—— 1957. A Note on Descent Groups in Polynesia. *Man* 57, No. 2, pp. 4-7.

—— 1963. Bilateral Descent Groups: An Operational Viewpoint. In Studies in Kinship and Marriage, ed. I. Schapera. Royal Anthropological Institute, Occasional Paper, No. 16.

Fortes, Meyer. 1953. The Structure of Unilineal Descent Groups. *American Anthropologist* 55:17-41.

—— 1959. Descent, Filiation, and Affinity. *Man* 59, No. 309, pp. 193-97; No. 331, pp. 206-12.

Goodenough, Ward. 1955. A Problem in Malayo-Polynesian Social Organization. *American Anthropologist* 57:71-83.

Goody, Jack. 1959. The Mother's Brother and the Sister's Son in West Africa. *Journal of the Royal Anthropological Institute* 89:61-88.

Gouldner, A. 1960. The Norm of Reciprocity: A Preliminary Statement. *American Sociological Review* 25:161-78.

Homans, George C. 1958. Social Behavior as Exchange. *American Journal of Sociology* 63:597-606.

—— 1961. Social Behavior: Its Elementary Forms. New York, Harcourt, Brace & World.

Homans, George C., and David M. Schneider. 1955. Marriage, Authority, and Final Causes. Glencoe, Ill., The Free Press.

Josselin de Jong, J. P. B. de. 1952. Lévi-Strauss's Theory on Kinship and Marriage. Leiden, E. J. Brill.

Kirchhoff, Paul. 1959. The Principles of Clanship in Human Society. Reprinted in Readings in Anthropology, Vol. II: Cultural Anthropology, ed. Morton H. Fried. New York, T. Y. Crowell Co.

Lane, Barbara. 1961. Structural Contrasts Between Symmetric and Asymmetric Marriage Systems: A Fallacy. *Southwestern Journal of Anthropology* 17:49-55.

—— 1962. Jural Authority and Affinal Exchange. *Southwestern Journal of Anthropology* 18:184-97.

Lane, R. 1962. Patrilateral Cross-Cousin Marriage: Structural Analysis and Ethnographic Cases. *Ethnology* 1:467-99.

Leach, E. R. 1951. The Structural Implications of Matrilateral Cross-Cousin Marriage. *Journal of the Royal Anthropological Institute* 81:23-55. Also in E. R. Leach, Rethinking Anthropology. London School of Economics Monographs in Social Anthropology No. 22. London, 1961.

—— 1954. Political Systems of Highland Burma. Cambridge, Mass., Harvard University Press.

—— 1957. Aspects of Bridewealth and Marriage Stability among the Kachin and Lakher. *Man* 57, No. 59, pp. 50-55.

—— 1958. Concerning Trobriand Clans and the Kinship Category Tabu. In The Developmental Cycle in Domestic Groups, ed. Jack Goody. Cambridge, Cambridge University Press.

—— 1960. Descent, Filiation and Affinity. Letter in *Man* 60, No. 6, pp. 9-10.

—— 1961a. Rethinking Anthropology. In Rethinking Anthropology. London School of Economic Monographs in Social Anthropology, No. 22. London.

—— 1961b. Asymmetric Marriage Rules, Status Difference and Direct Reciprocity: Comments on an Alleged Fallacy. *Southwestern Journal of Anthropology* 17:343-51.

Lévi-Strauss, Claude. 1944. Reciprocity and Hierarchy. *American Anthropologist* 46:266-68.

—— 1949. Less structures elementaires de la parente. Paris, Presses Universitaires de France.

—— 1953. Social Structure. In Anthropology Today, ed. Alfred Kroeber. Chicago, University of Chicago Press.

—— 1957. The Principle of Reciprocity. In Sociological Theory, eds. L. Coser and B. Rosenberg. New York, Macmillan.

—— 1960. On Manipulated Sociological Models. *Bijdragen tot de Taal- Land- en Volkenkunde* 116:45-54.

—— 1963. Structural Anthropology. Tr. by Claire Jacobson and Brooke Grundfest Schoepf. New York, Basic Books, Inc.

—— 1965. The Future of Kinship Studies. (The Huxley Memorial Lecture 1965.) Proceedings of the Royal Anthropological Institute of Great Britain and Ireland for 1965.

—— 1969. The Elementary Structures of Kinship. Rev. ed. by J. H. Bell, J. R. von Sturmer, and R. Needham. London, Eyre and Spottiswoode; Boston, Beacon Press.

Lounsbury, F. G. 1962. Review of *Structure and Sentiment: A Test Case in Social Anthropology,* by Rodney Needham. *American Anthropologist* 64: 1302-10.

Mauss, Marcel. 1920. L'extension du potlatch en Melanesie. *L'Anthropologie* 30:396-97.

—— 1925 (1954). The Gift. Tr. by Ian Cunnison. London, Cohen and West.

Maybury-Lewis, David. 1960. The Analysis of Dual Organizations: A Methodological Critique. *Bijdragen tot de Taal-, Land-, en Volkenkunde* 116:2-44.

Murdock, George P. 1949. Social Structure. New York, Macmillan.

—— 1960. Cognatic Forms of Social Organization. In Social Structure in Southeast Asia. Viking Fund Publications in Anthropology, No. 29. Chicago, Quadrangle Books, Inc.

Murphy, Robert. 1963. On Zen Marxism: Filiation and Alliance. *Man* 63, No. 21, pp. 17-19.

Needham, Rodney. 1958. The Formal Analysis of Prescriptive Patrilateral Cross-Cousin Marriage. *Southwestern Journal of Anthropology* 14:199-219.

—— 1960. Patrilateral Prescriptive Alliance and the Ungarinyin. *Southwestern Journal of Anthropology* 16:274-91.

—— 1961. Notes on the Analysis of Asymmetric Alliance. *Bijdragen tot de Taal-, Land-, en Volkenkunde* 117:93-117.

—— 1962. Structure and Sentiment. Chicago, University of Chicago Press.

—— 1963. Symmetry and Asymmetry in Prescriptive Alliance: Further Comments on an Alleged Fallacy. *Bijdragen tot de Taal-, Land-, en Volkenkunde* 119:267-83.

Richards, Audrey. 1950. Some Types of Family Structure among the Central Bantu. In African Systems of Kinship and Marriage, eds. A. R. Radcliffe-Brown and Daryll Forde. London, Oxford University Press.

Sahlins, Marshall. 1965. On the Sociology of Primitive Exchange. In The Relevance of Models for Social Anthropology. A.S.A. Monographs, No. 1. London, Tavistock Publication.

Schneider, David M. 1965. Some Muddles in the Models; or, How the System Really Works. In The Relevance of Models for Social Anthropology. A.S.A. Monographs, No. 1. London, Tavistock Publications.

Schneider, David, and Kathleen Gough, eds. 1961. Matrilineal Kinship. Berkeley, University of California Press.

ETHNOGRAPHIC WORKS

Barbeau, Marius. 1917. Growth and Federation in the Tsimshian Phratries. Proceedings of the Nineteenth International Congress of Americanists, Washington, D.C.

—— 1929. Totem Poles of the Gitskan, Upper Skeena River, British Columbia. National Museum of Canada, Bulletin 61, Anthropological Series No. 12. Ottawa, Department of Mines.

—— 1957. Haida Carvers in Argillite. National Museum of Canada Geological Survey, Bulletin 139, Anthropological Series No. 38. Ottawa, Department of Northern Affairs and National Resources.

—— 1959. Totem Poles. National Museum of Canada, Bulletin 119, Anthropological Series No. 30.

—— 1961. Tsimsyan Myths. National Museum of Canada, Bulletin 174, Anthropological Series No. 51. Ottawa, Department of Northern Affairs and National Resources.

Barnett, Homer G. 1938a. The Nature of the Potlatch. *American Anthropologist* 40:349-58.

—— 1938b (1968). The Nature and Function of the Potlatch. Published by the Department of Anthropology, University of Oregon, Eugene, Oregon.

Belshaw, Cyril. 1965. Traditional Exchange and Modern Markets. Englewood Cliffs, N.J., Prentice-Hall.

Benedict, Ruth. 1934 (1959). Patterns of Culture. Boston, Houghton Mifflin Company.

Birket-Smith, Kaj. 1964. An Analysis of the Potlatch Institution of North America. *Folk* 6:5-13.

Boas, Franz. 1886. Mittheilungen über die Vilxula-Indianer. Original Mittheilungen aus dem Kaiserlichen Museum für Volkerkunde, pp. 177-82. Berlin.

—— 1888. The Houses of the Kwakiutl Indians, British Columbia. Proceedings of the U.S. National Museum, 11:197-212. Washington, D.C., Smithsonian Institution.

—— 1889a. Indians of British Columbia. Proceedings and Transactions of the Royal Society of Canada for the Year 1888, Vol. 6, Section 2.

—— 1889b. Preliminary Notes on the Indians of British Columbia. Report of the 58th Meeting of the British Association for the Advancement of Science for the Year 1888. London.

—— 1890. First General Report on the Indians of British Columbia. Report of the 59th Meeting of the British Association for the Advancement of Science for the Year 1889, London.

—— 1891. Second General Report on the Indians of British Columbia. Report of the 60th Meeting of the British Association for the Advancement of Science for the Year 1890. London.

—— 1894. Sagen der Indianer an der Nordwest-Küste Americas. Zeitschrift für Ethnologie 26:281-306.

—— 1895a. Sagen der Indianer an der Nordwest-Küste Americas. Zeitschrift für Ethnologie 27:189-234.

—— 1895b. Fifth Report on the Indians of British Columbia. Report of the 65th Meeting of the British Association for the Advancement of Science for the Year 1895. London.

—— 1896. Sixth Report on the Indians of British Columbia. Report of the 66th Meeting of the Association for the Advancement of Science for the Year 1896. London.

—— 1897. The Social Organization and Secret Societies of the Kwakiutl Indians. Report of the U.S. National Museum for 1895. Washington, D.C., Smithsonian Institution.

—— 1898. The Mythology of the Bella Coola Indians. Memoir of the American Museum of Natural History, Vol. 2.

—— 1899a. Social Organization of the Haida. Report of the 68th Meeting of the British Association for the Advancement of Science for the Year 1898. London.

——1899b. Summary of the Work of the Committee in British Columbia. Report of the 68th Meeting of the British Association for the Advancement of Science for the Year 1898. London.

—— 1902. Tsimshian Texts. Bureau of American Ethnology, Bulletin 27. Washington, D.C., Smithsonian Institution.

—— 1909. The Kwakiutl of Vancouver Island. Memoir of the American Museum of Natural History, Vol. 8, Part 2; Publication of the Jesup North Pacific Expedition, Vol. 5, Part 2.

—— 1910. Kwakiutl Tales. Columbia University Contributions to Anthropology, Vol. 2. New York, Columbia University Press.

—— 1912. Tsimshian Texts. Publications of the American Ethnological Society, Vol. 3. Leiden, E. J. Brill.

—— 1916. Tsimshian Mythology. Thirty-first Annual Report of the Bureau of American Ethnology for the years 1909-1910. Washington, D.C., Smithsonian Institution.

—— 1920. The Social Organization of the Kwakiutl. *American Anthropologist* 22:111-26.

—— 1921. Ethnology of the Kwakiutl. Thirty-fifth Annual Report of the Bureau of American Ethnology for the Years 1913-1914, Parts I and II. Washington, D.C., Smithsonian Institution.

—— 1925. Contributions to the Ethnology of the Kwakiutl. Columbia University Contributions to Anthropology, Vol. 3. New York, Columbia University Press.

—— 1930. The Religion of the Kwakiutl Indians. Columbia University Contributions to Anthropology, Vol. 10. New York, Columbia University Press.

—— 1932. Bella Bella Tales. American Folk-Lore Society, Memoir 25, New York, G. E. Stechert & Co.

—— 1934. Geographical Names of the Kwakiutl Indians. Columbia University Contributions to Anthropology, Vol. 20. New York, Columbia University Press.

—— 1935. Kwakiutl Culture as Reflected in Mythology. American Folk-Lore Society, Memoir 28. New York, G. E. Stechert & Co.

—— 1940. The Social Organization of the Tribes of the North Pacific Coast. In Race, Language, and Culture. New York, Macmillan.

—— 1966. Kwakiutl Ethnography. Ed. Helen Codere. Chicago, University of Chicago Press.

Boas, Franz, and George Hunt. 1905. Kwakiutl Texts. Memoir of the American Museum of Natural History, Vol. 5; Publication of the Jesup North Pacific Expedition, Vol. 3.

—— 1906. Kwakiutl Texts: Second Series. Memoir of the American Museum of Natural History, Vol. 14, Part 1; Publication of the Jesup North Pacific Expedition, Vol. 10, Part 1.

Codere, Helen. 1950. Fighting with Property. Monographs of the American Ethnological Society, No. 18. Locust Valley, N.Y., J. J. Augustin.

—— 1956. The Amiable Side of Kwakiutl Life: The Potlatch and Play Potlatch. *American Anthropologist* 58:334-51.

—— 1957. Kwakiutl Society: Rank Without Class. *American Anthropologist* 59:473-86.

Collison, William Henry. 1915. In the Wake of the War Canoe. London, Seeley.

Curtis, E. S. 1916. The Haida. The North American Indian, Vol. 11. Cambridge, Mass., The University Press.

Dawson, George M. 1880. On the Haida Indians of the Queen Charlotte Islands. Report of Progress for 1878-1879 of the Geological Survey of Canada. Montreal.

—— 1887. Notes and Observations on the Kwakiool People of the Northern Part of Vancouver Island and Adjacent Coasts, Made during the Summer of 1885, with a Vocabulary of about 700 Words. Proceedings and Transactions of the Royal Society of Canada for the Year 1887, Vol. 5, Section 2.

—— 1889. Notes on the Indian Tribes of the Yukon District and Adjacent

Northern Portion of British Columbia. Annual Report of the Geological Survey of Canada for the Year 1887-1888, Vol. 3, Part 1.

De Laguna, Frederica. 1952. Some Dynamic Forces in Tlingit Society. *Southwestern Journal of Anthropology* 8:1-12.

—— 1960. The Story of a Tlingit Community. Bureau of American Ethnology, Bulletin 172, Washington, D.C., Smithsonian Institution.

Drucker, Philip. 1939. Rank, Wealth and Kinship in Northwest Coast Society. *American Anthropologist* 41:55-65.

—— 1951. The Northern and Central Nootkan Tribes. Bureau of American Ethnology, Bulletin 144. Washington, D.C., Smithsonian Institution.

Drucker, Phillip, and Robert Heizer. 1967. To Make My Name Good. Berkeley, University of California Press.

Duff, Wilson, ed. 1960. Histories, Territories and Laws of the Kitwancool. Anthropology in British Columbia, Memoir No. 4. Victoria, British Columbia Provincial Museum.

Durlach, Theresa M. 1928. The Relationship Systems of the Tlingit, Haida and Tsimshian. Publications of the American Ethnological Society, Vol. 11. New York, G. E. Stechert & Co.

Emmons, G. T. 1911. Native Account of the Meeting Between La Perouse and the Tlingit. *American Anthropologist* 13:293-98.

Ford, Clellan S. 1941. Smoke from Their Fires. New Haven, Yale University Press.

Freeman, John F., comp. 1966. A Guide to Manuscripts Relating to the American Indian in the Library of the American Philosophical Society. American Philosophical Society, Memoir 65.

Garfield, Viola E. 1939. Tsimshian Clan and Society. University of Washington Publications in Anthropology, Vol. 7, No. 3. Seattle, University of Washington Press.

—— 1947. Historical Aspects of Tlingit Clans in Angoon, Alaska. *American Anthropologist* 49:438-52.

Garfield, Viola E., Paul S. Wingert, and Marius Barbeau. 1951. The Tsimshian: Their Arts and Music. Publications of the American Ethnological Society, Vol. 18. Locust Valley, N.Y., J. J. Augustin.

Hazard, Thomas P. 1960. On the Nature of the Kwakiutl Numaym and Its Counterparts Elsewhere on the Northwest Coast. Paper presented at the American Association for the Advancement of Science meetings, December.

Herskovits, Melville. 1952. Economic Anthropology. 2d ed. New York, Alfred A. Knopf.

Holmberg, Heinrich J. 1856. Ethnographische Skizzen über die Volker des russichen Amerika. *Acta Societatis Scientiarum Fennicae (Helsingforsiae)* 4:281-421.

—— 1859. Ethnographischen Skizzen über die Volker des russichen Amerika. *Acta Societatis Scientiarum Fennicae (Helsingforsiae)* 7:37-101.

Hunt, George. 1906. The Rival Chiefs: A Kwakiutl Story. In Boas Anniversary Volume. New York, G. E. Stechert & Co.

—— n.d. George Hunt Manuscript Materials. Archives of the American Philosophical Society, Philadelphia, Pa.

Hunt, George, and Franz Boas. n.d. George Hunt–Franz Boas Correspondence. Archives of the American Philosophical Society, Philadelphia, Pa.

Jacobsen, Fillip. 1894. Indianska sagor. *Ymer, Tidskrift utgifven af Svenska Sällskapet för Antropologi och Geografi* 14:187-202.

—— 1895. Sissauch-dansen. *Ymer, Tidskrift utgifven af Svenska Sällskapet för Antropologi och Geografi* 15:1-23.

Koppert, Vincent A. 1930. Contributions to Clayoquot Ethnology. The Catholic University of America Anthropological Series, No. 1. Washington, D.C.

Krause, Aurel. 1956. The Tlingit Indians: Results of a Trip to the Northwest Coast of America and the Bering Straits. Tr. by Erna Gunther. Published for the American Ethnological Society by the University of Washington Press, Seattle.

Lévi-Strauss, Claude. 1943. The Art of the Northwest Coast at the American Museum of Natural History. *Gazette des Beaux-Arts,* 6th Series, 24:175-82.

McIlwraith, Thomas F. n.d. Field Notes on the Bella Coola. University of Toronto Library.

—— 1948. The Bella Coola Indians. 2 vols. Toronto, University of Toronto Press.

Mayne, R. C. 1862. Four Years in British Columbia and Vancouver Island. London, John Murray.

Murdock, George Peter. 1934a. The Haidas of British Columbia. In Our Primitive Contemporaries. New York, Macmillan.

—— 1934b. Kinship and Social Behavior among the Haida. *American Anthropologist* 36:355-85.

—— 1936. Rank and Potlatch among the Haida. Yale University Publications in Anthropology, No. 13. New Haven, Yale University Press.

Newcombe, C. F. 1907. The Haida. Congrès International des Américanistes, 15th Session, Vol. 1.

Niblack, A. P. 1890. The Coast Indians of Southern Alaska and Northern British Columbia. Report of the U.S. National Museum for 1888. Washington, D.C., Smithsonian Institution.

Oberg, Kalervo. 1934. Crime and Punishment in Tlingit Society. *American Anthropologist* 36:145-56.

Olson, R. L. 1967. Social Structure and Social Life of the Tlingit in Alaska. University of California Publications in Anthropological Records, Vol. 26. Berkeley, University of California Press.

Piddocke, Stuart. 1965. The Potlatch System of the Southern Kwakiutl: A New Perspective. *Southwestern Journal of Anthropology* 21:244-64.

Portlock, Nathaniel. 1789. A Voyage Around the World. London, J. Stockdale and G. Goulding.

Sapir, Edward. 1911. Some Aspects of Nootka Language and Culture. *American Anthropologist* 13:15-28.

—— 1915a. The Social Organization of the West Coast Tribes. Proceedings and Transactions of the Royal Society of Canada, Series 3, Vol. 9.

—— 1915b. A Sketch of the Social Organization of the Nass River Indians. National Museum of Canada, Bulletin 19, Anthropological Series No. 7. Ottawa, Department of Mines.

—— 1920. Nass River Terms of Relationship. *American Anthropologist* 22:261-71.

—— 1921. The Life of a Nootka Indian. *Queen's Quarterly* 28, No. 3, pp. 232-43; No. 4, pp. 351-67.

—— 1922. Sayach'apis, a Nootka Trader. In American Indian Life, ed. E. C. Parsons. New York, B. W. Huebsch, Inc.

—— n.d. Nootka Ethnographic Field Notes. Unpublished.

Sapir, Edward, and Morris Swadesh. 1939. Nootka Texts: Tales and Ethnological Narratives. Philadelphia, Linguistic Society of America.

—— 1955. Native Accounts of Nootka Ethnography. Indiana University Research Center in Anthropology, Folklore, and Linguistics Publications No. 1.

Service, Elman. 1958. The Nootka of British Columbia. In A Profile of Primitive Culture. New York, Harper & Brothers.

Sproat, Gilbert. 1868. Scenes and Studies of Savage Life. London.

Suttles, Wayne. 1960. Affinal Ties, Subsistence, and Prestige among the Coast Salish. *American Anthropologist* 62:296-305.

Swadesh, Morris. 1948. Motivations in Nootka Warfare. *Southwestern Journal of Anthropology* 4:76-93.

—— n.d. Unpublished Nootka Ethnographic Notes. Archives of the American Philosophical Society. Philadelphia, Pa.

Swan, James G. 1870. Indians of Cape Flattery. Smithsonian Contributions to Knowledge, Vol. 16, No. 220, Article 8. Washington, D.C., Smithsonian Institution.

—— 1876. The Haidah Indians of Queen Charlotte's Islands, British Columbia. Smithsonian Contributions to Knowledge, Vol. 21, No. 267, Article 4. Washington, D.C., Smithsonian Institution.

Swanton, J. R. 1905a. Contributions to the Ethnology of the Haida. Memoir of the American Museum of Natural History, Vol. 8, Part 1; Publication of the Jesup North Pacific Expedition, Vol. 5, Part 1.

—— 1905b. Social Organization of the Haida. Proceedings of the International Congress of Americanists, 13th Session, Easton, Pa.

—— 1905c. Haida Texts and Myths. Bureau of American Ethnology, Bulletin 29. Washington, D.C., Smithsonian Institution.

—— 1908a. Social Condition, Beliefs, and Linguistic Relationship of the Tlingit Indians. Twenty-sixth Annual Report of the Bureau of American Ethnology for the years 1904-1905. Washington, D.C., Smithsonian Institution.

—— 1908b. Haida Texts—Massit Dialect. Memoir of the American Museum of Natural History, Vol. 14, Part 2; Publication of the Jesup North Pacific Expedition, Vol. 10, Part 2.

—— 1909. Tlingit Myths and Texts. Bureau of American Ethnology, Bulletin 39. Washington, D.C., Smithsonian Institution.

—— 1911. Haida, an Illustrative Sketch. Handbook of American Indian Languages. Bureau of American Ethnology, Bulletin 40, Part 1. Washington, D.C., Smithsonian Institution.

Vayda, Andrew P. 1961. A Re-examination of Northwest Coast Economic Systems. Transactions of the New York Academy of Sciences, Series 2, Vol. 23, No. 7, pp. 618-24.

Wike, Joyce. 1952. The Role of the Dead in Northwest Coast Culture. In Indian Tribes of Aboriginal America, ed. Sol Tax. Selected Papers of the 29th Congress of Americanists, Vol. 3. Chicago, University of Chicago Press.

INDEX